A Community Called G.R.A.C.E.

The Ten Core Values of Neighborhood Ministries

Kit Danley

Neighborhood Ministries
Phoenix, Arizona

To my beloved community of

G.R.A.C.E.

*who live in these pages and whose stories testify
of all Ten Core Values*

CONTENTS

INTRODUCTION

*An organization's core values signal its bottom line. They
dictate what it stands for, what truly matters, what is worth-
while and desirous. They determine what is inviolate for it;
they define what it believes is God's heart for its ministry.*
–Aubrey Malphurs, *Value Driven Leadership*

WELCOME
...to this booklet on the *Ten Core Values of Neighborhood
Ministries*. Thanks for joining us on this journey. After thirty
years of doing urban ministry and training many along the way,
we desired to codify the contribution our work makes to the body
of Christ and to its kingdom mission. The values of Neighborhood
Ministries (simply referred to as *Neighborhood* in this book) serve
to tell our specific story; they also serve a larger function of keeping our mission focused on Jesus, the kingdom of God and service
to the poor in our city. Unpacking these values could very well
keep us purposed for another thirty years.

WELCOME
...to the co-laborers inside the Neighborhood Ministries'
family. This booklet is for you. It comes from the heartbeat to pass
on the core messages that God has given us to the next generation.
There is nothing new about this. The Apostle Paul wrote to Timothy, his protégé, with the strongest desire to keep him rooted and
grounded in the unwavering truths he had been mentored within.
Paul's epistles to Timothy were written for many reasons, but one
of the primary ones was to keep Timothy from veering down theological rabbit-holes, he wanted to keep Timothy focused on what
mattered the most (2 Cor 11:12-14). Timothy was a co-laborer; he
bore the responsibilities of the larger work with Paul (2 Cor 1:1).

He was put in charge of passing on truth to others so that they would live well (1 Tim 6:19; 2 Tim 2:1). He was invited to bear the calling of the work, though it would indeed bring suffering (2 Tim 1:8,9; 2 Tim 2:3; 2 Tim 2:10). And he was asked to protect what had been entrusted to him, these words, these patterns and sound principles (2 Tim 1:13; 2 Tim 2:14,15). Timothy would also participate in mentoring the generation under him (Titus 1:4). Paul wanted Timothy to stay the course and pass on clearly what he had been given. Paul was hungry for Timothy to become all he was supposed to be for the cause of the kingdom of God.

This desire of mine to give what has been given to us to the next generation comes from a similar place which I imagine Paul having. Watching leaders develop at Neighborhood, I want to give you the tools to carry on, to stay the course, to bear the calling, to protect what has been entrusted, to pass on clearly what has been given to you. Though it could be argued that our core values are discussed frequently and are in the "air we breathe," I learned long ago that though more is caught than taught, we need words to describe what we are catching.

WELCOME

...to friends from the larger body of Christ, especially the next generation. We believe that our pain and hard work have taught us some important lessons which are worth passing on. God's heart is for the poor and his desire is for many to risk everything to follow Him, where He is.

THE GOAL IS TRANSFORMATIONAL LEADERSHIP

The mission of Neighborhood Ministries (NM) is: "to be the presence Jesus Christ, sharing his life-transforming hope, love and power among distressed families of urban Phoenix, igniting their passion for God and his kingdom."

Our end game as stated in our mission is to see kingdom minded leaders develop. This mission drives just about everything we do. NM's ten core values are the tracks this mission runs on. They are the template, if you will, of how leaders develop here. Unpacking and developing them gives us a tool that will accompany the hands-on mentoring that leaders receive. Our desire is to see transformational leaders emerge out of our mission for our community, for our city, our state and for the world.

We identify leaders by their calling. Six of the ten core values begin with, "we are called:" called to incarnational love, called to leadership development, called to the work of reconciliation, called to be the church as well as support the church, called to the work of justice, and called to holistic ministry. Underneath these callings is a substratum of theology that identifies us with the cause of Christ. We are Christians sent out to love and be loved inside a community that God claimed, and we recognized that our calling was to join him there.

To live these values requires a commitment to be "at the ground" and to look at Jesus and his calling "from below." That means our urban poor community gets to influence how we integrate and teach truth so that the gospel is truly good news to the poor. We know from what we have learned over the years that our traditions can drive our ministry models and direct our message. Many parts of these traditions have come from an "outside" place where the church was culturally captive. In order to live these core values we need an alternative construct for our Christian practice, a different way of doing things. The rest of the values, the other four, emphasize that different way and the reforming role they play in our regular, everyday kingdom perspective. They begin, "we value:" we value community, we value relationships, we value learning and we value partnerships. These ten values communicate a life of service, where the "good news to the poor" brings transformation not just to our community but to the power structures and influencers in our city. That message is prophetic.

TEN CORE VALUES

This booklet is structured in a particular way. The first chapter contains the biblical and theological foundations of the work out of which the core values emanate. The next ten chapters are given to the values, each chapter tackling one. And each chapter has three parts. The first part has to do with how the value lives at Neighborhood and its biblical and theological underpinnings with stories to illustrate. Then each chapter has a way in which the work of the grace of God informs that value. The third part has some spiritual direction that helps us live that value; this part will be found in the back of the booklet in an appendix.

THE TWO OVERLAYS

The second and third parts are called overlays and as already stated, they accompany the examination of each core value. They are important in order for these values to be useful for transformation. No Christian needs a new list of things to do or be; that would be burdensome. None of us needs a new legalism. These two overlays function to suggest how we might live these values.

Grace Rules

The first is the overlay of grace. What does grace have to do with a mission to the poor's core values? The answer is, "Everything." There is idealism inside our values which could be argued is over-reaching, aspiring as we do to follow Jesus' way among the poor could result in unhealthy perfectionisms, burn-out and hypocrisies. Therefore, this great challenge to live inside these values calls for an extraordinary focus on grace. One, to prevent any of us from slipping into an unwitting trap of a new legalism; the old one was bad enough. The other, to continually remind us all that we are mere humans, flawed and always in process. These particular messages of grace which sit inside each value are fondly called "rules." Why? Because grace can rule as well as law. It can guide, direct and provide the bottom line. But grace will offer its truth differently, reminding us ultimately that we are loved by a God who promises to never leave us or forsake us. At the beginning of every "Grace Rule" will be this reminder: *A grace rule is the way grace rules. This rule describes a lavish gift from God as experienced in our community. By receiving it, grace rules – leading us further into love and action.*

Inside Out

And the second is the overlay of spiritual direction. It's impossible to live a counter culture value system with an upside-down-kingdom theology without the mind of Christ and a developed sense of the work of the Holy Spirit enabling the follower to live so unusually. These spiritual tools are gifts to the believing community from Christendom, in some cases the ancient church. Christians have been working out their spiritual formation for two thousand years and these tools keep us in the game here, where life is rugged and spiritual mentoring is needed. I call this over-lay "Inside Outs" because these spiritual directions ultimately reveal the spiritual life inside us that is there for the blessing and benefit of others. I have repurposed the words "Inside Out" from the core value of Incarnational Love.[1] At the beginning of every "Inside

Out" will be this message: *When God's life inside of us spills out onto others, it is recognizable. Its source is from an upside-down kingdom value system. Choose to cultivate these expressions of God.*

VOICES OF THE INTERVIEWEES

I interviewed thirteen long time Neighborhood Ministries' family members, asking them questions pertaining to all ten values. Most of them have been with the mission for more than a decade, many of them almost all their lives. They understand the values and live them. Their voices are interspersed throughout the chapters. They add real life perspective and a depth of understanding to how and why we live these values. Though three are of my generation, all the rest represent the generation receiving these values who will carry on the work.

Sarah Leon – Sarah Leon began volunteering at NM right out of grade school and came on staff as the youngest two year intern to date, at just 18. She held many positions in the ministry. Our greatest influence in her life was to get her to consider college. We were successful; Sarah is now in Austin, Texas working on a graduate degree in poetry.

Ian Danley – As his surname indicates, Ian is our second child and only son. His story of growing up in the neighborhood is something everyone should know. He is married to Shiloh, works in the ministry as the director of the outreach department with kids and youth, spearheads leadership development initiatives, and directs all matters of social justice that emanate from the mission.

Malissa Geer – Malissa found us when we first moved onto the property in 2001. She was searching for a place to serve representing the mega church she was attending at the time. It wasn't long before she came onto our staff in the education department. And like so many others, she began to dream again about her own future, went back to college and pursued graduate work. Malissa became a great advocate for NM at ASU when she was Dean Debra Friedman's assistant. She is currently working on a PhD in community development at UIC (Chicago).

Marcos Márquez – Marcos grew up in the neighborhood and in our outreach programs. He was from one of the families that attended our first Kids Club in 1987. We have watched him grow up, grieved when he was in prison for many years, celebrated his coming back to the ministry and growing as a leader, suffered when he was imprisoned again unjustly, and joyfully see him and his wife and child everyday in their different participations in the mission. Currently, Marcos is a key employee at Opportunitees, our t-shirt business.

Panda Coral – Panda was about nine years old when she wandered into our lives and into the ministry. She and her nine siblings lived across the street from the church. Once they began coming, they brought their cousins and other relatives. We counted at one point, identifying over 65 family members from the Medrano clan that had participated in our programs. Panda is a mother of three and today works as a teacher in our preschool, *Katy's Kids*.

Jorge Macias – In 1987, our outreach teams decided that it was time to begin focusing on Spanish speaking adults. A bible study was begun and Jorge and Rosalinda Macias began attending. As Jorge grew in Christ through this process, and as his family became more involved in the ministry, he stepped into leadership positions. Jorge has served on our staff for over a decade and is the pastor of our Neighborhood Church.

Susan Leon – Susan is Sarah's mom. She began volunteering in our Mom's Place program when Sarah was young and on staff. As the program developed and needed a new director, Susan stepped into that role, leaving a career path she had been with since a young woman. Susan has just recently moved into the neighborhood, something she has desired for a very long time. She has two grown children, Sarah and Joseph.

Jeremy Wood – Jeremy found NM while he was attending a mega church in the East Valley of metro Phoenix. His first step into the ministry was as a mentor. Shortly afterwards, became a two year intern. During that time, he married Jessica, a long time volunteer with us since high school. Jeremy graduated through our education department and now is the director of that department. Jeremy influences the direction of the ministry through his leadership and perspective. Jeremy and Jessica have one child, Rubi, who they adopted.

Alex Canéz – Alex is one of the older cousins from an extended family, most of who are involved in the ministry. He became more and more involved in the ministry as he made the decision to leave an old lifestyle of gangs and drugs. He is a husband and father of three amazing children.

Francisco Mendoza – Francisco has lived in the neighborhood most of his life. He works for Katy's Kids everyday, helping with the set up and tear down of meals and other logistics. He attends church and helps with other programs.

Isiah Oakes – Isiah has a long standing reputation for work with urban youth in the city, dating back to the 1970's. He joined us in the early 1990's, has been a volunteer, a board member, was a part of our Neighborhood Church and helps with our workforce development department. He has been the lone African American presence on our board for years. We are correcting that.

Claudia Sanchez – We met Claudia and her siblings through Kids Club when she was just six years old. Together, we have done just about every part of life together. We have watched her grow up. She has three delightful children who are doing well in life and school and she is finishing her RN program at Phoenix College. She recently received her resident visa, which has been one of her long standing life goals.

Gumecinda Medrano – We call Gumecinda "Googoos", it is her childhood nickname. She is Panda's older sister. Googoos was a child mother to her only son Luis, who is now in college. Googoos is second in command in our Moms' Place program serving teen moms. We have watched Googoos tackle many life goals and have cheered her on. She has completed her GED after six years of trying and is trying to purchase her own house.

G.R.A.C.E.

You may be curious as to the nature of the acronym G.R.A.C.E. Like our community, the words that form the acronym are still being decided upon; both are still in process, still in formation. Do you have some ideas? I would like to hear them, but read this booklet through first. Though the final words that fill out this acronym are forthcoming, I do have a metaphorical story that is a reference point for me, regarding grace and how it breaks down. Rewind all the way back to the early 1990s. I was teaching the older kids class for Kids Club. Marcos was in the class and I must have been stumbling over how to describe God's amazing grace through Jesus' life and death to the first generation in our mission. Most of them would either die or go to prison in the next five years. Smart and intuitive, Marcos helped me out. High went his hand with all five fingers extended, each finger taking on one letter. "Grace," he said, "can be learned this way: **G** od, **R** escues, **A** t, **C** hrists, **E** xpense. Grace." Most of you know how his and our story would play out over the next nineteen years.[2] It is about real people experiencing what it means to live inside the grace of God together. I've thought about the acronym this way – maybe it stands as a placeholder for all the words we don't have and are still searching for to tell it like it is. It might be enough to simply be – a community called G.R.A.C.E.

God bless you journeyers. For yours is the kingdom of God!

– Kit Danley

NOTES

1. The fact that God so loved the world that he entered into our reality allows us through that love to follow him by standing with the poor and vulnerable on the ground in under-resourced communities, ministering with, not to or for, committed to an *inside-out* approach, not relying on an outside-in perspective.

2. To get caught up, ask us for a copy of *The Relentless Pursuit, A Story of Love, Hope and Grace in the Neighborhood,* by Amy Sherman.

CHAPTER ONE

FOUNDATIONS

*I am recovering the claim that Jesus was not crucified in a cathedral
between two candles, but on a cross between two thieves; on a town
garbage heap; at a crossroad of politics so cosmopolitan that they
had to write His title in Hebrew and in Latin and in Greek ... and
at the kind of place where cynics talk smut, and thieves curse and
soldiers gamble. Because that is where He died, and that is what He
died about. And that is where Christ's men ought to be, and
what church people ought to be about.*
– George MacLeod[3]

The Word Made Flesh
The Word of God
The Kingdom of God

There is a teaching phrase we use here at Neighborhood Ministries. It is "Jesus with skin on". This phrase captures what we want to be about. We desire for Jesus to be revealed in what we say, what we do, in the love given away, in all kinds of relationships. We hope that an encounter with us will cause people to have an experience with Jesus, Himself in some way. *Jesus, with our skin on.* This idea is foundational to an understanding of how all ten or our core values operate here. The core values, when all is said and done, are about who Jesus is, what the Bible says about Him and His work, and the invitation He gives us to join Him in the adventure of living inside His Core Value, the kingdom of God. This chapter lays out these three foundations of Neighborhood Ministries for its ten core values.

THE WORD MADE FLESH AND THE WORD OF GOD
Jesus Christ is the Word made flesh and that the Bible bears witness to that.

Jesus is the revelation of the God who created heaven and earth.[4] The Apostle John writes "the Word became flesh and blood, and moved into the neighborhood. We saw the glory with our own eyes, like Father, like Son, generous inside and out, true from start to finish."[5] The all-powerful God became a human being, born as a vulnerable baby. Born of the Virgin Mary[6] they named him Jesus which means YHWH saves, because he would save his people from their sins.[7] He came from the Father[8], and was the human face of the living God. Who understands this? In the *Nicaraguan Peasants' Mass* we hear other vulnerable people trying:

You are the God of the poor,
The human and sensitive God
THE God who sweats in the street

> The God with a sun-scorched face
> That is why I speak to you
> Just as my people talk,
> For you are the God who labors
> You are the worker, Christ.[9]

Jesus revealed the glory of the Father's only Son. He is the image of the invisible God, the firstborn of all creation.[10] And who from the beginning of his public life received his Father's approval and unquestioned love: "You are my beloved Son; with you I am well pleased."[11] Jesus is Emmanuel, meaning God with us. He is the God-with-us king for his kingdom has come on earth as it is in heaven.[12]

God's son Jesus came into the world because of love and for love. "For God so loved the world, that He gave His only Son, that whoever would believe in him would not perish but have everlasting life."[13] He loved tax collectors and sinners,[14] he loved prodigals,[15] he loved guilty adulteresses,[16] he loved the poor,[17] he loved his enemies,[18] he loved his friends, his followers[19] and he loved His Father.[20] This love compelled him to preach and teach, to heal and restore, to comfort and serve.[21] He became the servant of all proclaimed so beautifully in the *Hymn of Christ*:

> His state was divine
> yet he did not cling
> to his equality with God
> but emptied himself
> to assume the condition of a slave,
> and became as we are;
> and being as we are,
> he was humbler yet,
> even to accepting death,
> death on a cross.[22]

He showed his love and compassion. He healed the sick,[23] he preached good news to the poor,[24] he forgave sinners,[25] he cast out demons,[26] he welcomed the outsiders and the unwanted,[27] he prayed for strength to do so.[28] And he taught us to do the same, to humble ourselves[29] to lose our life for his sake and the sake of the gospel,[30] to make ourselves little as a child in order to be greatest in the kingdom of heaven,[31] to take up our cross and follow him,32 and to love our enemies.[33]

He suffered and died on the cross, carrying our guilt and shame.[34] He rose again on the third day[35] and revealed himself to his friends,[36] and is seated at the right hand of the Father37 and will come again someday.[38] And we say with the author, "Come, Lord Jesus."

The Bible, the Word of God, bears witness to all of this. "For the word of God is living and active and sharper than any two-edged sword, and piercing as far as the division of soul and spirit, of both joints and marrow, and able to judge the thoughts and intentions of the heart."[39] This word is alive and will lead us to the truth and as it teaches us, the truth will set us free. It will lead us to Jesus, who said He is the Truth, and it will lead us on the path of righteousness and justice. The word is filled with testimonies of the saints who have plodded this way before us, of Jesus, who we fix our eyes on, the author and perfector of our faith[40] which makes possible our testimony. This word has enabled us to be born again "not of seed which is perishable but imperishable, that is through the living and abiding word of God…the word of the Lord [which] abides forever. And this is the word which was preached to you."[41] The word of God provides a way to know the truth of God and a way forward, for "you received from us the word of God's message, you accepted it not as the word of men, but for what it really is the word of God, which also performs its work in you who believe.[42] And that performance happens in all the real places we live and in all the real locations our world suffers so that God's will would be done through us.

> If we are to take seriously the public dimension of interpretation that we find in the pages of the Bible itself, we will need to consider moving our primary training grounds for interpretation from the classroom to the places where people live – homes, businesses, executive parks, malls, and the streets. If biblical interpretation is to have vitality and power in relations to the social structures, economic systems, and political institutions of our own day, it must be set free from the social and spatial confinements imposed by the academy and the structures of the institutional church. We must learn to read the Bible in new places.[43]

And the Word of God is our weapon against all evil, against our adversary, against the principalities and powers. It is the sword of the Spirit, the word of God.[44]

> In the face of death, live humanly. In the middle of chaos, celebrate the Word. Amidst babel...speak the truth. Confront the noise and verbiage and falsehood of death with the truth and potency and efficacy of the Word of God. Know the Word, teach the Word, nurture the Word, preach the Word, defend the Word, incarnate the Word, do the Word, live the Word. And more than that, in the Word of God, expose death and all death's works and wiles, rebuke lies, cast out demons, exorcise, cleanse the possessed, raise those who are dead in mind and conscience.[45]

We base our work of loving this community on Jesus, the

Word made Flesh and on the Word of God, the Bible. Loving our community in Jesus name is our theological aim. We want to live what we know about God. We desire a lived...a living kingdom theology. These three Bible stories inform the way we see Jesus in our neighborhood.

Can we see you, Jesus? *Matt 25:31-46* – The Parable of The Sheep and the Goats

The Son of Man will come in all his glory. All the angels will come with him. Then he will sit on his throne in the glory of heaven. All the nations will be gathered in front of him.

He will separate the people into two groups. He will be like a shepherd who separates the sheep from the goats. He will put the sheep to his right and the goats to his left.

Then the King will speak to those on his right. He will say, 'My Father has blessed you.

Come and take what is yours. It is the kingdom prepared for you since the world was created. I was hungry. And you gave me something to eat. I was thirsty. And you gave me something to drink. I was a stranger. And you invited me in. I needed clothes. And you gave them to me. I was sick. And you took care of me. I was in prison. And you came to visit me.'

Then the people who have done what is right will answer him. 'Lord,' they will ask, 'when did we see you hungry and feed you? When did we see you thirsty and give you something to drink? When did we see you as a stranger and invite you in? When did we see you needing clothes and give them to you? When did we see you sick or in prison and go to visit you?'

The King will reply, 'What I'm about to tell you is true. Anything you did for one of the least important of these brothers of mine, you did for me.'

Then he will say to those on his left, 'You are cursed! Go away

from me into the fire that burns forever. It has been prepared for the devil and his angels. I was hungry. But you gave me nothing to eat. I was thirsty. But you gave me nothing to drink. I was a stranger. But you did not invite me in. I needed clothes. But you did not give me any. I was sick and in prison. But you did not take care of me.'

They also will answer, 'Lord, when did we see you hungry or thirsty and not help you? When did we see you as a stranger or needing clothes or sick or in prison and not help you?'

He will reply, 'What I'm about to tell you is true. Anything you didn't do for one of the least important of these, you didn't do for me.'

Then they will go away to be punished forever. But those who have done what is right will receive eternal life.

We are instructed by Jesus in this kingdom parable about where he can be seen and found. He is in disguise among the least, last and lost. His choice is to be identified with people in society's most difficult places. This parable tells us volumes about our God and his humility.[46] And is another biblical image of his compassion.[47] The authors of the book *Compassion* recognize this identification with suffering people:

> They moved him; they made him feel with all his intimate sensibilities the depth of their sorrow. He became lost with the lost, hungry with the hungry, and sick with the sick. In him, all suffering was sensed with a perfect sensitivity. The great mystery revealed to us in this is that Jesus, who is the sinless son of God, chose in total freedom to suffer fully our pains and thus to let us discover the true nature of our own passions. In him, we see and experience the persons we truly are. He who is divine lives our broken humanity not as a curse (Gn 3:14-19), but as a blessing. His divine compassion makes it possible for us to face our

sinful selves, because it transforms our broken human condition from a cause of despair into a source of hope.[48]

Jesus Christ reveals God's solidarity with us. In and through Jesus we know that God is for us. This identification has not been lost on other theologians. Howard Thurman wrote the important work called *Jesus and the Disinherited* during the Civil Rights era. He taught his African-American brethren that the Lord Jesus was born to poor parents, among oppressed and persecuted people in Palestine. Thurman's audience needed reminding that Jesus was of a class that had been disinherited of all power and position like them, controlled by others like them, a people whose "backs were against the wall". Jesus was born identifying, born to take the part of the lowest. The author of the book of Hebrews says He had "to be made like his brethren to become a merciful and faithful high priest" or "we do not have a high priest who cannot sympathize with our weaknesses."[49]

Virgilio Elizando in *A God of Incredible Surprises* affirms Thurman's premise. He describes his own marginal Mexican-American story and the commonness he discovered with this Jesus of Galilee.

> Who, humanly speaking, was Jesus of Nazareth, and why did God become this very particular, stereotypically marked human being in order to be the savior of the world? What is the saving element of his earthly identity? After all, God did not begin the salvation of humanity by belonging to the great conquering and colonizing empires of this world, but through the marginal poor of the colonized peoples of the world. Yet he did not convert the colonized into colonizers but allowed them to initiate something new that would go beyond the categories of the colonizer-colonized.[50]

We see you Jesus; through a discernment you give us in the Word, that recognizes you in the low places. This is the Jesus we follow, for we long to discover you *where you are.*

Do we understand your message, Jesus? *Luke 4:14-21* – Unrolling the Isaiah 61 Scroll

> *Jesus returned to Galilee in the power of the Holy Spirit. News about him spread through the whole countryside. He taught in their synagogues, and everyone praised him. Jesus went to Nazareth, where he had been brought up. On the Sabbath day he went into the synagogue as he usually did. And he stood up to read. The scroll of the prophet Isaiah was handed to him. He unrolled it and found the right place. There it is written,*
>
> > *The Spirit of the Lord is on me.*
> > *He has anointed me*
> > *To tell the good news to poor people.*
> > *He has sent me to announce freedom for prisoners.*
> > *He has sent me so that the blind will see again.*
> > *He wants me to free those who are beaten down.*
>
> *And he has sent me to announce the year when he will set his people free.(Isaiah 61:1,2) Then Jesus rolled up the scroll. He gave it back to the attendant and sat down. The eyes of everyone in the synagogue were staring at him. He began by saying to them, "Today this passage of Scripture is coming true as you listen.*

Jesus identifies with the least, last and lost. The message of this identification is embedded in all that God is, and was recorded as prophecy in the Old Testament. So when Jesus inaugurated his mission in Nazareth, it was natural for him to turn to the scriptures, open them up to the place where it was described what God would look like when he walked on earth. The prophets foretold how God's people would recognize the Messiah. He would be focused on his mission which he called *the kingdom of God*, and the recipients would be the broken and beat up, disregarded and disinherited. The Old Testament not only rehearsed over and over again a God who preferred the poor, who disciplined his people for their neglect of those most precious to him, but also let us see the heartbeat alive in Emmanuel, God with us.

"I know where Jesus would be if he were in my city"[51] people commonly report. "It's the rough part of town. Drugs and prostitution are visible. Kids drop out of school and get involved in trouble. The mentally ill and homeless live on the streets there. People are out of work and there aren't many businesses. The community has given up on itself. It's not a place where most church people want to go or are." "But," they say, "this is EXACTLY where Jesus would go, this is his kind of place, these are his kind of people." The Jesus they believe is in the Bible is the Jesus that goes to the very worst neighborhood in our world's cities and makes his home there.

In the passage we are looking at, Jesus is in Nazareth. This is his first time back to his own hometown synagogue since the Holy Spirit came upon him in the River Jordan and anointed him to begin his ministry. This church synagogue is filled with people who have watched him grow up. He isn't Jesus the Christ, to them. He is Jesus, the son of Joseph the carpenter, the laborer. When you are in your own hometown, people don't see you as special, you are familiar. Sometimes, so familiar, they hardly see you at all.

Today, he is there to tell all his hometown people that salvation has come to the earth. The tradition of ancient synagogue preaching was to speak from a passage in the sacred scriptures. Jesus asked for the scroll that came from the volume of Isaiah and it was handed to him, he unrolled it until he came to the prophecy written in Isaiah 61 about the Messiah and his mission. God in the flesh – doing God things – acting in God ways. So here is Jesus, preaching in his own hometown, to the very people who hadn't noticed him yet, and his objective was to open their eyes. God was in their midst.

And he reads: "The Spirit of the Lord is on me." This old prophecy stood ready. Once the Messiah would walk on earth, everything about him would be filled up with God Himself. The Holy Spirit would compel him to go here, to say this, to heal with power this person or that. God the Father, would give His power, through His Spirit, to His Son. And he would be anointed for his work, his God-job. Jesus, full of the Holy Spirit, was anointed to tell the good news to poor people. Not any good news…like a job, or a good health report from cancer, or getting counseling or help with a marriage, though those are all things filled with beautiful and good news. This anointing to preach good news to the poor is about the greatest good news.

First, who are these poor? These are the literal poor, who are so beloved by God. When Jesus talked about the poor, this wasn't a code word for some other kinds of people whose souls were poor. We know this by studying the Bible. Here is an example of Jesus and his preaching good news to the literal poor.

When John the Baptist was in prison, and it looked like Herod was going to take his life soon, John sent his closest friends to find Jesus and ask him if He indeed was the Messiah. If He was, John could die in peace, as he was able to say that he had done his job for God, by announcing successfully that the Messiah was here. "Are you the Messiah, the expected One, or should we be looking somewhere else"? John's friends asked Jesus. Instead of saying," no worries friends, of course I am the Messiah. Tell John that I am 'He.'" Jesus told them instead, tell John what you see (what only the Messiah would be doing, what only the Messiah could do). He told them "Go and report to John what you have seen and heard: the blind receive sight, the lame walk, the lepers are cleansed, and deaf hear, the dead are raised up, the poor have the good news preached to them."

What is this good news? This good news is spiritual, it is physical, it is economic, it is about the forgiveness of God for our sins, and it is also about the kingdom of God, that makes all things new, that brings restoration, healing and hope. What will help us understand the good news a little better is the very last line: "To proclaim the favorable year of the Lord", or as the above translation says – "and he has sent me to announce the year when he will set his people free (vs. 19)." *What is this favorable year, this important year where God's people are set free?* The year Isaiah is referring to, of which Jesus says the good news proclaims, is the year of Jubilee. A year God designed for his people Israel, where if they practiced it, they of all the peoples on the earth would become a people of justice and righteousness. For every 50 years, Israel, if they practiced this year of Jubilee would do three important things that would change everything for the poor who worked for them, who lived with them and who suffered in their land. First, the year of Jubilee required that Israel free all its slaves. Second, all debts were eliminated and third, everyone got their family's land back, which would have been taken from them to pay their debt. The imagery of the good news proclaimed to the poor sits inside the beauty of the Jubilee year. Do you hear the physical, holistic message of God's good news? It sounds like this: In Jesus, he frees you, from guilt, shame, disobedience, self-centeredness – in Jesus, you get to dream again, of everything your life should have been about. You are smart, resourceful, capable, you had things taken from you, yes, but God wants to give you back your life, fully respectable, full of dignity. Though the world treated you as a slave, took your land, and handicapped you with debt, in Jesus, his message to you is hope and freedom and promise. His is a Jubilee salvation!

We talk about the year of Jubilee when we describe "the kingdom of God". The good news we preach, is the message of the gospel of the kingdom of God. Jesus is king; his kingdom is to come on earth as it is in heaven. In his reign, we get our lives back. We get a do-over! Jesus came to preach good news to all broken humanity in addition to the poor: "He has sent me to announce freedom for prisoners. He has sent me so that the blind will see again. He wants me to free those who are beaten down."

Can you see it? Can you see why everyone, no matter the city, language or culture, why they see Jesus walking in that infamous neighborhood. He carries a message of salvation that is so whole, and so complete and so needed and so wanted, that the people who need it the most are the ones who get it first. "Wherever his spirit appears, the oppressed gather fresh courage; for he announced the good news that fear, hypocrisy, and hatred, the three hounds of hell that rack the trail of the disinherited, need have no dominion over them."[52]

Will we respond as you ask us to, Jesus? *Luke 10:25-37* – The Parable of Accidental Righteousness

Jesus identified with the least, last and lost. He lived what he taught, and then he told his followers what loving God with all their hearts, minds and souls meant, so they could live what He taught. Neighbor love, living theology! We know this famous story; it's the parable about *The Good Samaritan.* I like the way MLK, Jr. teaches this kingdom parable:

Let us develop a kind of dangerous unselfishness. One day a

man came to Jesus; and he wanted to raise some questions about some vital matters in life. At points, he wanted to trick Jesus, and show him that he knew a little more than Jesus knew, and through this, throw him off base. This conversation could have easily ended up in a philosophical or a theological debate. But Jesus immediately pulled that question from mid-air, and placed it on a dangerous road between Jerusalem and Jericho. And he talked about a certain man, who fell among thieves. You remember that a Levite and a priest passed by on the other side. They didn't stop to help him. And finally a man of another race came by. He got down from his beast, decided not to be compassionate by proxy. But with him, administered first aid, and helped the man in need. Jesus ended up saying, this was the good man, this was the great man because he had the capacity to project the "I" into the "thou," and to be concerned about his brother. Now you know, we use our imagination a great deal to determine why the priest and the Levite didn't stop...But I am going to tell you what my imagination tells me. It's possible that these men were afraid. You see, the Jericho road is a dangerous road... It's a winding, meandering road. It's really conducive for ambushing. In the days of Jesus it came to be known as the Bloody Pass. And you know, it's possible that the priest and the Levite looked over that man on the ground and wondered if the robbers were still around. Or it's possible that they felt that the man was merely faking. And he was acting like he had been robbed and hurt, in order to seize them over there, lure them over there for quick and easy seizure. And so the first question that the Levite asked was, 'If I stop to help this man what will happen to me?' But then the Good Samaritan came by. And he reversed the question: 'If I do not stop to help this man, what will happen to him?'

To live a followership of the Lord Jesus we must grasp this kingdom parable and be able to comprehend and answer the question of "who is my neighbor?" We are implicated by being unable to "see" the one beaten down in front of us. Conversely, we are also implicated by our ability to have compassion, the kind that commands us to stop and get involved, though it will be costly and inconvenient, "for the love of Christ controls us"[53] the Bible says.

> *Beloved, I am writing you no new commandment, but an old commandment that you had from the beginning. The old commandment is the word that you have heard. At the same time, it is a new commandment that I am writing to you, which is true in him and in you, because the darkness is passing away and the true light is already shining. Whoever says he is in the light and hates his brother is still in darkness. Whoever loves his brother abides in the light, and in him there is no cause for stumbling. But whoever hates his brother is in the darkness and walks in the darkness, and does not know where he is going, because the darkness has blinded his eyes.*[54]

THE KINGDOM OF GOD

Jesus said, "I am the Way, the Truth and Life, no one comes to the Father except by Me."[55] And he showed us the way, not just to the Father, but to the Father's ways. There is a path to follow when following Jesus. Jesus revealed it through all his teachings about the kingdom of God. It was his central message. The kingdom of God captured all of what Jesus was about. It captured the Father's will and design for all of creation. It captured all of the Old Testament teachings of God to his people Israel, that they might be a light to the nations and a people after His own heart. It captured all that Jesus was about on earth, the heartbeat of his mission, his core values, if you will. And as a result, it captured the desire Jesus had for his followers. That they might "show up" in all their activity representing him and the kingdom of God.

PARABLES

Jesus taught about the kingdom of God. And he revealed the kingdom of God through his works (miracles) and interactions with people. In teaching about the kingdom, Jesus used parables, which unless interpreted, sounded very mysterious to his listeners. Jesus didn't invent the use of parables, but he certainly took a common method of storytelling to the next level. A parable was used to help people understand something difficult, like an abstract concept (the kingdom of God) and put flesh and bones on it by using ordinary experiences people are familiar with. Parables are stories Jesus could deliver in a few minutes time and which would be easy to remember and pass on. In his parables he was showing in minute detail exactly how the kingdom of God operates and how we operate within it. The kingdom of God is the spiritual world pressing into and transforming the natural world of the here and now. To illustrate this, Jesus would usually begin his stories this way: "What shall we say the kingdom of God is like, or what parable shall we use to describe it?"[56] About one-third of what Jesus taught was through parables and he never defined what he meant by kingdom of God.[57] So these parables become the definitions through which to view different aspects of the kingdom; and when taken all together a big picture begins to form. Kingdom parables are scattered throughout this booklet because our core values are kingdom values. *Look for them, like a hunt, like a treasure hunt.*

THE ALREADY AND THE NOT YET

A part of the mystery is that the kingdom is both "already" and "not yet". Jesus' friends had trouble understanding this.[58] They wanted the kingdom that they believed was prophesied, where the Messiah would come with power to overturn their oppressors. It was clear quickly that Jesus' definition of the kingdom was different from theirs. *What was the reign of God?* A definitive answer to what the reign of God is cannot be given. But two elements in the Old Testament give a glimpse. The first is the law that God gave to guide Israel in living according to God's kingdom design. Robert Linthicum, in *Transforming Power,* reminds us that the book of Deuteronomy is the clearest statement in the Bible of the world as God intended it to be. In effect, Israel had a constitution. Deuteronomy means "the second telling of the Law", and this book presents a summarization or a systematic presentation of what was haphazardly fashioned throughout Exodus.

> The premise of Deuteronomy is that if the nation and its people are in love with God, it will inevitable be a nation that loves its people. And why? Simply because God is in love with the people: God loves the strangers, providing them food and clothing. You shall also love the stranger, for you were strangers in the land of Egypt". (Deut 10:18-19). A culture that places its primary value on relationship to God must also be a culture that places primary value on People and their well-begin. So the Deuteronomic intention to build a society on a love relationship with God and each other must inevitable move that society to shape its political system in conformity to those love relationships.[59]

The second glimpse into God's kingdom design in the Old Testament was through the prophets. The prophetic forecasts and the prophet's expectations can be summarized in the prophetic vision of shalom.

It envisions a world characterized by peace, justice, and celebration. Shalom, the overarching vision of the future means "peace", but not merely peace as the cessation of hostilities. Instead, shalom envisions the full prosperity of a people of God living under the covenant of God's demanding care and compassionate rule. In the prophetic vision, peace such as this comes hand in hand with justice. Without justice, there can be no real peace, and without peace, no real justice. Indeed, only in a social world full of a peace grounded in justice can there come the full expression of joy and celebration.[60]

The fulfillment of the reign of God *begins* with Jesus. He embodied the reign of God by living under its rule (Deuteronomic Covenant) thereby obeying all that the Father gave him to be and do. And as Prophet, he described and revealed the kingdom through his words and deeds, he embodied *shalom*. That is "the already". The "not yet" is when Jesus comes back and the kingdom comes in its final and most completed form. "But to each in his own order: Christ the first fruits, then at his coming those who belong to Christ. Then comes the end, when he hands over the kingdom to God the Father, after he has destroyed every ruler and every authority and power."[61] "The future rule of God breaks in ahead of time as a harbinger of the world's future to be fully and finally reconciled to God."[62] When He prayed, "thy kingdom come, thy will be done on EARTH as it is in heaven", he was saying, "the time is fulfilled, and the kingdom of God has come near; repent, and believe in the good news."[63]

Jesus did not suffer and die to leave things as they were but, rather, to bring a new order of life. He both proclaimed and embodied the kingdom of God, the new order of love,

freedom, justice, and peace which aims at the total transformation of history and demands a radical conversion
as condition for participation in it. To incarnate Christ
in our world is to manifest the transforming presence of
God's kingdom among the victims of sin and evil. It is to
make possible a process of transformation from personal
sin and corporate evil to personal and collective freedom,
justice, and well being.[64]

GOD'S PEOPLE REPRESENT THE KINGDOM REIGN

To incarnate Christ in our world is to manifest the transforming presence of God's kingdom among the victims of sin and evil.
We follow Jesus, not a blueprint for the kingdom; we follow him
to a real realm, a space that may be inhabited. In fact the New
Testament uses the words *receive* and *enter* to describe the ways in
which God's people engage the kingdom of God.[65] "Truly I tell
you, whoever does not *receive* the kingdom of God as a child will
never enter it (Lk 18:17)." In that same context Jesus notes how
hard it is for those who have riches to *enter* the reign of God (vv.
24-25), and he assures the disciples that there is no one who has
left mother or father, houses or land, for the gospel's sake, who will
not *receive* one hundredfold (vv. 29-30). "These two verbs represent dominant image clusters embedded throughout the New Testament's discussion of the relationship between the people of God
and the reign of God. Taken together they indicate the appropriate
way for a community to live when it has been captured by the presence of God's reign."[66]

THE SIGNS AND FORETASTE

What is the role then, of God's people as it relates to the kingdom of God. "By its very existence then, the church brings what
is hidden into view as sign and into experience as foretaste. At

the same time, it also represents to the world the divine reign's character, claims, demands, and gracious gifts as its agent and instrument."[67]   The church becomes the divine reign "with skin on" signaling what this reign looks like. "But the divine reign is distinguishable from us. It is something we can be in and something we can possess. But it is ultimately something other than who or what we are, and it can never be captive and owned by us in the sense of being controlled by us."[68] "The church cannot be more than a sign."[69] "Our being, doing, and speaking are signs that his coming is 'already' and 'not yet.'"[70] God's people are to be a distinctive community birthed by God's reign revealing its unusual counterculture, supernatural characteristics.[71] Things, transformational things, ought to be happening when the Holy Spirit filled people of God[72] (cf. Matt 28:18-20); how they live is upside down from the world's systems and values.[73]

"Broken though they may be, the signs persist in the world by the Spirit's insistence, and they spell hope for the renewal of the human community in the final reconciliation of all things to God through the Lord Christ. In this respect, the church is the preview community, the foretaste and harbinger of the coming reign of God."[74]

IN THE KINGDOM OF GOD THERE IS PREFERENCE FOR THE POOR

This preview community is living, doing, and speaking specifically out of a kingdom theology. It is what provides the signs that his coming is 'already' and 'not yet'. These signs point back to Jesus and what God is like with distinct markers or indicators.

> Theology for God's sake is always kingdom-of-God theology. Gustavo Gutierrez maintains that every healthy, fruitful liberation theology is embedded in the theology of the kingdom of God, and the same is true for political

theology in all is different guises. As the theology of God's kingdom, theology has to be public theology: public, critical and prophetic complaint to God – public critical and prophetic hope in God.[75]

At Neighborhood Ministries, a theology of the kingdom of God and it's revelation that God's heart is for the poor has led us thus far and guided our theologizing and our questions:

- Where are we going? And how does our theology direct us?
- How does our theology help us discern the voice of God in our community?
- How does our theology help us determine what impacts in our work are important and which ones are not?
- What is it God is asking us to do when all is said and done?

The answer for us, as suggested before, has been found in the Bible. Something happens to us when we listen to the whole Bible for a message that threads itself from beginning to end. That message is strong and powerful and changes us. We can call that long and deep thread, a theology; at least modern academics call it that. There is a thread which weaves itself from the law, through the prophets, through all that Jesus said and did and in through the church.[76] It is the message of God's heart for the poor. Some theologians followed the poor in South America; the poor themselves had in their difficult and oppressed circumstances discovered this message. Together they named this theology "A Preferential Option for the Poor."[77]

The message of God's heart for the poor is what drives us to do what we do in our city, in our neighborhood, on our campus. It has embedded itself inside our comings and goings and alerts us to a theologizing moment when our community is in trouble and God is trying to wake up his church. I'd like to think that the process is "Barthian"[78] the Bible in one hand and the community we know and love in the other. While the community presses in on us, educating us, alerting us to its suffering, troubling us about things we would dismiss or wouldn't allow to agitate us, simultaneously the Bible speaks about that very thing. God is troubled, God is agitating, God is requiring the prophet to speak and address that very wrong. The Bible in one hand, the community in the other. The result is an exposed understanding of where God stands. We are constantly learning, from both our community and the Word of God. You will hear this theology, throughout this core values booklet and notice other theological connections to this overriding theme.

The theological journey of evangelicals as it relates to an understanding of a biblical preferential option for the poor is not unique to us. From my very first lesson from the thousands of verses of God's heart for the poor in 1975, our group of young evangelicals was challenged to formulate a lasting theology that took all the parts of the Bible that had been cut out and metaphorically glue them back in. And then, of course, live by them. In those days, we had very little direct knowledge of how influenced we were by an emerging liberation theology, from Latin America, from the African-American community and additional forms taking root among underrepresented peoples in oppressed conditions. Both streams were young and sorely needed. And both were misunderstood inside their birth places. It was called a new way of "doing theology" with "an attempt to look at the world in terms of involvement with the under-privileged and oppressed, and to find within the Christian gospel both the analytic tools and the energizing power to work for radical change in the world."[79] Latin American liberation theology, in many ways, gave substance to an already emerging contextual theology that would be taken up by others, like ourselves, in impoverished and marginalized places and translated into our conditions. Liberation and all it represented crossed over from its Roman Catholic beginnings and translate into other "Christian" and biblical orientations, even landing inside possibly the most uncommon of places, evangelical seminaries. Not to underestimate the differences that would develop over the course of the ensuing decades, what was at the base of both evangelical and Catholic urgings of biblical discovery was that God sides with the poor and the oppressed against the rich and powerful, and both had the Bible to prove it. Evangelical theologian Orlando Costas uses the term "radical evangelicals" to describe the evangelical counterpart to this duo.

> The word 'radical', as used by this group, refers to a cluster of ideas including: going to the root of things in our analysis; a renunciation of everything for Jesus; a total commitment involving every area of life; discipleship involving a total social realignment; an unconditional and all embracing response; costly and compassionate identification with the poor; and allowing commitment to God to shape all other decisions.[80]

In and among the poor, a two-pronged renewal was happening with Catholics and evangelical Protestants. At the Third Catholic Bishop's Conference, which met in Puebla, Mexico, in 1979, there was an acknowledgement that the poor are a key to an adequate understanding of the gospel; something evangelicals were also learning:

> The poor are the first addressees of mission – in Jesus and in His Church. And the poor have also a potential

for evangelization, because they question the Church constantly, calling her to conversion, and because many of them carry out in their lives the evangelical values of solidarity, service, simplicity and availability to receive God's gift.[81]

This radical evangelical tradition, though we could arguably say has always been in the minority or remnant, has been the theological contribution to our own "praxis" and holistic proclamation of the gospel. It's important to note that evangelicals have also been theologically influenced by the larger ecumenical church, and other racial minorities who we found solidarity with recognizing each other because we were all "singing the Lords song in a foreign land (Ps 137:4)."

A current example in our ministry regarding these Scriptures has to do with our Arizona political landscape. The Bible came alive, like a sign that read, *Trouble Ahead*. In the hundreds of passages that have to do with God's heart for the poor, three descriptors of these poor are repeated over and again: the widow, the orphan and the alien living in the land.[82]   And there was trouble for the alien living in the land, in our land. Immigration is a common theme in the bible; many of the bible's prime actors were immigrants, including Jesus when he was a child. But to the point of this focus, much of what God has to say in the Bible is to give guidance to his people about interacting with immigrants. Israel was told to remember their own immigrant story and therefore "welcome" the immigrant among them. And not just welcome, but never mistreat them, care for them as you would the native born, and love them as yourself.[83]   The vulnerability of the immigrant was the emphasis here, so God's people were to become as active on behalf of the immigrant as they traditionally would be with the widow or orphan, defending, making provision and advocating for them.

God's preferential option was also being taught "up the road a piece" in most of our cities. Brothers and sisters were instructing us out of their own struggle. Urban ministers in America have been theologically educated by African-American thinkers. We had to go them because the white evangelical church had lost its way for almost a century as it related to a biblical understanding of social justice. During that same century, the African-American church had been working out theologies of liberation, reconciliation of both the oppressed and the oppressor, an engaged ecclesiology of a missional church, all the while identifying with the historical suffering and current social disparities facing their own people. "The Catholic monk and writer Thomas Merton once described the civil rights movement as the greatest example of Christian faith in action in the social history of the United States."[84] And their theologians were accessible, some in person others in books: James Cone and Howard Thurman, Tom Skinner and John Perkins. Long before the white evangelical church knew how to craft theological language for justice and transformation, the African-American church was *theologizing*, preaching and practicing what it proclaimed. And the African-American church was positioned inside communities as the dispenser of biblical truth and the deployment of transforming action. The African-American church was teacher, mentor and model of a theology lived.

FOUNDATIONS

This foundation of *Jesus*, the Word made Flesh, *the Bible*, the Word of God, and *the Kingdom of God* lay as the soil within which the ten core values of NM have grown. It would be impossible to understand them, much less live the core values without reckoning with its substratum. Jesus described the role a solid foundation plays: "Therefore everyone who hears these words of mine and puts them into practice is like a wise man who built his house on the rock (Mt 7:24)." And as the child's song goes, when the rain came down, the house stood firm.

NOTES

3. Ronald Ferguson, *George MacLeod, Founder of the Iona Community,* (London: Collins, 1990).
4. Hebrews 11:3.
5. John 1:14, Message Translation.
6. Luke 2:7.
7. Matthew 1:21.
8. John 7:28-29.
9. "Vos sos el Dios de los pobres," La misa campesina nicaragüense, por Carlos Mejia Godoy.
10. Colossians 1:15-20.
11. Luke 3:22 .
12. Matthew 28:18-20; Matthew 16:27-28.
13. John 3:16.
14. Luke 5:30; Luke 15:10.
15. Luke 15:24.
16. John 8:11.
17. Luke 4:18-19.
18. Luke 23:33-34.
19. John 15:13.
20. John 17.
21. Mark 10:42-45.
22. Philippians 2:6-8.
23. Matthew 11:15, 15:30; Luke 7:22.
24. Luke 4:18.
25. Mark 2:5.
26. Mark 1:37-39.
27. Luke 14.
28. Mark 1:35.
29. Luke 14:11.
30. Mark 8:35.
31. Matthew 18:4.
32. Mark 8:34.
33. Matthew 5:44.
34. John 12:23; Matthew 27:46; John 19:30; Mark 15:37; Luke 23:46.
35. John 20:19.
36. Luke 24:16-33.
37. Colossians 3:1.

38. Revelation 22:20.
39. Hebrews 4:12.
40. Hebrews 12:2.
41. 1 Peter 1:24, 25.
42. 1 Thessalonians 2:13.
43. Stanley P. Saunders and Charles L. Campbell, *The Word on the Street, Performing the Scriptures in the Urban Context*, (Grand Rapids: Eerdmans Publishing, 2000), 94.
44. Ephesians 6:17.
45. William Stringfellow, *An Ethic for Christians and Other Aliens in a Strange Land*, (Eugene: Wipf & Stock, 1973), 143.
46. "For you know the grace of our Lord Jesus Christ, that though He was rich, yet for your sake He became poor, that you through His poverty might become rich." 2 Corinthians 8:9.
47. Matthew 9:36; Matthew 14:14; Mark 8:2; Matthew 9:27; Mark 1:41; Luke 7:14.
48. Henri Nouwen, Douglas A. Morrison, Donald P. McNeill, *Compassion, A Reflection of the Christian Life*, (Garden City: Doubleday and Co., 1982), 17.
49. Hebrews 2:17 and Hebrews 4:15.
50. Virgilio Elizando, *A God of Incredible Surprises*, (Lanham: Rowman and Littlefield Pub., 2003), 6.
51. I teach these scriptures, all over the world. This question of where would Jesus be in my city and the answer of where, is always the same.
52. Howard Thurman, *Jesus and the Disinherited*, (Boston: Beacon Press, 1976), 29.
53. 2 Corinthians 5:14.
54. 1 John 2:7-11.
55. John 14:6.
56. Mark 4:30.
57. Thomas Purifoy, Jr. and Jonathan Rogers, PhD, "Parables, Living in the Kingdom of God," Vol. 1, (2008) Compass Cinema. http://modernparable. com/system/application/assets/pdfs/UnderstandingParables.pdf, (accessed April 7, 2012).
58. Matthew 13, Mark 4, and Luke 8, 13.
59. Robert Linthicum, *Transforming Power, Biblical Strategies for Making a Difference in Your Community,* (Downers Grove: InterVarsity Press, 2003), 29.
60. Darrell L. Guder, *Missional Church, A Vision for the Sending of the Church in North America*, (Grand Rapids, Eerdmans Publishing: 1998), 91.
61. 1 Corinthians 15:23,24.
62. Ibid.
63. Mark 1:14-15.
64. Orlando E. Costas, *Christ Outside the Gate: Mission beyond Christendom*, (Maryknoll: Orbis, 1982), 16.
65. Typical language heard in the North American church regarding the kingdom of God uses terms like *building* or *extending* the reign of God.

The images of building or extending arise from the combined effects of a Christendom heritage of power and privilege. Some use the words *establish, fashion,* or *bring about*. The reign of God in this view is perceived as a social project, placing the reign out there somewhere, so we go to construct is as it architects or contractors. Some use the terms of *spreading, growing,* or *expanding* treating the reign of God of something we promote, like CEO's or a sales force. (see Guder, *Missional Church*, 93).

66. Guder, 94.
67. Ibid., 102.
68. Ibid., 97.
69. J.C. Hoekendijk, *The Church Inside Out,* ed. L.A. Hoedemaker and Pieter Tijimes, tr. Isaac C. Rottenberg (Philadelphia: Westminster, 1966), 43.
70. Ibid., 108.
71. John 13:35 17:21; 14:9; 20:21.
72. They are breaking down dividing walls (Eph 2:11ff); they are a "sign" of God's wisdom to the cosmos as well as to the rulers and authorities in the heavenly places (Eph 3:10); they are (and behave as) co-workers for the kingdom of God (Col 4:11); they proclaim the mighty acts of the One who called them out of darkness into light (1 Pet 2:9); the church publicly announces the actions of God and the reign of God because it is an embassy full of ambassadors for the reign of God (2 Cor 5:20); but it is also a personal message, a call to conversion (Mark 1:15); is salt and light, represents the reign of God by its deeds (Matt 5:14-21).
73. The Sermon on the Mount and the beatitudes (Matt 5-7) contains a summary of Jesus' teaching for the reign of God, it is the New Testament constitution of the reign of God, or the manifesto for life under God's government that differs greatly from that of the dominant culture.
74. Guder, 108.
75. Jurgen Moltmann, *God for a Secular Society, The Public Relevance of Theology,* (Minneapolis: Fortress Press, 1999), 5.
76. I have heard reference to the number of verses in this theological thread from many hundreds to thousands. In the new Poverty and Justice Bible published by World Vision and the American Bible Society, they say "the evidence is there on almost every page of the book you're holding [the Bible] a concern for the poor and an emphasis on just and fair behavior … everywhere you go in this book, God's love for the poor and desire for justice leap out at you." (page 5 on insert) I have been teaching these verses for almost four decades and I just tell people to read the Bible with a desire to find them. Counting them isn't as important as letting them change your life and your life's work.
77. Gustavo Gutierrez is often called the Father of Liberation Theology, giving the emerging movement a construct through his book *A Theology of Liberation* (1971). He was influenced by a number of social teachings of the Catholic Church and some organizations including the Catholic

Worker Movement (Dorothy Day). Gutierrez also popularized the phrase "preferential option for the poor," which became a slogan of liberation theology. The biblical theme he emphasized was that the God of the Bible is revealed as having a preference for those people who are insignificant, marginalized, unimportant, needy, despised and defenseless.

78. Karl Barth is often quoted as saying that one should "read the Bible in one hand, and the newspaper in the other." Of course, suggesting that one would illuminate the other, although he would remind his audiences that it was the Bible first that would teach how to proceed inside the world. Perhaps the most clear statement on the record from Barth concerning these matters comes from a Time Magazine piece on Barth published on Friday, May 31, 1963. "[Barth] recalls that 40 years ago he advised young theologians 'to take your Bible and take your newspaper, and read both. But interpret newspapers from your Bible.'" http://libweb.ptsem.edu/collections/barth/, (accessed March 7, 2012).

79. Gerald H. Anderson and Thomas F. Stransky, C.S.P., *Mission Trends No. 4, Liberation Theologies,* (New York: Paulist Press and Grand Rapids: Eerdmans Pub., 1979), 3.

80. Ross Langmead, *The Word Made Flesh,* (Dallas: University Press of America, 2004), 97.

81. Ibid., 14.

82. Here are a few: Deut 10:18;14:29; 24:17-21, 26:Ex 22:21-24; 23:9; 27:19;Lev 19:33,34; Ps 146:9; Jer 7:6; Mal 3:5.

83. Leviticus 19:33-34.

84. Charles Marsh, *The Beloved Community, How Faith Shapes Social Justice,* from the Civil Rights Movement to Today, (New York: Perseus Books, 2005), 2.

"Front Porch" Nathaniel Gordnatta

CHAPTER TWO

We are Called to
INCARNATIONAL LOVE

Core Value #1

Definition: The fact that God so loved the world that he entered into our reality allows us to follow him by standing with the poor and vulnerable on the ground in under-resourced communities, ministering with, not to or for, committed to an inside-out approach, not relying on an outside-in perspective.

Those who believe in God can never in a way be sure of him again. Once they have seen him in a stable, they can never be sure where he will appear or to what lengths he will go or to what ludicrous depths of self-humiliation he will descend in his wild pursuit of man. If the holiness and the awful power and majesty of God were present in this least auspicious of all events, this birth of a peasant's child, then there is no place or time so lowly and earthbound but that holiness can be present there too.

And this means that we are never safe, that there is no place where we can hide from God, no place where we are safe from his power to break in two and re-create the human heart, because it is just where he seems most helpless that he is most strong, and just where we least expect him that he comes most fully.

– Frederick Buechner[85]

LIVING IN THE NEIGHBORHOOD

How do I begin the story of living in "the neighborhood"? After thirty years on the same block in the same house, with countless friendships and mission growth beyond all we could have imagined, what was it that brought our family to live and love incarnationally in our community?

It began in college with a supernatural meeting with God. I was converted, a Jesus encounter. What was unique, however, was my conversion came with a calling, one to the urban poor, to the central cities in our nation. I was twenty, being formed by young evangelicals in the theological foundations of all of this, the over three-thousand verses of God's Heart for the poor.

These became the construct out of which the nex thirty-eight years would play out. I was picked up by radical followers of Christ who were surprisingly inside a Baptist tradition that was recovering its soul from the previous fifty years, where the fundamentalism had wiped out one- hundred and seventy years of an evangelical social concern. Those predecessors were our inspiration. They were ardent social reformers, who were first evangelists; therefore their understanding of engagement in all social ills came from a conviction that social reform went hand-in-hand with revivalism. What led them to holistic concerns were the very needs of the people they were winning to Christ. The homeless had no beds. The men had no jobs. The women were stigmatized and needed a place of refuge to rejoin society. Eventually, these once only evangelists concerned themselves with changing, not just one life at a time, but the very things that made their dear ones lives so horrible in the first place. I was taught that these were the people I came from. And now it was our turn.

Wayne was involved in the concert evangelism work of the early 1970s Jesus movement. Music ministry was extremely satisfying on one hand, but the impersonal nature of mass evangelism left him wondering and wanting something more personal, more like Jesus. Still, when we would talk, he wondered how I had learned such beautiful and yet conceivably errant theology. I like to say, he married me anyway. The radical evangelicals I was being mentored by were teaching one another to follow a set of principles for these called-of-God to our nations poor: "move in" was the mantra, "live among." Wayne and I got married and five years later, he and I and our two small children sensed that God said NOW – to begin the ministry laid on our hearts. Our Jesus movement church had moved into the hood, because as old hippies, it was all they could afford.

For Wayne and I, it was the impetus to believe that it was time to move and begin to love and serve our neighbors. We bought an old run down house; it had twenty-six broken windows, carpet that had been used to change motorcycle oil, rats, roaches and paint that originally was brown, green or white, we couldn't tell which. Our little Heather said, "Mommy, why did we move from the pretty house to the ugly house?" That was 1982. That year we opened the first piece to the ministry, a food and clothing bank. That's how it began with us, but where did it really begin, this idea of incarnational missional living?

IT BEGAN WITH JESUS

This is the good news, God took on human flesh. The gospel of Matthew reads, "Now all this took place to fulfill the words spoken by the Lord through the prophet: 'The Virgin shall conceive and give birth to a son and they will call him Immanuel,' a name which means 'God-is- with-us (Mt 1:22-23).'" Gustavo Gutierrez says it this way in *Incarnation into Littleness*:

> Jesus was born in a particular place at a particular time.… He was born in Bethlehem, 'one of the little clans of Judah' (Micah 5:2), where at his birth he was surrounded by shepherds and their flocks. His parents had come to a stable after vainly knocking at numerous doors in the town, as the Gospels tell us.… There, on the fringe of society, the Word became history, contingency, solidarity, and weakness; but we can say, too, that by this becoming, history itself, our history, became Word.… To the eyes of Christians the incarnation is the irruption of God into hu-

man history: an incarnation into littleness and service in the midst of overbearing power exercised by the mighty of this world; an irruption that smells of the stable. The Son of God was born into a little people, a nation of little importance by comparison with the great powers of the time. Furthermore, he took flesh among the poor in a marginal area–namely, Galilee; he lived with the poor and emerged from among them to inaugurate a kingdom of love and justice. That is why many have trouble recognizing him. God has committed himself to live in solidarity with us, to suffer all of life with us.[86]

He is a God who moved in, who lived among us (Jn 1:14). God sent his only begotten Son into the world to redeem it, to reveal the foundation of His whole existence: holy love. "God's love," says P.T. Forsyth, "is love in holy action, in forgiveness, in redemption."[87] It is "God's movement toward his creatures for the purpose of communion."[88] This love that propelled God to earth to save and enfold mankind is the subject of *Exclusion and Embrace*[89] by Miroslav Volf. With this caveat, however, that Christians must learn that salvation comes, not only as we are reconciled to God, and not only as we learn to live with the ones around us, but as we take the dangerous and costly step of opening ourselves to "the other" of enfolding him or her in the same embrace with which we have been enfolded by God. It is the call by Jesus to follow him as disciples, that is, as those who learn from him how to live. We intentionally practice his methods and his forms. Sarah Leon remembers that she had to learn to enter the neighborhood with humility and respect, choosing to "be present" in a human way. She says:

> ...*it took a lot of practice to just feel normal here. Practicing incarnational living in St. Matthews's neighborhood was*

a lot of small steps in learning how to breathe in this new place. When I first moved in, I used to leave the neighborhood to find rest, or decompress in other neighborhoods that were "prettier". That seemed to do the trick, but then there was a season when that stopped working. So I tried to hang out in a normal organic way, like walk to the market, talk to a neighbor, sit on the porch, and I breathed better there. It started to become a part of who I was, walking and being open to a different way of receiving joy or rest. I kept on doing it, and it never changed. To this day I feel most at home in a neighborhood like this.

It's as if C.S. Lewis were tracking right along with Sarah. "Our imitation of God in this life," he says, "must be an imitation of God incarnate: our model is the Jesus, not only of Calvary, but of the workshop, the roads, the crowds, the clamorous demands and surly oppositions, the lack of all peace and privacy, the interruptions. For this, so strangely unlike anything we can attribute to the Divine life in itself is apparently not only like, but is, the Divine life operating under human conditions."[90]

Human beings going about life together, purposefully: this was the model that took us into the neighborhood. It wasn't long before we began to fall in love with our neighbors and our community. An Incarnational mission's model believes the way to do the work of serving a community is to live inside of it and to become one with it.

IT CAN GET COMPLICATED

In John 20:21, we hear Jesus say to his waiting friends soon after the resurrection, "As the Father has sent me, so I send you." He sends his children into the world, as the Father sent him. The Neighborhood Ministries family will hear through stories and the direct emphasis, "it is better to live in the neighborhood." Our ministry members are challenged by this, for different reasons. For some, the challenge is to leave the familiar and enter the world of the other with a heart open to an embrace, says Volf. Like Abraham. God told Abraham to leave his country and family and go to the land He would show him. From Genesis 12:1-3:

> The command to 'go forth' placed before Abraham a difficult choice: he would either belong to his country, his culture, and his family and remain comfortably inconsequential or risking everything, he would depart and become great – a blessing to 'all the families of the earth'. If he is to be a blessing he cannot stay; he must depart, cutting the ties that so profoundly defined him.; The only guarantee that the venture will not make him wither away like an uprooted plant was the word of God, the naked promise of the divine 'I' that inserted itself into his life so relentlessly and uncomfortably.

The Christian appropriation of Abraham's story comes through Paul who didn't leave family and land, but did leave genealogical ties and religious program to embrace the beauty of multi-culturality.

> Through faith one must 'depart' from one's culture because the ultimate allegiance is given to God and God's Messiah who transcends every culture. And yet precisely because of the ultimate allegiance to God of all cultures and to Christ who offers his 'body' as a home for all people, Christian children of Abraham can 'depart' from their culture without having to leave it (in contrast to Abraham himself who had to leave his 'country' and 'kindred'). De-

parture is no longer a spatial category; it can take place within the cultural space one inhabits.

According to Volf, this departing allows for the Spirit of God to re-create us into what he likes to call a "catholic personality", a personal microcosm of the eschatological new creation. "The Spirit unlatches the doors of my heart saying: 'You are not only you; others belong to you too.'" And these "others" are the particular ones that have been excluded, usually by our culture, often by us. They are the ones we've been told are alien to us, the ones who are a threat to the pristine purity of our cultural identity, the ones our culture stands in judgment against, the ethnic, religious, gender, racial otherness. Volf's theological treatment demands we accept that incarnational love particularly embraces the ones who have been excluded.

That is one kind of complication. Here is another. Some of our family can only look at the neighborhood through a perspective that has been colored by the hard things that happen in a community like ours and that happened to them. Marcos Marquez remembers the early years. "It was dangerous to live in the neighborhood, drugs, gangs, prostitution. The presence of Jesus Christ was felt very little, if at all. That's why all the negative stuff started happening, joining gangs, going to prison, deaths." Despite the trauma of the negative years, Marcos and his family have moved back into the neighborhood, they want to be a part of the presence of God in all he is doing.

Three terms circulate to describe the complex choices different ones have to live here intentionally: *relocators, remainers* and *returners*. A relocator is someone who comes from outside the community, and because of their desire to be authentically involved with the community, sharing its burdens and desires, moves in to make this place home. Susan Leon is a relocator. She describes her choice to move in:

I lived in a white middle class neighborhood for sixteen years. Before I moved out, I had a neighbor who came into my house for the first time in all those years. People don't talk to each other, they may wave; there is very little sense of living any kind of life together. Here I watch people live life together, maybe in each other's business, maybe in the best or worst possible ways, but they know each other; standing together in a tragedy, a celebration, sharing life together. It meets a need for me that doesn't get met any other way. I am the beneficiary of living incarnationally. The friends here in our neighborhood wave when we go down the street. Something about being known, that is really a powerful gift.

A remainer is someone who stays in the neighborhood. They are excelling people, taking advantage of all they can to become all they are designed by God to be. The messages they hear from outside our community are often exhortations to "get outta Dodge," "flee the bad influences" and retreat to the haven of an affluent area. "You've earned it, moving up means moving out." The remainer chooses instead to remain right where they are. Their excelling will bless and benefit their community. Though aware of the messages to leave, more of our community members are choosing to be remainers.

A returner is someone who did leave for various reasons, but has decided to come back. Marcos is a returner. So is Panda Coral, although she doesn't yet live in the neighborhood she works here, and has been here most every day for over a decade. She talks about why she came back. "I always looked at it as my life, what I have been called to do, trying to do it as best as I can. Ever since I was little, this church has always brought me back. I always knew I would give back, to other kids who are like me."

One last complication. And that has to do with moving out

or moving on. Ministry in our community requires a long-term commitment to long-term relationships. People will hear about that from the beginning from us. But how it all comes together for someone as they grow here is unknown at the start. I like the way in which different monastic orders structure the process of discovery for their initiates. There are stages of decisions that are made regarding their potential calling. Each stage prepares for the decision about whether or not they will move forward. We don't have that sort of process. How does someone move on, here at Neighborhood, when living in the community isn't working? Some missiologists, like Viv Grigg and Manuel Ortiz,[91] warn potential relocators, that a desire for a radical identification with a community is right and necessary, but be aware that people from privilege come into a community knowing they have a proverbial back door. The back door is what it sounds like: *options*. Something the poor don't have. Living in the community is a choice for wealthy people, and moving out is a similar choice. Grigg's point of view is that a back door will start to disappear the longer a person remains in a poor community. (He sees wealthy people becoming poorer the longer they live in a community, less connected occupation wise, less connected to an affluent power base.) Jeremy's opinion is that people from privilege always have options, and that makes moving into a community fairly risk free. Regardless, we've noticed that the importance of the conversation isn't about whether you use your back door, or whether its option diminishes over time, or whether only people of privilege have a back door. The point is how each person addresses their own back door once they move into the neighborhood. Let's agree to talk about it along the way.

HOW SHOULD WE THEN LIVE?

How we live in the community is equally as important. Missional living just begins when we move in, but the radical transformation happens when we allow the community to change us and our approach, once we've begun to do life here. There is a temptation "to fix" things here, especially people. That is dangerous and really ought to be seen as a violent act. We use the following prepositional phrases to locate the "how" of our ministry minds. Our incarnational motive is to minister **with**, not to, **among**, not for, **inside out**, not outside in. Susan reflects on this. "I see in Neighborhood's teaching this very equitable stance, not standing over others, not reaching down and towering over other people, but walking with them." Jorge Macias defines our incarnational work as work done together, with the community. "We don't do something for somebody, as John Perkins teaches. We work with them to find the solution; we don't tell them what they need to do. This is an unusual approach in comparison to other Hispanic ministries. Most other ministry leaders tell the people, 'you come to me and I will help you with your problem.'" Malissa Geer says it is about:

> ...reciprocal care and learning, in a political sense, in a spiritual sense, holistic, every one transformed by the other. There isn't one person who has the answers and therefore gets to go about ministering TO and FOR. We are all equal, suffering, experiencing redemption; no one has an upper hand or advantage, but each gets to grow up in the unique ways in which they are designed by God. That's the inside out part – inside each of us, is a unique story of redemption and when we are in touch with that we can have an outward expression of love. The fabric of community grows strong, because we are able to be in it together.

"If you're not with and among," says Ian Danley, "then you have little ability to understand the capacity of the community where you are working. The dominant narrative in the world is that poor people are a collection of problems and to the extent that you can solve those problems, you can see change happen. This is a destructive narrative. The counter narrative is the deep capacity of the community, whether exercised or latent. It is there, congealed, hidden, maybe, but it is there. Some of it is already exercised, demonstrated, in all kinds of ways, individual, communal, familial. You can see it if you are "serving among". If you're not "among", you are likely to be co-opted to the dominant narrative, that poor people are problems to be solved."

LOVE COMES FROM SEEING

One of the aspects of incarnational love is "seeing"; the practice of seeing the other. William Stringfellow in *A Private and Public Faith*[92] believes it is the Word of God that creates the space within us to see. The Word of God challenges us to fearlessly and obediently live truth despite the prevailing winds of Christian self-interests; to be "in but not of" for love of Christ, to bear the gospel message inside a world that God loves and died for. Stringfellow learned that a Christian way of life would be born out of being among the poor and seeing God present there, and discerning what God sees. This would overt a "hardness of heart" or a "paralyzed conscience", which he says is the peril of the church today: "Something of what I know of the presence of the Word of God in the life of the world I know from living and working in East Harlem."[93] Unearthing the understanding he possessed came through relationships. He tells a story about some gang kids in his neighborhood to illustrate his point: "The Word of God – the same Word uttered and observed in the sanctuary – is hidden in the ordinary life of these boys in gang society and in the violence of the streets which is part of their everyday existence. And so it is within the common life of the entire world."[94] Teaching the church to be in the world but not of it, to be outside the wall, to be fully aware of the presence of God in the places we live and act, to see holy ground differently and not a designated space, to live the Word of God allows us to see. Volf would agree and his challenge is to see the very ones others don't see, don't want to see or have been taught not to see. For Christians to allow human beings to be "excluded" – violated, murdered, destroyed, dismissed, disregarded, dehumanized, discarded, TO BE INVISIBLE – we must agree together that exclusion of the other is sin. I love watching each other see. Panda remembers being seen and discusses who she now sees:

> … *ever since I was little this church (Neighborhood) just stuck with me, just stuck by my side, helped me at my worst times to get through. I came here as a kid, lost and forgotten. I remembered this when I saw one little boy. He got in my heart the other day. I have had him in Kids Club the past two years. He always remembered my name and would greet me with a giant smile. Recently, I found out the craziness he is going through; to see him with the life inside of him, pushing forward, even though he has been going through so much. I prayed, Lord, please don't let his spirit be broken. That's what I love about our community. We see God all over it. He is getting this little boy by, just like he got me by. This bad life doesn't make this little child angry, although it makes me angry. Compassion, it wants to make me do what I am doing.*

A THEOLOGY OF PRESENCE

The Neighborhood Ministries mission statement begins "to be the presence of Jesus Christ…." All that we have been talking about regarding incarnational love has to do with this passionate commitment to be the presence of Christ. There are a few different ways Christians talk about incarnational mission,[95] and our language of being *the presence* is one of them. The distinguished modern theologian who has nuanced this distinctive understanding of presence as incarnational witness is Jürgen Moltmann. "What he contributes most distinctively is an emphasis on God's initiative in making incarnational mission possible through the saving and empowering *presence of Christ*."[96] He identifies five ways to understand the church's incarnational mandate as it continues Christ's mission in the presence and under the lordship of Christ:

1) The mission of Jesus proclaimed good news to the poor and called people to repentance, which is a message of joy, liberation and solidarity with the poor and weak.

2) Jesus calls us to follow him on the way of the cross, a way of self-surrender and public suffering. The church is called to a "public apostleship" and "public intervention on behalf of the lost and despised." The life of Christ is to be embodied and made transparent in our lives.

3) Christian existence is new life in Christ's sphere of influence, acknowledging Christ as lord through testimony, fellowship and living with a passion for life. The church exists only to the extent that it reflects this new life, in its internal relationships and in its public stance.

4) Jesus, our pattern for mission, which includes beauty, freedom, song and laughter. This is an important corrective to excessively ethical approaches to Jesus' lordship. Jesus is NOT the new law-giver. To live in the kingdom of God is to be guests at the feast of God.

5) Jesus calls us to open and public friendship. Though Jesus has many titles, which emphasize his uniqueness and difference from us, he also calls us friends (Jn 15:13-14), communicating his acceptance of us and solidarity with the unrighteous and despised. Jesus, friend of sinners (Lk 7:34).[97]

GRACE RULES – SOLIDARITY through LOVE

*A grace rule is the way grace rules. This rule describes a
lavish gift from God as experienced in our community. By
receiving it, grace rules – leading us further into love and
action.*

The grace rule we experience through the value of in-carnational mission, is solidarity through love. Incarnational mission brings us into a posture or a position to receive as well as to give. Though it could be argued that because giving costs something, it really doesn't qualify as grace, but when love is exchanged reciprocally in our community, most of us would agree that what we receive is far more, and far greater than what we give. Love opens us up to the grace of this exchange of shared life. Many of our loved ones suffer with very difficult things. Our shared life requires we respond. Solidarity develops as we stand together. Solidarity refers to "struggling on the side of" rather than simply to "suffer together with." A fully developed understanding of incarnational love affirms the theme of solidarity, for it underscores the activity of the Christian who has embraced the other in self-giving.

Solidarity is the word traditionally used when Christians stand with the poor. Archbishop Oscar Romero says it this way, "I am speaking of an incarnation that is preferential and partial: incarnation in the world of the poor."[98] For what purpose? So that the poor can benefit from the promises of democracy or the American Dream? Did Jesus ask us to follow him in solidarity among the "excluded" for liberation? No. Love, he declares, the greatest is love.

The father of Latin American Liberation Theology, Gustavo Gutierrez, was right to insist that love, not freedom is ultimate. The 'deepest root of all servitude, he stressed in his *Theology of Liberation*, 'is the breaking of friendship with God and with other human beings, and therefore cannot be eradicated except by the unmerited redemptive love of the Lord whom we receive by faith and in communion with one another.[99]

Over the years this gift of solidarity through love has expressed itself in multiple ways. One recent example is the choice we collectively made to stand with our immigrant friends as our city and state entered its dark and oppressive years. Laws were passed that made our friends criminals. Out of love for them, we have chosen solidarity in the cause of immigrant rights and immigration reform. We stand together because of love, and only love. The suffering of our friends has caused us to know a deep intimacy with them that we couldn't have known without the costliness of taking on their plight. And their stories of courage and faith have strengthened us. This experience in solidarity has been a true give and take.

We consider it amazing grace when the acts of incarnational love bring us into deep solidarity with one another. Shared life, shared love, shared hope, shared suffering. God's love births this grace to share all of this. "Inscribed on the very heart of God's grace is the rule that we can be its recipients only if we do not resist being made into its agents; what happens to us must be done by us."[100]

NOTES

85. Frederick Buechner, *The Hungering Dark,* (San Francisco: Harper, 1985).
86. Gustavo Gutierrez, "Incarnation Into Littleness" from *The God of Life,* (Maryknoll: Orbis, 1991), http://www.inwardoutward.org/author/gustavo-gutierrez (accessed March, 2012).
87. P.T. Forsyth, *Positive Preaching and the Modern Mind,* (London: Independent Press, 1954), 242.
88. John H. Rodgers, *The Theology of P.T. Forsyth: The Cross of Christ and the Revelation of God,* (London: Independent Press, 1965), 37.
89. Miroslav Volf, *Exclusion and Embrace, A Theological Exploration of Identity, Otherness, and Reconciliation*, (Nashville: Abingdon Press, 1996).
90. C.S. Lewis, *The Four Loves,* (New York: Harcourt, 1960), 6.
91. This discussion can be found in Grigg's *Companion to the Poor* and Ortiz' *Urban Ministry: The Kingdom, the City, and the People of God.*
92. William Stringfellow, *A Private and Public Faith*, (Eugene: Wipf and Stock Publishers, 1999).
93. Ibid., 58.
94. Ibid., 61.
95. For a very thorough theological treatment of incarnation ministry see *The Word Make Flesh, Toward an Incarnational Missiology,* by Ross Langmead, (University Press of America, 2004).
96. Ross Langmead, *The Word Make Flesh, Toward an Incarnational Missiology*, (Dallas: University Press of America, 2004), 143.
97. Ibid., 148.
98. Archbishop Oscar Romero, *Voice of the Voiceless, The Four Pastoral Letters and Other Statements*, (Maryknoll: Orbis, 1992), 179.
99. Volf, 105.
100. Volf, 129.

"Reconcile" Ralph Martinez

CHAPTER THREE

We are Called to the
WORK OF RECONCILIATION

Core Value #2

Definition: The breadth of reconciliation begins with God's saving work through Jesus Christ then expressed in our commitment to radically loving all people. The work of reconciliation, therefore, is to see our diverse community find a way back to one another, rich and poor, black, white and Hispanic, gang to gang, suburban and urban, Catholic and Protestant, Pentecostal to Baptist, young and old.

Jesus prayed: "I'm praying not only for them, but also for those who will believe in me because of them and their witness about me. The goal is for all of them to become one heart and mind— Just as you, Father, are in me and I in you, so they might be one heart and mind with us. Then the world might believe that you, in fact, sent me. The same glory you gave me, I gave them, so they'll be as unified and together as we are— I in them and you in me. Then they'll be mature in this oneness, and give the godless world evidence that you've sent me and loved them in the same way you've loved me (Jn 17:20-23, Message)."

The great desire of unity as expressed by Jesus in John 17 often appears illusive as we look at the global assault expressed in one tribal group against another or one culture dominating another. But the scriptures call us to "be reconciled" both to God and to one another. We obey God when we choose reconciliation. It has to begin with us, in our homes, in our cities, in our state, and in the U.S.

TWO RIVAL GANGS

When we began reaching kids and youth through our programs in 1987, we had no idea that these kids who we loved equally would be killing one another and going to prison for it a few years later. It could be that our programs were set up by God for such a time as this to give them help and hope as they would eventually suffer debilitating guilt, grief, and trauma. We were also unaware of the role we would play in teaching a message of reconciliation to these same young people. Who when given the chance, would make life changing decisions to forgive mortal enemies, and do so in front of an audience of rival homies.

Victor Lopez and Luis Lemus were two of these rival gang members in our mission. Victor remembers it this way:

> We both grew up in the neighborhood – with all the gangs and drugs and prostitutes. My homeboys were at 6th Avenue and Roosevelt. His gang hung around 12th Avenue and Roosevelt. When you get two gangs so close, you get pride and bad intentions and it leads to violence. My gang had a lot of problems with his; a lot of revenge. And his had a lot of revenge on mine. We had shootouts. We had rumbles. People died.

Both Victor and Luis were very involved in the youth programs at Neighborhood. So much so, they have distinct memories of avoiding each other. They remember they wouldn't have stopped to give a hand shake. They would have considered the other one non-existent, "I don't know you. ...You are invisible to me." This is not to be misunderstood as nonchalant. Luis remembers that he was taught to hate other gangs, the one that Victor was in, in particular. As the boys got older, the hate for each other's gang had grown to revenge. They were being tutored in stories of "payback" routinely.

Around age seventeen a series of deaths and a series of personal crisis' brought Victor to Christ. At youth group he heard a talk about forgiving your enemies. In a community whose enemies had taken the lives of family members the message was radical. One night, Victor told God he would forgive his enemies. Not too long afterwards, he followed me to Durango Jail, a juvenile prison. He had been locked up periodically as a youth and hoped to make sense of his own story by caring about kids in jail. We were visiting some NM youth; we got to a final visit and there sat Luis. Victor hadn't given his prayer to God much thought until now. Forgiving your enemies was a good idea, but here sat a real enemy in real time. Victor extended a handshake and a word of prayer, straight from the heart. For Luis, this visit was from God.

> *I knew there was a God out there, cuz who takes time to visit someone who the gang hated. That opened my eyes because Victor took a chance to visit me. I knew there was a God because this meant that people can change. That inspired me the most. If his friends would have found out, they would have said, 'that fool.' Knowing how Victor was back then ... that really got to me.*

When Luis was released months later and came to church, he walked up to Victor, hugged him and thanked him for visiting him in prison. A true friendship was born. They discovered quickly, they had more in common than differences. This began years of sharing ministry alongside each other in the very community where there had only been historic divisions.

Though this reconciliation happened over fourteen years ago, both Luis and Victor have said that it has rooted in them a capacity and pattern that has established the ability to forgive others in their lives. It reminds them of the will of God to love everyone and for Luis, he believes he couldn't have gone on with the ministry or God for that matter, if this particular reconciliation wouldn't have happened. He says, "You can't move on in your life in a positive way if you haven't forgiven what people have done in the past."

RECONCILIATION BEGINS WITH GOD

But where did all this reconciliation desire come from, with Luis and Victor? It started from a changed heart, one that God gave them. For their first reconciliation was with God, himself. I was there during the years they bowed the knee to their Savior, and I can't say that it was very complicated. "Let your prayer be very simple. For the tax collector and the prodigal son just one word was enough to reconcile them to God."[101]

Their confession of sin is theirs to tell, but what I can assure you is this, they would not have any need nor desire to reconcile with one another had they not found peace with God first. "For if while we were enemies we were reconciled to God through the death of His Son, much more, having been reconciled, we shall be saved by His life (Rom 5:10)." Maybe, I could share a little of my story here. I recognized my own guilt before God at a young age, which is strange, because I don't come from a very religious family. In fact, both my parents were off the path of the straight and narrow and didn't raise us with much of a code for right and wrong. Stranger still, was the constant drawing of my life to a place at the cross of Christ, first in the Episcopal church of my family, then through an outreach ministry called Young Life. I wanted and needed to know that my sins could be forgiven by God. Praying the sinners prayer was easy, for I knew I was not on God's side, how could I be, I did so many things that even I thought were disgusting. And then, one day in college, in a phone booth, I was ready to not just be a fallen and forgiven sinner, but a follower of Jesus. It was supernatural and still to this day, hard to describe, but I walked out of that phone booth changed forever. I tell you that story, because my reconciliation with God, led to a deep desire to put the broken relationships in my life back together. First reconciled to God, I desire to be reconciled to all those whose lives I was certain I had made miserable. Just a few short years later, I made a list and started visiting them, one by one. The hate and bitterness I knew for the people who had hurt me was changing into a very different emotion. I wanted them to forgive me.

All this is done by God, who through Christ changed us from enemies into his friends and gave us the task of making others his friends also. Our message is that God was making all human beings his friends through Christ. God did not keep an account of their sins, and he has given us the message which tells how he makes them his friends. Here we are, then, speaking for Christ, as though God himself were making his appeal through us. We plead on Christ's behalf: let God change you from enemies into his friends (2 Cor 5:18-20)!

ENMITY

Enmity is a Bible word used to describe the feelings Victor, Luis and I all knew as young people, taught to us by others. This word enmity describes deep-seated ill will. Enmity is hatred, like for an enemy. Enmity is hostility; it is antagonism, which is a hostility turned to action. Enmity is animosity which leads to bitter resentment. Enmity is rancor, the seedbed of revenge. Jesus put enmity to death.

> For He Himself is our peace, who made both groups into one and broke down the barrier of the dividing wall, by abolishing in His flesh the enmity, so that in Himself He might make the two into one new man, thus establishing peace, and might reconcile them both in one body to God through the cross, by it having put to death the enmity (Eph 2:14-16 NIV).

Luis has experienced the death of enmity, and knows the blessing of it.

You don't have to worry about that guy, backstabbing you, killing you. There is freedom; you don't have to worry about walking down the street, seeing him at the store. When you build a relationship with a person you hated in the past, it completely changes everything. A real person is inside your enemy, you see the funny side, the deep inside, he is really a great guy. Not everyone can be bad their whole lives, people change, honestly, if I hadn't reconciled with him I wouldn't be the same person. If I hadn't reconciled with him I wouldn't be who I am in the ministry. Now I can see him and hang out at the church. You will never again hide in the shadows.

AN EVEN BIGGER PROBLEM

Susan remembers watching this reconciliation take place with Luis and Victor. She says, "They talked about their reconciliation in front of all of us, won in this place and in their lives, from their warring gang backgrounds. They were brothers now, reconciled into a new family." Her own story of reconciliation into this community has to do with a bigger problem, that of a dominant white society out of which she comes. She confesses though she grew up in a Hispanic community in Tucson, "[Reconciliation] is so much harder than I thought it would be." There is, in our culture and in our city, a bigger problem of hate and division than rival gangs pose, unfortunately. And this bigger problem affects us all every day. There is no doubt that America suffers deep racial divisions, and what some call the problem of being racialized.[102] Social experts say it is probably the most entrenched social problem we face in America today. "Worse in the church" many say, so captive to its own culture[103] that little has changed in this regard. H. Richard Niebuhr made this stinging indictment in 1954, still so true today: "The color line has been drawn so incisively by the church itself that its proclamation of the gospel of the brotherhood of Jew and Greek, of bond and free, of white and black has sometimes the sad sound of irony, and sometimes falls upon the ear as unconscious hypocrisy – but sometimes there is in it the bitter cry of repentance."[104]

If you are of color or live in an ethnic community and do ministry there, you trip over our racialized society everyday. It is unavoidable. We must be determined to face it and talk about it, and work to dislodge its hold, in our own ministries, communities and churches. We must have a response, and not be afraid of its prophetic message. Racial reconciliation should be a labor of the church, locally and globally. Michael Emerson and Christian Smith in *Divided by Faith*[105] have provided us an intelligent look at this problem. They use responsible sociological theory and research to categorically argue the perpetuation of the racialization of America (exclusively studying black/white relations) and the role religion plays in this, primarily white evangelicalism. They explore "...the ways in which culture, values, norms and organizational features that are quintessentially evangelical and quintessentially American, despite having many positive qualities, paradoxically have negative effects on race relations."[106]   This study has the courage to look perceptively at the enigma of desire on the part of white evangelicals to transform the wrongs of the larger culture (injustice, inequality, racial discrimination) while actually continuing to be one of the major places that allow these systemic practices to remain entrenched.

According to Emerson and Smith, evangelicals have limited "religio-cultural tools" in their toolkit. And the tools they do have[107] prevent the acquiring of a broader theology that would override their built in cultural bias. Though they desire a color-blind society, instead "evangelicalism's cultural tools lead people in different social and geographical realities to assess the race problem in divergent and non reconciliatory ways. This large gulf in understanding is perhaps part of the race problem's core, and most certainly contributes to the entrenchment of the racialized society."[108]   Jeremy Wood and his wife, Jessica, came to Neighborhood from white, middle class backgrounds, and would agree with Susan that reconciliation is a hard topic to address for many reasons. "It's not enough to have ethnic friends; it's bigger than that," says Jeremy. He goes on to say,

> *Though we live in a new multi-blended society, we still get strange looks when we are out with our Hispanic daughter. There are boxes people expect things to be in. It is good to have the word <u>work</u> inside this core value. It's easy to say I am about the idea vs. the work of reconciliation, especially being white. White evangelicals can be blind to reconciliation. They have moved into power [politics], and the assumption is that power works for them. It is hard to see since it works for you, it should work for others.*

THE HARD WORK OF RELATIONSHIPS

Racially isolated people cannot *see* what injustices others face every day. How to help racially isolated people see the problem is the crux. Most people will start to see if they know someone with the problem. Relationship building is the hard work of reconciliation. When people live alongside friends and neighbors who suffer the consequences of a racialized society, the suffering of their friends changes them. They can no longer ignore it.

Isiah Oaks is one of our board members and has been a volunteer for going on two decades. As an African American, crossing racial divides has been his personal story for his nearly sixty-five years. He crossed a different racial divide when he joined us, the cultural and language gulf between African American and Latino. Building friendships here "you learn that people are all the same."

While at the same time, these relationships have brought the pain of the Latino community to his attention, and in his opinion, to the attention of other African American community leaders. In his opinion God has used Neighborhood Ministries to bridge the black and Hispanic community creating an opportunity for leaders to see the civil rights issues of our day which reside in the Hispanic community.

Relationships potentially open the conversation up to deep levels. But it must be remembered that "the collective wounds over race run deep. They need to be healed. And for healing to take place, there will have to be forgiveness. But before there is healing, different racial groups of Americans will also have to stop injuring one another."[109] There are vast inequalities, memories of oppression, segregation, unequal education in neighborhood schools, "and immense divisions between social networks, cultures, and religions that contribute to the rawness of these wounds."[110]

Jurgen Moltmann in *God for a Secular Society* reminds us that superficial relationships won't break down the racial divide. "Knowledge and community are mutually related. In order to arrive at community with one another we have to know one another, and in order to know one another we have to come closer to one another, make contact with another, and form [deep and lasting] relationships."[111]

RECONCILIATION AND HEALING FOR MYSELF

Brenda Salter McNeil in *The Heart for Racial Justice,*[112] teaches that this knowing of each other starts with knowing ourselves. We must understand biblically and embrace personally our God-intended identities, and with determination abandon destructive ethnic identities that have carried negative messages about us and others.

Ian shares vulnerably about this part of his reconciliation journey as a white kid raised in a Hispanic neighborhood. "No one was harder on me in life than youth in this neighborhood. To come back to work with the youth in this neighborhood, first for a couple of years as a volunteer, and now as the Youth Pastor, trying to get them to accept me, and for me to accept them, there is reconciliation going on there. The values that are developing in me, as I embrace the stigmas of my story, my culture, my race and then lead out of those stigmas, make me more attractive and allow us all to move past those stigmas."

Malissa shares her own personal story of healing and reconciliation:

> *On this core value, the work of reconciliation, I think if I would have been born in the barrio of Phoenix, I could have been one of the kids in the ministry. I found NM in my twenties. At that time I had been abandoned and neglected by my mom, living from home to home, homeless, foster homes, though not formally in the system. I came to Christ in the conservative church. The people and culture didn't match my own story. At Neighborhood I noticed the God I knew existed, the preferential God. I saw my upbringing. At that time I didn't have a relationship with my mom. When I would see her or she would try and contact me, in the beginning it was really uncomfortable. I knew God, and I knew that this relationship was unresolved. At NM, God loved the kind of person my mom was. I could love her through them from a distance. People didn't judge her; they affirmed the gifts she did have. But my own story of neglect and abandonment left me with pain and confusion. NM was able to love her, and me, by not pressuring me, allowing me to find a healing process of my own. By walking alongside my mom for her own healing and reconciliation, she began to come to church, though she had to drive from*

a hundred miles away. She drove a bus during Kids Club and helped with Mom's Place. I remember when Panda told me "your mom is so great". I couldn't believe it. That was a moment of reconciliation for me, when I realized my mom is loveable. It reconciled me to my mom. Today, she has an opportunity to be a grandmother to my kids and in some small way, a mother to me again. On that personal level, that story repeats itself over and over, a community of care and reconciliation; it doesn't have to be figured out, it is a real process ... God redeeming broken relationships.

USING YOUR GOD-GIVEN IMAGINATION

Walter Brueggemann in his influential work *The Prophetic Imagination*[113] suggests we can nurture an alternative consciousness to the dominant cultural influences through God's Spirit and God's vision driven by his Word. This idea of nourishing a prophetic imagination (an alternative perception from the dominant culture around us) toward reconciliation is profound and needed.

We must use our imagination, to see what it would look like to take someone else's part which is critical to reconciliation. Panda doesn't even know she is using her imagination when she chooses to be a reconciler. She takes the other person's part by imagining herself in them. She was used by God recently to bring two families together:

Well, in the beginning of our pre-school, there were two families that were struggling, and their children weren't allowed to go to school together. One of the kids was already here, and the other wanted to come but couldn't. I was the middle person, when one person was there I would talk to them, when the other came around, I would talk to them. Some way, some how, things got resolved, and both kids came to school. I said, 'we have got to all get along, we have to work together for our kids sake, let the past be the past, whatever happened, just think about the kids. I saw big reconciliation there, in the end, they made up and both kids got to be benefitted, got to come to school. Even the other teachers said it isn't possible, but I was thinking in my head, 'no we have to give every kid a chance'. We can't turn kids away. I think what made me understand that more, is because I was a parent here and my kids got to go to school here.

For Sarah, her imagination toward reconciliation comes from her own story as well, but was ignited in this neighborhood. She shares that

"... a lot of reconciliation has been happening with me, with all of humanity, especially when I think about the streets, pain, loss or atrocity. My deep connection with their pain comes from my own personal loss, especially with communities encountering these things. This reconciles me with them. Its like, my own story of loss, keeps on building, building more connections with others, with their own unique stories of loss. Though it can make me feel like I have to grieve over again, I still receive it as a reconciliation, as funny as that might sound."

Howard Thurman, the great Civil Rights theologian, spent a life-time considering how white and black communities could come together. He believed that God's love crosses all boundaries and an increased understanding of the other person can be arrived at by a disciplined use of the imagination.

We are accustomed to thinking of imagination as a useful

tool in the hands of the artist as he reproduces in varied forms what he sees beyond the rim of fact that circles him round. We recognize and applaud the bold, audacious leap of the mind of the scientist when it soars far out beyond what is know to fix a beachhead on distant, unexplored shores. But the imagination shows its greatest powers as the *angelos* of God in the miracle it creates when one man, standing on his own ground, is able while there to put himself in another man's place.[114]

THE HARD WORK OF THE CHURCH

Though this is all necessary, Christians must move past individual relationships and take on reconciliation corporately. We can call this the hard work of the church. Churches and church bodies must begin with Scripture to direct and navigate the conversation about decisions and actions toward reconciliation. The biblical word "reconciliation" though abused in some historical situations still carries the weight of the demands of Scripture. The radical claims in the Bible can be used by anyone, and therefore the challenge to "be reconciled" is for everyone. Marva Dawn directs us to see that our worship, along side the calculated use of the Scriptures function to do battle against the principalities and powers that are inside our broken unreconciled relationships:

> Christian worship involves many dimensions of the community's work in relation to the powers. Ideally, the sermon should name them and demonstrate their perversions. The offering attacks the power of money. The intercessory prayers remind us of our task to be agents of God's reconciliation and commit us to live out our faith in Christ's victory over the powers. The sacraments of baptism and the Eucharist give signs and seals that we partic-

ipate in the triumph of Christ so that the powers have no ultimate control over us. Karl Barth calls this the 'priestly function of the Church'"[115]

Curtiss De Young, a reconciliation partner, says there is hope, there is always hope, that the work of reconciliation is possible. "Reconciliation is 'our role in God's script' for the twenty-first century. When people of faith come together in relationship and common purpose for peace, they can inspire people of faith at all levels to build communities of peace."[116]

THE HARD WORK OF THE WORLD

Reconciliation is the hard work of the world. Miroslav Volf, in *Exclusion and Embrace,* argues for justice between cultures, which moves the work of reconciliation into the sphere of social change and systemic engagement. As a philosopher/theologian, it is no easy task imagining how warring cultures agree on what would bring justice and reconciliation to conflict which in some cases is ages old. Jeremy has led the way in our mission to bring in theological and sociological texts that look at the structural injustices that lopsidedly oppress poor ethnic communities; problems with the prison system, the courts, public education. He says, "Through friends you can see the deficits, but friendships won't make you do the work. Our commitment to justice for these friends is what will make us do the work of exposing, opposing and changing unjust systems that oppress."

'Anything short of love cannot be perfect justice', wrote Reinhold Niebuhr.[117] In a world of evil, however, we cannot dispense with an imperfect and therefore essentially unjust justice. The imperfect justice is the kind of necessary injustice with which people cannot be protected from violent incursions into their proper space. The weak, above all, need such protection. Unjust justice is therefore indispensable for satisfying the demands of love in an unjust world. It must be pursued relentlessly, above all for the sake of the oppressed. But this pursuit of justice must be situated in the context of love. Gustavo Gutierrez has argued in On Job that 'the gratuitousness of God's love is the framework within which the requirement of practicing justice is to be located.'[118]

Jorge's sense in all of this talk about reconciliation is that it must spill over into our all our loyalties. "As Hispanics we work for reconciliation with people from other Latin countries. For me, the hard work is with people from South America and Central America, though it is a little easier there. In this case, reconciliation looks like respect. Respect the culture, especially the culture. Be open, come with an open heart. Respect is critical too," he says "as Baptists and Pentecostals argue over how they do ministry. For me, it is always about respect, respecting both of them."

GRACE RULES – JESUS and OUR NEW IDENTITY

A grace rule is the way grace rules. This rule describes a lavish gift from God as experienced in our community. By receiving it, grace rules – leading us further into love and action.

Jesus' gift of a new identity allows us to participate as reconcilers in a world of enmity and dividing walls. Reconciliation is a problem for us when we don't know who we are, crippled by self-hate, stereotypes, victim mentality, shame, guilt and false sense of superiority. These negative self perceptions rip us off, robbing us of who God says we are in Christ. Brenda Salter McNeil sees this identity problem as pivotal to being able to do the *work of reconciliation*: "self acceptance is a great human and Christian virtue. It is the recognition that you are created in the image of God and that you are ultimately good. You have intrinsic worth because God made you. Further, God gave you and your people – your ethnic group – the gifts and capacities to create a culture that brings glory to God."[119] We hear our new identity in this Bible passage:

> in reference to your former manner of life, you lay aside the old self ... and be renewed in the spirit of your mind, and put on the new self, which in the likeness of God has been created in righteousness and holiness (Eph 4:22-24).

Marcos has become a reconciler, where once he had enemies, today he looks for peace. This desire to bring reconciliation comes from a new identity he has chosen to live within: *When I was younger, I believed what a lot of people think:*

"poor me, I have been dealt a bad hand, if there was a God why would he allow all these bad things to happen in my life." I made a terrible mistake, the good I had done, couldn't override the bad. I blamed others while I was in prison. The Lord didn't put me in prison, I had to accept responsibility for the decisions I made, something I have learned in the last couple of years. Even when I feel distant from the Lord, for whatever reason, it is me that is going astray. In the bottom of my heart, he is always there in the presence of something working in the sidelines, he is doing something. I have learned to trust the Lord. With people in general, I have learned patience. Taking time to spend with myself, and with prayer, I can assess situations better, and with mediation with a friend, who is more mature spiritually, I can make peace with the situation and I can make good with anyone.

Jesus taught a story about a son who asked for his inheritance early, left home and squandered it all on loose living, landing in a pig pen. If occurred to him to crawl back home, in all his shame, and ask his father to forgive him and install him as a servant for the rest of his life. Instead, the Father was waiting every day for the son who was "lost" and "dead" to come home. And when he did, the Father ran to him, embraced him and gave him back his identity as son.

We are able to be reconcilers, because we are fully loved, fully accepted, fully known and fully received as the Father's beloved. We accept and receive our culture, our story and our ethnicity as gifts from God. We replace the old self-understanding that pits us in competition or opposition with others with the new self which is purposed toward love, peace and unity.

NOTES

101. Quote from John Climacus, *The Ladder of Divine Ascent*, Kathleen Norris, *Amazing Grace, Vocabulary of Faith*, (New York: Riverhead Books, 1998), 69.

102. Michael Emerson and Christian Smith, *Divided by Faith*, (New York: Oxford University Press, 2000), 9. Emerson and Smith define "racialization" – "It understands that racial practices that reproduce racial division in the contemporary United States, 1. Are increasingly covert, 2.are embedded in normal operations of institutions, 3. Avoid direct racial terminology, and 4.are invisible to most Whites."

103. Miroslav Volf, from Exclusion and Embrace, 36: "The slide into complicity with what is evil in our culture would not be nearly as easy if the cultures did not so profoundly shape us. In a significant sense we are our cultures and we find it therefore difficult to distance ourselves from the culture we inhabit in order to evaluate its various elements. The difficulty, however, makes the distancing from our own culture in the name of God of all cultures so much more urgent. The judgments we pass need not be always negative, of course. As I have argued elsewhere, there is not single correct way to relate to a given culture as a whole; there are only various ways of accepting, transforming, rejecting or replacing various aspects of a given culture from within. (Volf 1995, 371ff.; Volf 1996, 101).

104. H. Richard Niebuhr, *The Social Sources of Denominationalism*, (Hamden: The Shoe String Press, 1954), 263.

105. Michael O. Emerson and Christian Smith, *Divided by Faith*, (Oxford: University Press, 2000).

106. Ibid., ix.

107. The authors contribute a great deal to our understanding of the inability of evangelicals to deal with structural evil and sin by assessing these tools: "Accountable free will individualism", "relationalism" (attaching central importance to interpersonal relationships), "anti-structuralism (inability to perceive or unwillingness to accept social structural influences.)," 76.

108. Ibid., 91.

109. Ibid. 171.

110. Ibid.

111. Jurgen Moltmann, *God for a Secular Society*, 135.

112. Brenda Salter McNeil, *The Heart for Racial Justice*, (Downers Grove: InterVarsity, 2004), 57.

113. Walter Brueggemann, *The Prophetic Imagination,* (Philadelphia: Fortress Press, 1978).

114. Walter Earl Fluker and Catherine Tumber, Editors. *A Strange Freedom, The Best of Howard Thurman on Religious Experience and Public Life,* (Boston: Beacon Press, 1998), 183.

115. Marva Dawn, *Powers, Weakness and the Tabernacle of God*, (Grand Rapids: Eerdmans, 2001), 134-5.

116. Curtiss Paul DeYoung, *Living Faith, How Faith Inspires Social Justice*, (Minneapolis: Fortress Press, 2007), 151.
117. Reinhold Niebuhr, "Christian Faith and Natural Law," *In Love and Justice.* Selection from the Shorter Writings of Reinhold Niebuhr, edited by D.B. Robertson, 46-54. (Cleveland: The World Publishing Company, 1967), 50.
118. Gustavo Gutierrez, *On Job: God-Talk and the Suffering of the Innocent.* Translated by Matthew J. O'Connell. (Maryknoll: Orbis, 1987), 89.
119. Brenda Salter McNeil, 77.

"Jireh"
Hope Thru Art

CHAPTER FOUR

We are Called to
HOLISTIC MINISTRY

Core Value #3

Definition: As Jesus did, we address the needs of the whole person, spiritual, physical, emotional, economic, psychological, educational and relational. Our programs and our church live out this focus with children, youth and adults, birth to grave and multi-generational.

"Sometimes I would like to ask God why He allows poverty,
suffering, and injustice when He could do something about it."
"Well, why don't you ask Him?"
"Because I'm afraid He would ask me the same question."
– Anonymous

Thirty years ago, when we began our outreach to the poor community that surrounded our church, it was a big deal to "preach the gospel holistically". In 1982 evangelical churches borrowed more from their fundamentalist theological legacy than their neo-evangelical reformers, at least ours did. Our first effort to serve the community was through a food and clothing bank. Our church building was on a walking path for many homeless and inside a neighborhood infamous for its poverty and decline. When we submitted our request to the elders of our church for this initiative, our pastor let me know that he had an "aha" moment as he was digesting this new concept. Holistic ministry was unfamiliar to him and so this "aha" had to do with trying to figure out *why* we would feed people. He told me that we must be feeding people as an evangelistic technique. "So, food is like the bait," he said. He couldn't imagine that we should care about hunger and do something practical simply as a way to love and serve our neighbors. His confusion stumped me. I had no answer to this; it would take me a few more years to find the words. As you can see by the developed ideas inside this core value, we have found words that describe why we do holistic ministry. Susan speaks for us:

> We do holistic ministry because we are whole persons; God created us as whole people; he cares about how many hairs are on our head. He deeply, deeply cares about all aspects of our lives. Why would we not do so the same with each other?

WHAT IS HOLISTIC MINISTRY?

I was twenty when I first heard the message of the scriptures regarding God's heart for the poor. In the young evangelical world of the early 1970s, theologians and urban missiologists were instructing us on a whole gospel, challenging us to learn that the Bible asks us to meet the needs of the whole person in Jesus' name. Many Christian leaders, associations and denominations, covenants and convocations[120] have since then drafted statements regarding the nature of a whole gospel message, a holistic view of people, a holistic view of time and even a holistic state of mind on the part of the practitioner. This theological work pushed the pendulum to swing back to a time when good deeds weren't separated from the good message, a message that is also whole.

> We have to keep the whole story in mind and avoid the temptation to reduce it to the gospel story only. The biblical narrative is a whole story that spans creation, the call of Israel, the exile, Jesus and his death and resurrection, the church, and the end of history with the second coming. The biblical narrative is a story of a seamlessly related world of material and spiritual, of persons and social systems. If we truncate this story, we rob it of much of its life and meaning. The full story of Jesus begins at creation and ends with his second coming.[121]

Isiah comes from a church tradition that is still operating with a gospel message that is focused only on the spiritual life of a person.

> *God gave this vision [to NM] of holistic ministry, which is more than preaching the gospel in salvation words. When people come to a saving relationship with Christ and don't have homes, with lots of social problems ... over the course of time, over the years, God has taught Neighborhood that you can't walk away. You can't pretend you didn't see or hear this.*

Holism is the idea that the parts are understood in relationship to the whole. To see something holistically is to see both its whole and the interdependence of its parts. Christian ministry is intended to be holistic – seeking to bring healing and restoration to every area of brokenness in the community. Jesus' ministry while on earth was whole, preaching, teaching and healing (Mt 4:23). Jesus was continually moved to compassion as He encountered the lame, the sick, the widow, and the orphan. As Jorge says:

> *The Scriptures show us Jesus among people. Now when they were hungry, as Jesus was ministering to the crowd, he fed them – a person was sick for years, and he healed him. He did good deeds, healings, helping people holistically. Jesus saw their whole needs, and took care of them. His was a holistic ministry.*

THE COMPASSION OF GOD

Jesus is described in the book of Isaiah as "a man of sorrows ... acquainted with grief" (Isa 53:3). Could it be that Bob Pierce, the founder of World Vision, got it right when he prayed, "Lord, let my heart be broken by the things that break YOUR heart,"?[122]

How is it that our holistic ministry expression is defined by the Lord's own broken heart for the suffering in our communities, and his desired response to those things? Jeremy responds to this question this way:

> *Maslow's hierarchy of needs would say, 'when people are starving its hard to have a real conversation about where they are at in life'. But as a Christian, we should care about whether or not someone is hungry, that is the conversation! When Jesus says, "I was hungry and you didn't feed me" this is mystery in which God works – not Maslow's hierarchy of needs (although there is some sense to this as all humans need to eat) – that is the gospel, there isn't a bottom level in order to get to the top level. An understanding of the mystery is this, when you feed someone and they're hungry, they believe that God is providing, they see this as coming from God.*

St. Teresa is well know for this poem which directly connects us to the compassion of God:

Christ has no body on earth but yours,

No hands but yours,

No feet but yours.

Yours are the eyes through which

Christ's compassion for the world is to look out;

Yours are the feet with which He is to go about doing good;

And yours are the hands with which He is to bless us now.

– St. Teresa of Avila[123]

A THEOLOGICAL JOURNEY FOR EVANGELICALS

As mentioned earlier, coming from an evangelical tradition when we did, our story of holistic ministry captures a time when evangelicals were just emerging from a period of fifty years where a holistic gospel was uncomfortable language and a challenging theology. Our ministry was "out there" so to speak and we were attempting to learn not just how to do holistic work, but how to speak about it theologically. We found like minded Christians who had established theological foundations for a generation of evangelicals in this regard. Ron Sider, a well known writer and practitioner was one. His book *Good News and Good Works*,[124] a "full blown biblical theology that affirms both personal and social sin, both personal conversion and structural change, both evangelism and social action, both personal and social salvation, orthodox theology and ethical obedience,"[125] a theology for the whole gospel.

Sider begins his treatise at the great fundamentalist/modernist controversy to establish the backstory for the reasons we bring the two parts back together again (this is his signature contribution to the discussion for 40 years). Sider helps the reader grasp a biblical concept of "the kingdom of God". It is the kingdom foreshadowed by the law, the calling of a chosen nation and one anticipated by the prophets. Jesus would fulfill all the law and the prophets in word and deed, and the kingdom would be viewed for the first time as both present and future.

And its ethics and its power would be lived out inside a forgiven and forgiving community. This "disturbing kingdom community" as Sider calls it would live out a radical understanding of followership convinced that the gospel is not just forgiveness of sins, but is filled with an understanding of a whole gospel that is good news to the poor. How do we understand this rendering here in the ministry? Malissa explains:

> *Holistic ministry is modeled after how Christ came to earth, he walked alongside people in all of the whole ways people live and are created. It is important that the church cares about the whole person. When we don't have a sense of*

continuity of care, we isolate parts of our lives, and they become barriers or obstacles. It becomes a defect when we don't know what it means to be whole. Here are ways I see holistic ministry through NM images:

- *Many people who live in our neighborhood have never left the city – we take kids and sometimes their parents from our ministry up to Mt. Meadows, to see stars and pine trees for the first time. Imagine taking a teenager to go on a trip to the ocean for the first time, the doors that simple activity opens.*
- *A whole person needs to be educated, and education alone gives a person a much bigger worldview and a host of opportunities to grow.*
- *A whole person needs health care.*
- *Young people who struggle with homelessness need housing.*
- *Neighborhood welcomes the parents of our kids to become leaders on Monday nights; whole people have a need to be treated with dignity and to contribute.*
- *At Neighborhood we recognize the felt needs that people have and we are doing the best we can to provide for those felt needs. We go beyond the space of survival, opening up people to something they never would have had – that is wholistic, to open up the world. Now they have seen the stars! When whole people in survival meet their needs in isolation there is often a temptation to give up and never dream again. NM provides an alternative. Holistic ministry provides the gift and joy of dreaming again.*

WHAT HOLISTIC MINISTRY COMMUNICATES TO A COMMUNITY IN SEARCH FOR GOD

There is a need for models of incarnational kingdom mission everywhere, which is what Sider is appealing for. We have found that holistic ministry is a critical way in which disaffected people can see and feel and hear the love of Jesus for the broken places in our world. It is one of the best ways to do evangelism today. "Kindness has converted more sinners than zeal, eloquence, or learning."[126] Panda believes this. She says, "we start with those things [meeting felt needs] to show people the love of God; it shows them what He is really like. I think that when we serve this way we represent God and people can see God through all the work." Jeremy agrees.

> Holistic ministry provides lots of access points in how our faith is developed and where we find hope. It's a touch from God by getting a job, or understanding our value when we get an education, sometimes we meet God through mental health care. God meets us in lots of different places, why shouldn't the church do the same. There are lots of different ways to access God, why shouldn't the church believe that way and act that way?

One way to look at holistic ministry is that we become partners with God in the work of the kingdom, going about the Master's business, carrying the good news through our word and deeds. N.T. Wright in *Surprised by Hope*, takes a stab at describing what it might look like when Christ returns, as he surveys the work of his body that was done in His name:

> But what we can and must do in the present, if we are obedient to the gospel, if we are following Jesus, and if we are

indwelt, energized, and directed by the Spirit, is to build for the kingdom. This brings us back to 1 Corinthians 15:58 once more: what you do in the Lord is not in vain. You are not oiling the wheels of a machine that's about to roll over a cliff. You are not restoring a great painting that's shortly going to be thrown on the fire. You are not planting roses in a garden that's about to be dug up for a building site. You are – strange through it may seem, almost as hard to believe as the resurrection itself – accomplishing something that will become in due course part of God's new world. Every act of love, gratitude, and kindness; every work of art or music inspired by the love of God and delight in the beauty of his creation; every minute spent teaching a severely handicapped child to read or to walk; every act of care and nurture, of comfort and support, for one's fellow human beings and for that matter one's fellow nonhuman creatures; and of course every prayer, all Spirit-led teaching, every deed that spreads the gospel, builds the church, embraces and embodies holiness rather than corruption, and makes the name of Jesus honored in the world – all of this will find its way, through the resurrecting power of God, into the new creation that God will one day make. That is the logic of the mission of God.[127]

What does holistic ministry communicate to people looking for God? Speaking from the community's point of view, Alex and Francisco say it says:

> We care. We care for the future of the children, to help kids stay out of trouble, to give them a better perspective of life. We care for the future of our people, the next generations, we care that the community gets better. We care about work

and helping people find jobs. We want them to come when-
ever they are feeling bad. We're a helping hand. God helps
us love each other and care about each other and we help
God by keeping the love growing and growing.

A NATURAL MINISTRY PROGRESSION

Holistic ministry, by its very nature, is progressive. Once practical felt needs are met, there is an increased awareness of the bigger picture, and that opens the ministry up to a new horizon. We have matured in our understanding of the ways in which holistic ministry is done, what works and doesn't work, and how to measure a successful effort in serving our neighbors. We have also matured in recognizing that relationship centered holistic ministry targets a certain kind of transformation, while broader efforts bring systemic transformation. The diagram below describes the progression and the layers of holistic ministry that have developed over time here at Neighborhood. One thing to note: Progression doesn't mean leaving one for the other. It does mean two other things, however. As we moved from one stage to the next we were learning. Sometimes we stopped doing things from the previous season. It also means that we were combining strategies. A new season opened up ways in which the previous one could be done better. (These following short descriptions condense 30 years of holistic ministry learning into sentences. For a more detailed look at the story of our mission's development, see *The Relentless Pursuit, Stories of God's Hope, Love and Grace in the Neighborhood,* by Amy Sherman)

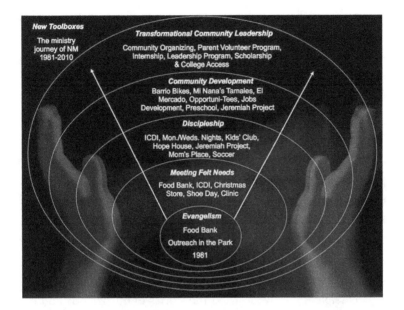

Evangelism – Our ministry started on the heals of an evangelistic revival called *The Jesus Movement*. Many of us, including the leaders in our church, were formed during this time. As recipients of this formation, it seemed very natural for us to begin a relationship with our community first as evangelists. There was eventual tension between caring for someone by meeting a real, tangible need and feeling obligated *every encounter* to share the gospel message. This was especially true if the "witness" was careless about loving the receiver of the food or other physical help. The gospel message in those cases sounded judgmental and the intention to share it, legalistic. These early lessons were critical, and helped develop more natural ways to both love our neighbors and verbally share Christ. We were learning that what we both wanted, evangelist and potential convert was really a true friendship. This learning helped us grow new expressions of the work.

Meeting Felt Needs – Still handicapped by a religious culture that preferred spiritual activity over addressing the needs of whole people, we strained to hear how our friends "needed" us and what our response might be to the chronic problems in the community. Though we still wanted people to come to a saving knowledge of Jesus, we were running into all the obstacles they practically faced and the loss of hope it created: the systems that labeled them ("You will be a drop-out."); the destinies they claimed ("I will go to prison."); the identities that determined their futures ("You will be a gang member or you will be a teen mom."). The ministry's growth was therefore around the felt needs of the community; life enriching programs for kids and youth; back to school shoes and Christmas presents; Bible studies for adults in Spanish and eventual worship services; a medical clinic for many underserved; and the early stages of educational programs, targeting kids who came families where older siblings had dropped out of school.

Discipleship – we learned the stories of our friends and entered into their lives, we discovered that the depth of these friendships was changing the direction within which we served. It is painful to admit today that we carried a positional arrangement with our friends. We were the church people who gave ministry, and they were the community who received. These friendships were changing us. As a result, our programs took on a depth that would look at someone's life journey in a more whole way. We felt good about calling this kind of programming *discipleship* as we learned that we were all growing up in Christ holistically, not just our friends. Young teen moms were learning parenting skills; kids and youth were getting good resources to stay in school and develop peer relationships that changed the trajectory of future thinking; college readiness was on the map; job skills training, mental health resources and relationship curriculums started filling tool boxes with life skills that would keep people in the game of life.

People need real resources to take their lives back, things that are definite rungs on a ladder of progress, things that work. As an organization we were maturing by realizing that very particular resources when offered in the context of trusted relationships really do make a difference. Patterns and models were being created in some of our programs that were tested, recreated, discontinued, reformed, studied and measured. We used the term "best practice" to describe what we were looking for, functional programs that worked. By this time, whole clans had been influenced through Neighborhood, and as a result negative, debilitating messages inside whole families were changing. Our community had a different perception about itself.

Community Development – Though we were, in many ways, still primarily relationship oriented in terms of looking at impact, we recognized that pieces inside the community had to experience more large scale efforts for a more widespread message of hope to capture the community we love. We thought and studied the problems of gentrification; we recognized that our zip code had the most CPS calls in the state and one of the worst employment statistics. There was little to no affordable rentals in our neighborhood and we had more than our fair share of absentee landlords. The very presence of our campus in this neighborhood suggested that the physical community itself was one of our community transforming objectives and the ministry elements confirmed it. Our pre-school sent a message to our friends that we were putting our money where our mouth was and investing in a way for change to happen systemically in lives and families through the role that early childhood classrooms play. We opened up a bike shop, with specific ways in which youth can learn to build and take care of their own bikes, a common form of transportation in our community. We went from job skills development to creating a position for a jobs developer to help people get employment and then opened up some businesses of our own, for internal sustainability as well as job creation. The economic landscape of our community mattered and we were trying to do something about it. Meanwhile, we entertained the possibility of engaging in the conversation of affordable housing.

Transformational Community Leadership – The next and maybe final phase of movement inside holistic programs, is a move from holism into social justice and transformational community leadership. Moving to this stage was also very intentional and in some ways had begun a decade or so earlier when we finally put our foot down and said "no more free stuff". Recognizing that dignity robbing hand-outs were not only dependency laden but really didn't tell our friends clearly the message of God's love or ours, we initiated what we called at the time "the big new idea". Sadly, it should have been an idea we had from day one. It began with what we called "giving Christmas back to the parents". After years of free hand-outs of all kinds of things and years where we spent weeks during the holidays with Christmas present delivery, we stopped being one of the charities in town that distributed free Christmas. We began the Parent Volunteer Program that exchanges parent's work hours at The Neighborhood Center for an in- house paycheck that today can be redeemed for items in our mercado, NM's thrift store. That has led to other approaches that empower the community members to see themselves as the change agents, building access to power and introducing leveragable opportunities. This progression is further described in the core values of Justice and Leadership Development.

THE EIGHT DEPARTMENTS AND OTHER HOLISTIC EXPRESSIONS OF NEIGHBORHOOD MINISTRIES

The direct activity of these holistic expressions is described below and fills out how holistic ministry looks today at Neighborhood. I will give a brief description of the department or expression and then mention how it ministers in both word and deed the gospel of good news to our community.

Kids Outreach (*Kids Life; Kids Club; Kids Camp*) – All year long kids from the ages of 5-13 participate in a weekly program of Bible lessons, learning activities (sports, arts and crafts, industrial arts projects, dance and other life enlarging opportunities). The summer version of this school year program includes field trips, swimming, a BIG carnival and a whole day at a local lake. For the older kids who have been integral throughout the year, a week up in the mountains at summer camp is included. This outreach program is where the kids in our ministry first hear about a relationship with Jesus and what it looks like to be a Christ follower for the rest of their lives. It is also the program where relationships with kids and leaders begin, and where whole families get involved in participation and service.

Youth Outreach (*Youth Group, Leadership Development*) – As with the kids outreach, the youth outreach, ages 13-20, happens all year long as well. The weekly gathering has an additional focus on youth leadership development which has a good attendance. The curriculums for this leadership development are sophisticated and bent toward community organizing and youth empowerment. Participants vie for summer internship positions earmarked for this age group. When the new classroom building is finished, the youth will have an entire floor dedicated as a youth drop-in center, with computer lab, college access department, leadership and discipleship classroom, hang-out space and tutoring rooms.

Ian Danley, Youth Pastor, reminds us,

"Young people in distressed communities are often the people God has a tendency to choose as his agents of change in the neighborhood. As in so much of scripture, God chooses the unlikely ones

to be transformative leaders rather than those who meet the world's criteria. Leadership development is the heartbeat of Christian Community Development as it seeks to restore justice to our broken world using those on the margins as the restorers."

Education Department – (*Katy's Kids; Mentoring; College Access; WKD Scholarship*) – The determining factor of whether or not a child grows to have a different future than their family histories is by staying in school and completing post high school education of some sort, i.e. college or career skills training. We have learned key principles in this regard. The first has to do with early childhood education. Zero to five education focused programs change the futures of children in marginalized communities. There is significant research supporting this. As a result, we are building an early childhood wing inside a newly renovated education building. The second has to do with mentoring. Many of the children in key NM families are matched with one-one mentors, some of who stay matched with their kids for a number of years. Again, research shows that an additional caring adult invested in a child's life is more apt to help that child stay in school, as compared to after school tutoring or other more impersonal help. During and post high school, our education department offers a range of college access services, from college tours, filling out FAFSA's and support help when college gets tough. DREAM Act students (undocumented) can apply for an in-house college scholarship. These students would not be able to attend college without this. The cycle of poverty is being broken in countless households because of these education programs and love of God is exchanged in all relationships involved, from teachers and mentors, to tutors and advisors.

Teen Mom Mentoring and Parenting Support (*Moms' Place*) – Moms' Place is a weekly program where teen moms inside the

Neighborhood Ministries family receive resources to help them successfully parent their children. Many of these young women begin their parenting while still children themselves, and with the resources and mentoring which Moms' Place provides, can move forward into becoming good mothers, despite their early entrance into parenting.

Susan Leon, Director of Moms' Place, captures their heart for young moms with this Bible verse,

"Because we loved you so much, we were delighted to share with you not only the gospel of God but our lives as well." 1 Thessalonians 2:8

Skills Development Workshop/Metal, Wood and Bikes (*Barrio Workshop; Barrio Bike Shop*) – This workshop provides access to important training in the use of metal and wood tools and guidance in projects for our young people during program nights. During the week the bike shop is open for business, offering high end training in bike repair and bicycle building. Incentivized, kids earn points for working on a bike during bike shop hours, which can earn them their own bike. Young people in our ministry find their skill set niche using their hands, their creativity and develop know-how creating a growing sense of empowerment and potential entrepreneurship.

Chris Williams, Barrio Works Director, likes to teach that:

In the book of Exodus, God poured out His Spirit on artisans and craftsmen, filling them with skill, ability, and knowledge of workmanship to build the tabernacle - the center of worship for a newly liberated people. In the same vein, Barrio Works seeks to learn, practice and teach skills and be filled with ability. We want to encourage creativity, provide access to the resources required to act on it, and take

*part in creating a community center where, once again, a
newly liberated people worships God together.*

**Residential Home for Young Women and Community
Garden** (*Hope House; Hope House Farms*) – We have learned that
a chaotic, traumatic childhood often results in a semi-homeless
teenager and young adult. Hope House was established for young
women (and on occasion their children) in our ministry who have
periodic seasons of unstable living and who desire those patterns
to change. The home not only provides a stable and supportive
living environment, but cultivates habits of living with others in
peace and co-dependency (the good kind). The house is settled in
the neighborhood and so offers one more way of retelling the story
that living in the community can be a positive experience. Hope
House's property is also a rich and lush garden space with over 100
fruit trees, a prolific vegetable garden and contains play space and
a swimming pool for children and the direct community.

Here is how Johnny and Stephanie Garippa, Hope House Directors, describe it:

> *At Hope House, we seek to love and guide our young
> women, many of whom have suffered severe instability and/
> or trauma from early childhood, into the maturity of adult-
> hood with all its responsibilities and possibilities; as Jesus
> became our Good Shepherd and called God the Father of us
> all, so we at Hope House seek to incarnate His love through
> the role of shepherd and good parent, leading the women
> in our care and home to streams of living water spiritually,
> emotionally, physically, and vocationally.*
>
> *Jesus ate, and when people were hungry he shared food
> with them. He called the splendor of Solomon drab in com-
> parison with the beauty and simplicity of the sparrows. He*

spoke in parables of planting seed and reaping its harvest. Many of his references to creation make sense to parents who grew up rurally but are lost on our hyper-urban kids who are growing up playing on concrete and video gaming systems, eating processed convenience store foods, and not knowing that eggs come from chickens or peaches from trees. At Hope House Farms, we live a lifestyle of farming and celebrate food creation as we seek to re-engage our community in the ability to appreciate and cultivate beauty from the earth. We seek to supply our community – which has no decent grocery stores within walking distance – with fresh, organic, and affordable produce at our soon-to-be on-site farm stand. And we recognize that to love our neighbors as ourselves, we must advocate for food and land justice, because "no matter how urban our life, our bodies live by farming; we come from the earth and return to it, and so we live in agriculture as we live in flesh (Wendell Berry)."

Workforce Development *(Neighbors at Work)* – Jobs and job skill development are some of the most critical needs in our community. Neighbors at Work provides our community with job accessing resources and case management for those looking for work. It also establishes relationships with businesses and employers who want to serve the community by hiring from us. In addition, apprenticeships are established where someone from our community is selected by a company for the express purpose providing training in that trade.

In-kind Barter Economics *(Parent Volunteer Program)* – This full on barter program exchanges hours that our kid's parents work for redeemable in-house dollars in our thrift store. This is real work, maintenance, repair and landscaping for our property and buildings, security, meal preparation and child care for our programs and office work. Work gives dignity and ownership; free giveaways build dependency and walls of differentiation between people.

Small Businesses *(El Mercado de la Comunidad; Opportuni-Tees, Mi Ñañas Tamales; Barrio Bikes; Hope House Farms)* – There is nothing quite like the role that businesses play in the overall design of a holistic mission. Successful businesses create economic health for people (both employer and employee) and for the ministry. They are potentially an income engine for the ministry while at the same time providing hope, growth, stability and vision for the employees in the businesses. A good job, in a good business, with good mentoring and leadership can change a person's life.

El Mercado de la Comunidad is our thrift store and also serves as the place where commodities are exchanged for work earned in the Parent Volunteer Program.

OpportuniTees is an embroidery and silk screen business, serving with entry level to management positions exclusively for our community.

Mi Ñañas Tamales is a Mexican food catering and holiday tamale business run by previous and current Parent Volunteers.

Barrio Bikes sells refurbished bikes and bike parts and is the exclusive vendor for a branded street cruiser called the "Barrio Bike".

Hope House Farms markets their home grown fruits and vegetables at the local farmer's market and also sells home-spun craft items made by and for the residents of Hope House.

Marcos describes what it means to work for one of our small businesses:

> *"Someone can help me spiritually, emotionally, and that is good, but when I started working for **OpportuniTees**, things*

really changed for me. I had worked in a few other jobs and didn't respect authority in those work places. When I started working here, I also butted heads with my boss, especially in the beginning. Alan has allowed me to keep that job with **OpportuniTees.** *I have developed a relationship with my boss. Through learning the Word, I am practicing reconciliation and humility. With bible study, speaking with my friends, I have used those practices in the work place, and realized that this job has the potential to be so much more. In this season, I am the sole provider, in my family. It makes me feel good, it makes Martha and my son feel good, I am paying my bills, and as a man, it is so fulfilling for me. My family can see that I am a working man. I am humble, and happy with what I have. I could make a whole lot more doing this that or the other but that is negative thinking. I am putting into practice in my everyday life at* **OpportuniTees** *the stuff I have learned in my bible studies, humility, respect, and reconciliation.*

Addressing Hunger *(The Food and Clothing Bank)* – The grandfather of our holistic programs, the food and clothing bank is still open once a week distributing food boxes. One of the roles of the parents in the PV Program is to facilitate this operation, taking the applications, interviewing the clients and putting the food and clothing together for the day's distribution.

Medical and Dental Services *(The Neighborhood Christian Clinic)* – The clinic is a separate non-profit from NM. This important medical and dental clinic cares exclusively for the medically uninsured and serves as a primary care facility for many of our neighbors. The clinic is an example of holistic ministry done through partnerships.

Paul Lorentsen, the medical director for the clinic on our

campus says this:

> *When Jesus walked this earth, he intentionally healed phys-*
> *ical illnesses, and many put their faith in him on the basis*
> *of his power to heal. At the clinic, we care for the body,*
> *knowing that it was His priority, and that it opens the door*
> *to the soul.*

Mental Health Services (*Mercy Minds*) – Mercy Minds is a new and growing component at Neighborhood, matching volunteer therapeutic professionals with people in our community who are struggling with mental health issues. Like the medical clinic, it will eventually become a separate non-profit due to medical malpractice legalities and for ease in which to serve clients and volunteer professionals.

Jan Hamilton, Exec. Director for MM shares this:

> *In the spirit of Jesus, we want to be the hearing ears and*
> *watchful eyes and compassionate voices in our work with*
> *the emotional and mental health needs of those with so few*
> *resources. What a privilege to be included in God's work of*
> *healing in the hearts and minds of those He loves.*

Sports Teams (*Soccer*) – Sports teach kids and youth important life lessons facilitating the development of a whole person. The most obvious is the growth that happens to a person physically through sports. But sports also help youth grow in character – qualities like tenacity, sportsmanship, leadership and self-discipline. Sports can win a kids heart for the difficult but good lessons of life unlike any other opportunity. It must be remembered that our public schools are offering fewer and fewer team sports options and community clubs are expensive and therefore off limits to most of our kids.

Kristen Nunley, who founded the soccer program, reminds us of the role of coaches in a program like this:

> *A Coach steps in as the Father, who sets boundaries with rules and consequences. Our kids have desperately needed this loving structure.*

The Arts (*Dance, Guitar*) – The lessons of life that the Arts bring to young people's holistic development are similar to those of sports. Both the arts and sports help a person learn about themselves and what they are made by God to be and do. It is unfortunate that many of our community's young people learn they are artists in prison, spending years designing "prison art" which though really beautiful and nuanced, is the wrong place to learn about who you are. Imagine instead finding your talent as a child, in church, and under God's supervision growing into the full person you were designed by God to be. In addition, the arts provide healing emotionally. A young author writing a poem, a street artist creating a message, a painter describing their inner demons, all these methods and more can give expression to the whole story of someone's life.

Affordable Housing (*The Casitas*) – A new venture for NM is the purchasing and rehabilitation of some slum housing units which sit to the west of our property. We have learned over the years that stable housing is one of the greatest gifts a mission can give to a community. And housing that is most needed in our neighborhood are affordable rentals. Most of our family members will not be able to become home owners, but that shouldn't prevent them from finding decent housing that is both affordable and available in our neighborhood.

One of the LLC members who supervises this endeavor is Rick Malouf, an NM Board member. He says that:

> *Affordable housing is so necessary to empower parents and provide a stable sense of "place" to raise their families. Housing is a significant contributor to a family's dignity and cohesiveness.*

GRACE RULES – PROVISION

A grace rule is the way grace rules. This rule describes a lavish gift from God as experienced in our community. By receiving it, grace rules – leading us further into love and action.

The message a holistic ministry sends to its community is that there is a God in heaven who cares about your whole life. He cares about the intricate ways in which you have been formed; he cares that you eat, have a decent place to live and can raise your children in health and safety. He is a God who provides for you. Jesus told a parable about this.

> *Therefore I tell you, do not be anxious about your life, what you shall eat or what you shall drink, nor about your body, what you shall put on. Is not life more than food, and the body more than clothing? Look at the birds of the air: they neither sow nor reap nor gather into barns, and yet your heavenly Father feeds them. Are you not of more value than they? And which of you by being anxious can add one cubit to his span of life? And why are you anxious about clothing? Consider the lilies of the field, how they grow; they neither toil nor spin; yet I tell you, even Solomon in all his glory was not arrayed like one of these. But if God so*

clothes the grass of the field, which today is alive and tomorrow is thrown into the oven, will he not much more clothe you, O men of little faith? Therefore do not be anxious, saying, 'What shall we eat?' or

'What shall we drink?' or 'What shall we wear?' For the Gentiles seek all these things; and your heavenly Father knows that you need them all. But seek first his kingdom and his righteousness, and all these things shall be yours as well (Matthew 6:24-34 and Luke 12:24-27).

We have been watching God supernaturally provide for this ministry for going on three decades. This Bible passage reminds us that, as his children, we ought to learn to rely on his providential care. God is utterly reliable. In the Lord's Prayer we are taught that God is our provider when we pray: Give us this day our daily bread. Trust in his grace and mercy, trust in his goodness, trust in his loving care. God knows our needs even before we ask and he gives generously to those who trust in him. We have many stories of how God has provided for this holistic mission, too many to mention in this short space. But I want to describe three:

The Neighborhood Center—Open Door Fellowship moved from its original location where NM was begun. Our mission was homeless. We needed to raise $2.2 M in order to establish a future location for the ministry. We had never raised money before. There was an old dilapidated feed and seed mill we fell in love with but it wasn't for sale. We prayed for nine months. One of the patriarchs of the family who owned the property for over 100 years woke up one morning and told his wife, 'I've decided to sell and I don't know why". He was the hold out. People came *along, money was raised. That was 15 years ago, and we contin-ue to watch all the things the Lord is doing through this campus.*

Hope House – *Research was done by an ASU graduate student for us about the problem of homeless youth in our min-istry. The findings and some internal stories caused us to begin praying for the first of three residential houses for our young peo-ple. A donor heard the vision alongside other reports of ministry growth. During a session at her spa she heard the Lord say, "Tell Kit you'll buy it." She had no idea we were (privately, off the mar-ket) just offered an incredible property in the neighborhood, the oldest Victorian house in Phoenix which remained a residential property. Today HH houses young women and produces a glo-rious garden. The lot next door is envisioned to become one of the foremost community gardens in the city.*

Katy's Kids – *The City of Phoenix told us they were discon-tinuing their funding for specialized "niche" Head Start class-rooms, which ours had been for about seven years by that time. Nothing could have been more disheartening as pre-school at the Center was changing lives. As an embedded classroom among "wrap-around" services, we knew there was nothing like it in the city. We began praying to be able to open up a privately funded classroom. The Lord directed all around. First with bringing forward professional staff, getting AZ licensed and then fund-ing coming through from AZ Tobacco Tax money earmarked for early childhood initiatives. Today, we have not one, but two classrooms, serving over 30 pre-schoolers.*

We know our God to be Jehovah Jireh, "the God who himself provides."

NOTES

120. Possibly one of the most famous is the statement that came out of the International Congress on World Evangelization at Lausanne in 1974: http://www.lausanne.org/en/gatherings/issue-based/easneye1986. html?id=26 (accessed March 21, 2012).

121. Bryant L. Myers, *Walking with the Poor*, (Maryknoll: Orbis Books, 1999), 135.

122. Pierce, Bob. http://www.goodreads.com/quotes/show/45537 (accessed March 23, 2012).

123. St. Teresa of Avila, http://www.journeywithjesus.net/PoemsAndPrayers/ Teresa_Of_Avila_Christ_Has_No_Body.shtml (accessed March 23, 2012).

124. Ronald J. Sider, *Good News and Good Works*, (Grand Rapids: Baker Books. 1993).

125. Ibid., 10.

126. Quote from Frederick W. Faber, found in *The Hole in our Gospel*, Richard Stearns, (Nashville: Thomas Nelson, 2009), 13.

127. N.T. Wright, *Surprised by Hope: Rethinking Heaven, the Resurrection, and the Mission of the Church*, (New York: Harper Collins, 2008), 208.

"Birth Pangs at the Bus Stop" Kyle Matthews

CHAPTER FIVE

We are Called to
BE THE CHURCH AS WELL
AS SUPPORT THE CHURCH

Core Value #4

Definition: The church is families and individuals coming together as the new community that Jesus ushered in as an expression of his kingdom. When the church as the body of Christ is a prophetic voice in a community advocating for and expressing love for change and transformation, God's "shalom" can be expressed in that local community. We value the local church because of what it represents in that location: compassion, solidarity, spiritual and physical transformation, hope and the activity of the life of Christ.

> "The church is the only society on earth that exists for
> those who are not its members."[128]
> –William Temple

Wayne and I fell in love with a Franco Zeffirelli film called *Brother Sun, Sister Moon* (1972) when we were young. Through its signature Zeffirelli style, the movie tells the story of St. Francis of Assisi (1181-1226) from his spoiled youth to his calling by God and service to the poor. As Francis (Francesco) leaves his old life to begin a walk with God, he goes toward the ruins of the chapel of San Damiano, where he hears God's voice asking him to restore it. Much to the dismay of his family, friends and the local bishop, Francesco gradually gains a following among the poor and the suffering. His childhood friends admiring Francesco's new life style as a beggar help him rebuild the chapel of San Damiano. There is a scene when the chapel is finished and all the poor from throughout the area are walking to church. Following them or in their arms are all kinds of animals, representing God's creation which Francis becomes famous for treasuring. These animals sit serenely on the altar and others roam freely in the small sanctuary.

This scene is part of my memory bank and will sometimes overlay a Sunday morning at Neighborhood, especially the mornings when a small dog is part of our worshipping community, either in the arms of a distressed person, a neighborhood child or running around trying to adjust their homeless status. Zeffirelli's image is Hollywood, ours is reality. But it resonates; a church that accepts me just as I am; a congregation that breaks out the front door around the same time of the morning and walking to church, a noisy place that doesn't shut down just because babies are squawking or dogs are loose, a church built especially for the one who struggles just to get there on a Sunday morning, so that the grace of God can roam freely amidst their sufferings.

Panda says, "Whenever I hear the song, 'Follow You'[129], I think of what we are doing here in church. It's so hard to describe, I'm barely trying to answer to God's calling, living my life for him and for our people. Sometimes I try to describe our church to others, it's hard. We're different. We just want to help; we want to be there for each other." Jorge adds, "We show up at church with an open heart for all of our community, whoever comes, open hands, open arms. No membership, we don't set rules that say, *who is in and who is out*, a church for the blessing and benefit of the community."

What is the church at Neighborhood? We're past thinking anyone is talking about a building. When our community says "church" referring to our mission, they could be affectionately talking about anything that happens on our eight acre campus from Monday through Sunday. Our kids outreach to six-hundred kids is called Monday Night Church, our pre- school called Katy's Kids is held at "church." The food bank, medical clinic, English classes, organizing for immigration reform, Mercy Minds counseling, youth group, Moms' Place for teen moms, the bike shop, the businesses, all happen at church or take place in a form that feels like and acts like church to them. But we also have a Sunday morning worship service that is a church in the traditional sense, performing all the services and sacraments, believers baptism (in a portable swimming pool and a lake), communion every Sunday, funerals (too many), weddings (too few), preaching the Word and bringing worship bilingually, Spanish and English. We call this the big "C" and little "c" church at Neighborhood. Both are church within our community. Susan comments, "I love our church, big 'C' and little 'c'. The big 'C' is where people are loved, supported, protected, welcomed, it happens all week long. But when I talk about the Sunday gathering, it is something special altogether, very precious and needs to be protected; here we are together as family, bilingually, in worship and celebration."

WHAT IS THE CHURCH FROM THE STANDPOINT OF THE BIBLE?

The church is a people whom the Spirit is forming together into a community for the purpose of modeling the kingdom of God, pointing out the future God has in store for all creation. God's kingdom is "bigger" than the church of course; the church is [simply] "constituted by those who are entering and receiving the reign of God. It is where the children of the reign corporately manifest the presence and characteristic features of God's reign."[130]

Therefore, the church derives its purpose from God's activity in the world, not just for today, but as a proclamation of the coming reign of God.

A definitive answer to the question, 'What is the reign of God?' cannot be given. But we can at least sketch some of its contours by listening to the Old Testament's prophetic forecasts of the coming day of God and the prophets' expectations of God's intended future for the world. In lectures given in the early 1980's philosopher Arthur Holmes summarized that prophetic vision as shalom. It envisions a world characterized by peace, justice and celebration. Shalom, the overarching vision of the future, means 'peace', but not merely peace as the cessation of hostilities. Instead, shalom envisions the full prosperity of a people of God living under the covenant of God's demanding care and compassionate rule. In the prophetic vision, peace such as this comes hand in hand with justice. Without justice, there can be no real peace, and without peace, no real justice. Indeed, only in a social world full of peace grounded in justice can there come the full expression of joy and celebration.[131]

THE BELOVED COMMUNITY AND GOD'S SHALOM

The church expresses God's reign by living differently, by living as a distinctive covenant community. What does that mean? Charles Marsh and John Perkins take on this question in their book *Welcoming Justice, God's Movement toward Beloved Community*.[132] Their reference point is the Civil Rights Movement and the promises of the beloved community. And according to our authors, the goal remains; it is the unfinished business of the movement. MLK, Jr. said, "The end is reconciliation, the end is redemption, the end is the creation of the beloved community."[133] And here we are, still trying to figure out how our churches get outside their own walls, still trying to figure out how to love our neighbor, how to be a relevant presence of justice in an unjust world. Can we attain to God's purpose for us as a community? The authors answer this way:

> [Beloved Community is the very goal of God's movement in the world]. God gathers us into the family of faith not only for our own sake, but also so that we might welcome justice and build beloved communities for the sake of the world. That is the purpose that drives followers of the risen Christ. It is the movement of the Spirit that began at Pentecost and has continued in faithful communities of disci-

pleship throughout every generation. It is the theological vision that we need desperately to reclaim in our time.[134]

For the authors, community, justice and racial reconciliation are interconnected. And its underpinnings are theological, a "lived theology", where theology has a place ... where it lives. The Civil Rights activists longed for this community, they were sustained by its vision, and its anchor was the church who proclaimed this theology. The vision was the work of "organizing and building communities in distressed and excluded places, it was about celebrating the common grace of women and men, black and white, the privileged and the poor, who found themselves together, miraculously, working in common cause for a more just and human social order."[135] When the Civil Rights movement became detached from its homes in the church it lost its spiritual and moral focus, its moorings. It was the church that bore the vision. Civil rights is a spiritual Kingdom idea, it does not find its roots in politics. With out the kingdom ideal politics can only make laws.

Ian and Ricardo just came back from Alabama and Mississippi. They made this pilgrimage to hear from the Civil Rights leaders of yesterday, their message for the church leaders of today. Ian describes:

Well, when I was in Alabama and in Mississippi, I was able to imagine firsthand the work those churches did, the voter registration drives, the recall efforts, the marches, etc. All these were driven and organized inside the churches. I knew that; but to be in those church basements and walk along the march's paths, I was struck that churches and church people were doing all of that. I would pray that our church would find an identity inside that history, and be an active and ag-

gressive community that defends and fights for justice. I'm not sure, if it's even likely, my expectation is that it won't happen; people who go to church today don't want those kinds of things. The hyper individualism and the theology that has been individualized is a disease. It is all about our own personal walk with Christ, our personal issues are what we hope will be addressed. Our volunteer work is really like a holy huddle, we aren't fighting the larger issues, and the church only serves as a support group. Changing the way we see people, building the kingdom, in contrast, it is the community which becomes our support and buttress for our work. Is it possible to be that kind of church? I don't know. But I choose hope, as Cornell West would say.

What can we learn from the Civil Rights movement? What was its biblical message that energized and sustained the desire of people to bring a redemptive presence in the world ... *in their communities?* ... a beloved community built with the intention of bringing a witness to broken and lost places. "The church," John Perkins says, "is the only institution I know of that offers the basis for a discipline, a commitment, a hope, a truth that is stronger than racism and stronger than any institutional form that clothes racism."[136] The beloved community is God's movement of the coming activity of *shalom* – peace, justice and joy in the Holy Spirit.

THE CHURCH THAT LONGS TO BE THE BELOVED COMMUNITY

But we must remember, that the church that longed to be the beloved community, also proclaimed the reign of Christ. It was Jesus' mission to put into words what was true about his presence and his deeds. It is a message of welcome, all are invited, and all are forgiven! "To all who received him, who believed in his name, he gave power to become children of God (John 1:12)."

We love the Church, the entire body of Christ. There is a role for the whole body of Christ in our community that joins the movement of the coming activity of *shalom*. This longing to be involved in the lofty vision of the kingdom of God is from the Holy Spirit. There is a new wave of interest in the church to engage in social justice and community ministry. This is good, but it is important for the church to enter humbly, searching for partners that have been inside hurting places for a long time. This intentionality is covered in more detail in the core value of partnerships, but it is important to note here, that the true beloved community of Christ followers isn't one local church, but a biblical community that stands together for the blessing and benefit of distressed and marginalized places. Our desire has always been to welcome and receive our brothers and sisters in the body of Christ, no matter the denomination or affiliation, to join together in the work God has called us all to.

As a local church in a distressed and marginalized place, we also long to be a beloved community in our context, looking to the example of those rugged faith dwellers before us. In one way, we have an advantage. We are never lethargic about the issues of race or justice, we are not able to be apathetic or disconnected. We are a church perpetually "outside the walls" so to speak. But there is an underside to that beautiful advantage. There is a great challenge in being the church of and for the community; our members have complicated lives. Our church is filled with people who are climbing out of difficult stories and most days exhausted from the battle. We are a people clinging to the hope we find in Jesus. Participating in our church requires a determined effort to be disciplined, as Dr. Perkins suggests, to the work at hand. It's further challenging here at Neighborhood, being a big "C", little "c" church, when folks from either one of the C's doesn't play a part in the other. As Jeremy reflects, "the tricky part [as the beloved community] is when people come exclusively to be served versus being a member of the community that also gives their lives away. The tension is with those who come because they want someone to teach them as opposed to coming as a learner in order to join the team and to lead. We ask everyone, what will you give, what will you create here?"

DEFINING THE ADVANTAGES AND CHALLENGES IN THIS
LOCAL BELOVED COMMUNITY

If we want to get the core value of church right, talking about our local beloved community, we have to admit that this is the most difficult thing we attempt here at Neighborhood, and the most outrageous when it comes to vision and resolve. It's never perfect, ever. And it can be really heartbreaking and unsettling. It is a paradoxical celebration of grace and true grit that when seen through a life loved, a hard fought battle, and even a miracle or two can't help but bring pure joy. For almost twenty years in one form or another we have been on the journey toward being the church inside a mission. Below are some of our convictions on what our church is as it attempts to live inside it's destiny as the beloved community, where we really are each other's beloved.

A Church in Mission – Unapologetically, we are a church inside a mission. This is on purpose and for a purpose, actually a few purposes. The earliest ideas about church inside our mission had to do with the bonding that was occurring because of the relationships of outreach. People were converted; natural discipleship began and so we had to ask where our friends were going to go to church? Church, in the beginning, was for the converts of the work, who we loved, and where family was already growing. Then, a thought developed that our church should also exist for the workers, which ideally was all of us, a weekly place of worship and respite from the frontline battles. Here in worship are gathered the progress and set backs of our lives lived, and where every week, the jailhouse convert can come home, the political battleground can be described, the struggle with every ailment and cancer can be prayed for and the limping, sprinting and strolling through life can be investigated and celebrated.

A church in mission is conversely NOT a church in competition in the supermarket of choices, as established by our consumer culture. You probably wouldn't choose us if you were looking for the splashy high tech program or intricate menu of services some other churches offer. That can lead to a bout of insecurity, but like the flu, we get over it; because we know who we are. We are a church smack dab in the middle of "real life" and we are particularly suited to be that kind of church. We know this is unique. Isiah recalls that [until attending church here] he hadn't ever gone to a church in a neighborhood he lived in, even though for a time he lived directly across the street from one. Church wasn't for or with the community. "It was totally impersonal that way," he thought.

A Church for the Community – What does that look like? Well, if we consider this statement: that "the Church is where natural enemies gather…,"[137] then our gathering every week is bringing people together into one family who, apart from this beloved community wouldn't have any reason to be one. Church must function then, as the location where people are working out reconciled relationships, attempting to overcome the things that divide us: culture, language and social barriers. We have to do intentional things because of this. Like make sure up front leaders represent the dominant culture. And make every effort for the preaching and the focus of the messages, informal and formal, to be about the very things the community is dealing with. The worship should bring suffering people into the presence of God. And the importance of our togetherness should be leveraged: organizing against oppression and for action; teaching truth about where God stands in light of our struggles, becoming the community's pulpit; building a theology together that instructs principalities and powers. How are we doing? If and when these are true, we become a prophetic and controversial place, unfamiliar ground for those looking for a place to worship in the supermarket. We are neither the coolest place for young evangelicals, or prosperous enough for the newest wave of evangelicalism from Latin America and because we are ministering with and not to we do not provide easy or quick answers.

A Simple Church – We like to say that the mission and values of our church can be simply captured in the great commandment, to love God and neighbor. Isn't that what we are doing? ... with worship on Sunday morning, Bible studies and healing groups during the week ... evangelism, outreach and service through word and deed and converts encouraged to grow up in Christ. But one thing church isn't ever, and that's simple. It isn't simple to care for a diverse flock that has unwieldy needs. It isn't simple to decide on things like church polity or women in leadership. It isn't simple to pull together a budget, decide whether or not the church is a separate entity from the mother ship or a necessary and critical source of mission health. And it isn't simple to pull together a bulletin every week. I don't think it's possible to be a simple church.

A Church inside a Holistic Approach – As covered in the core value on Holistic Ministry, our mission meets the needs of whole people. In many ways, that takes the pressure off the church to provide the necessary resources that allow people to become all they desire to become, as God inspires them to dream and grow. So what is the function of the church itself as an entity of its own, designed by God for its unique purpose? Emotional support and healing? Friendship, fellowship and community? Evangelism? Preaching of the word? Leadership development? Celebrations? Shared sufferings? Our church continues to determine before God and each other, its particular role in growing people into the likeness of Christ.

A Church for all of Life/Birth to Grave – Church, as we've come to understand it, isn't for a certain time in life: childhood, teenagers, college; it is for all people at all ages and for whole families. Though NM looks and feels like a para-church organization, it carries the heartbeat of a church. From the beginning of our relationships we people, we wanted to know people their whole lives, their kids and their kids, kids. And it is happening. By God's grace, we are getting to love the next generation, the children of those we loved in the beginning. And many come to "church", some all week long. But most are probably talking about a program happening at Neighborhood Ministries; and yes, this is church in a large wonderful sort of way; but Sunday morning church has a particular function in growing us up in Christ. There is a spiritual discipline called going to church that first generation Christians are still learning in our community.

The Unique Role that Worship Plays in a Suffering Community – Under the banner of a loving, powerful God, worshippers come together every week agreeing that God desires to show up inside their common and collective pain. This is a mystery best understood in the space of collective worship. Our problems are too big for us, we need God desperately, and so we draw near to God, knowing that when we do, he draws near to us. The solidarity we share with each other in our common humanity joins us together under the banner of love. And that leads us to pray. And so we pray together, cry together, grieve together and find that in the end, we find God together in our suffering. There is a biblical and theological understanding of the suffering church, of which we are learning to become.

GRACE RULES – A SUFFERING CHURCH

A grace rule is the way grace rules. This rule describes a lavish gift from God as experienced in our community. By receiving it, grace rules – leading us further into love and action.

Suffering is a grace word. What? Most of the time, in suffering, we ask where God is in all of it. It can't possibly be a gift of God. As with many paradoxes, or two truths, with suffering we don't have to disavow the pain to receive the gift embedded in it. But consider what also happens to people in pain. They look for help or at least some of us try to. "Cry out", the scriptures teach us. Cry out to God, and locate what puny, insignificant faith you can muster to believe that He hears and delights in showing up in the midst of your darkness. It is the promise of the presence of God. Where is he in suffering? He is present in it. His presence is promised, we are not alone, "I am with you always," says Jesus.

This is the grace shared in a suffering church, the knowledge that our God is a fellow sufferer. "In the Cross God is revealed not as One reigning in calm disdain above all the squalors of earth, but as One who suffers more keenly than the keenest sufferer – 'a man of sorrows, and acquainted with grief.'"[138]

A suffering church sees its own personal sufferings as gifts for each other, for without them we couldn't enter into an understanding or have compassion for the burdens that the other one carries. Without our pain we cannot love each other with grace. "We have learned to see for once the great events of world history from below – through the perspective of the

barred, the suspects, the badly treated, the powerless, the oppressed, the scoffed – in short the perspective of those who
suffer – we see that personal suffering is a more suitable key, a
more fruitful principle, than is personal good fortune for exploring the world by observation and action."[139]

As fellow sufferers, we are living examples that our pain
isn't the final word. We can teach through our own stories that
pain will be redeemed, that it is never wasted in God's economy, and that though there is deep darkness for awhile, we
illustrate this truth, "hope in God, for I will yet praise Him."
Underneath the chaos lies the grace of God, this is the mystery,
his provision through suffering.

And as a suffering church we remind each other that suffering teaches endurance,[140] the ultimate lessons of our faith.
"For power is perfected in weakness."[141] MLK, Jr. believed this
for his beloved community and so spoke about this power on
their behalf:

> We will match your capacity to inflict suffering with our
> capacity to endure suffering. We will meet your physi-
> cal force with soul force. We will not hate you, but we
> cannot in good conscience obey your unjust laws. Do
> to us what you will and we will still love you. Bomb
> our homes and threaten our children; send your hooded
> perpetrators of violence into our communities and drag
> us out on some wayside road, beating us and leaving us
> half-dead, and we will still love you. But we will soon
> wear you down by our capacity to suffer. And in win-
> ning our freedom we will so appeal to your heart and
> conscience that we will win you in the process.[142]

NOTES

128. Archbishop of Canterbury William Temple, quoted in *Feasting on the Word*, Year A, Volume 1, Advent through Transfiguration, (Westminister: John Knox, 2010), 336.
129. Leeland, performer and songwriter of "Follow You." And I'll follow you into the homes that are broken/Follow you into the world/Meet the needs for the poor and the needy God/Follow you into the World.
130. Darrell L. Guder, *Missional Church, A Vision for the Sending of the Church in North America*, (Grand Rapids: Eerdmans Pub., 1998), 99.
131. Ibid., 91.
132. Charles Marsh and John Perkins, *Welcoming Justice, God's Movement Toward Beloved Community*, (Downers Grove: Intervarsity Press, 2009).
133. Ibid., 17.
134. Ibid., 18.
135. Ibid., 23.
136. Ibid., 34.
137. Rocke, Kris. "The Gift of Desperation," http://geographyofgrace.com/2010/08/18/the-gift-of- desperation/. (accessed April 20, 2012).
138. Oswald Chambers, *The Place of Help*, (Grand Rapids: Discovery House Publisher, 1989).
139. Dietrich Bonheoffer, "After Ten Years," *Letters and Papers from Prison* (Eberhard Bethge, ed. New York: The Macmillan Company, 1971).
140. Rom 5:3.
141. 2 Cor 12:9.
142. Martin Luther King, Jr., *Stride Toward Freedom*, (http://www.hopemn.com/MLK.htm) (accessed April 22, 2012).

"No Limits" Nikki Villegas and Ximena Perez-Danley

CHAPTER SIX

We are Called to
LEADERSHIP DEVELOPMENT

Core Value #5

Definition: We value all leadership and believe that the best solutions to our community's problems are generated from with the community by local, indigenous leaders, those affected, owning and responding to the pain of injustice, oppression and poverty. We recognize our role in developing future leaders for the church, for institutional, non-profit, political and marketplace leadership.

"Show me the suffering of the most miserable;
So I will know my people's plight.
Free me to pray for others;
For you are present in every person.
Help me take responsibility for my own life;
So that I can feel free at last.
Grant me courage to serve others;
For in service there is true life.
Give me honesty and patience;
So that I can work with other workers.
Bring forth song and celebration;
So that the Sprit will be alive among us.
Let the Spirit flourish and grow;
So that we will never tire of the struggle.
Let us remember those who have died for justice;
For they have given us life.
Help us love even those who hate us;
So we can change the world."
–The Prayer of Cesar Chavez[143]

It was 1993-1994 and our kids outreach was surfacing a problem. The kids were getting older and our programs were set up for children. What were we going to do with the youth? In those days, we were still operating out of the Anglo church where we had begun the ministry. But our kids operation had become a separate entity several years earlier because the white church kids and the ethnic outreach kids weren't on the same cultural planet. It wasn't going to work for "our kids" to attend "their" youth group. We sized up the problem this way. *Our kids need a leader who understands them and their street ways. They need someone who they can identify with, culturally and socially. Our families look to us as their church, it is time they had someone who can come alongside them and remind them that God can raise up leadership from inside the very places they live and identify as home.*

This was also a very dangerous time for youth in our neighborhood. Gang violence and gang affiliation had grown considerably, and our community had a number of rival gangs who lived within blocks of each other, and in some cases their gang's boundaries overlapped. Shootings were routine, and young people in our ministry were involved in the escalating violence. We were a young ministry. I was the only staff, and worked another job. Our ministry workers were mostly volunteers. The volunteer crew was complemented by a few expatriated missionaries, who were helping with the Spanish speaking congregation. We wrote up a job description, which was really more of a flyer. It stated our need and profiled who we were looking for. YOUTH GUY WANTED – Hispanic, Christian, bilingual, loves kids, is experienced working with street youth, trained in outreach ministry…"

The flyer and I went everywhere together, beginning with our friends in Phoenix. We had been arm in arm in partnership with urban Young Life, and I felt like our work was a perfect next step for one of their developing leaders. Problem is, they only had one and Young Life wasn't ready to part with him. No one else was doing urban youth outreach in our city, and there was hardly anyone doing Hispanic church planting. So, I took the search on the road, and as I did, I realized that though it might not discover our needed youth guy, I was learning about leadership development which was still not occurring in Hispanic communities outside of traditional forms; I was pointed to places like LABI (Latin American Bible Institute) which was the Bible school for the Spanish Assemblies and HBTS (Hispanic Baptist Theological Seminary) which was Southern Baptist. I visited and made a presentation at LABI, the only Anglo there that day. Instead of wearing the ankle length skirt as the other women on campus, I made my presentation in jeans and a sleeveless blouse. Clearly, I hadn't gotten the dress code memo. I was out of my cultural league, and I was beginning to think that this whole search was starting to reflect the LABI debacle. I made friends with the director at the HBTS in San Antonio, and we discussed at length what the landscape was for developing Hispanic leaders. He admitted, NO ONE was developing leaders for Christian ministry to street gangsters. Hardly deterred, I followed every lead from every cold call, from Boston to L.A. If any of them had a developing leader in their organization that fit my profile, the ministry had developed them themselves, and I was told to "keep my grubby paws off."

Then I heard the refrain of this funny, weird "youth guy search" song. I remember it first, sung by Jesse Miranda, who was the President of the Spanish Assemblies in those days, a powerful national leader. He told me, "Kit, who you are looking for, doesn't exist. Churches aren't doing the kind of work you do, and therefore those they are raising up can't serve in a work like yours. In addition, the work of leadership development in Hispanic communities among protestant evangelicals isn't well developed. It is churchy and old fashioned. I'm going to tell you what you will start hearing from around the country. You must develop your own. The leaders you need are in your community. Your job is to find them, and grow them up." Well, of course he was right, on both accounts. I did start to hear this refrain, which had begun to sound a bit like a broken record. That's when I stopped looking. It was 1998 and we launched our first leadership development process with TWO two-year interns to run our youth work.

During the four years of looking, we were able to wrangle a part-time youth staff through our friendship and partnership with urban Young Life. Those were dark years for all of us. We lived through multiple shooting deaths of our youth, facilitated funerals with a local fire and brimstone pastor who was finding fame from doing gang funerals and had our own fair share of on-campus violence and lock-downs from threatened drive-byes.

While all this was going on, we had begun church planting. Joining me was an extended family that had spent the first leg of their life in Bolivia; they brought on another seconded missionary from their same agency. They spoke Spanish and were trained in the kind of work we were doing. We were relationship building in those days and enjoying the early stages of introducing people to Bible studies. As the church work began, the missionaries did what they had been trained to do. They took the lead. They led the Bible studies and eventually the worship services. A friend of mine, who was working in our same church, had been with OM (Operation Mobilization) for twenty years running both ships, the *Logos* and the *Doulas*. He introduced me to a famous church planter from Latin America who by that time was reputed to have planted more than 350 churches. He had a mantra that I'm sure he shared with thousands by this late stage in his life. "Begin with the community, your leaders are there. Don't lead with missionaries. Put your community members up front. If they don't know the Word well yet, just read scripture. If no one can sing, don't sing. The Word, the sacraments and an offering. (The church needs to pay for itself.) That's it, those three" … "Also", he almost forgot to add, "You've made too many mistakes so far. Shut everything down and begin again. This church will never live." I would have traded that bad news for another day at LABI in a sleeveless blouse. I had one more important encounter during these years. I was re-entering the CCDA (Christian Community Development Association) world. The movement was "browning" and I was lonely and isolated, I needed them. The few Hispanic leaders at CCDA welcomed me, it was a precious homecoming. This national conference was in the city where I had begun urban ministry in 1975. I had an afternoon to talk with my original mentor in urban work there. We talked about indigenous leadership development, the only thing on my mind. He is older than me and had war wounds still oozing on the subject. "They," meaning these emerging leaders, "won't make it." It was vitriolic. "They will have all kinds of personal problems and take your church down with them. I won't train local leaders anymore." I can't remember anything else we talked about. Walking back to the convention center from his home, I think I was having trouble breathing.

Even as I write this, I am reflecting on how much ground has been covered in the past two decades. Following are some of the lessons that have developed into *our mantras* and even birthed some systems that are in place. As we are prone to say, though all ten core values influence the direction of the mission in their own unique ways, the core value of leadership development guides the vision of the mission unlike the others. Therefore, it could be said, that this core value defines our end game the clearest. There are five defining features that characterize leadership development at Neighborhood Ministries: *Servant Leadership, An Open Door, Indigenous Focused, Empowerment* and *Process.* We will look at all five, here, but will begin with a brief overview of *Transformational Leadership.*

TRANSFORMATIONAL LEADERSHIP

For over forty years, the study of leadership remains compelling. Whether one finds it elusive or enigmatic, the concept itself has become the topic of enormous interest. Judging by the number of books on leadership that are currently on the market, there has never been greater interest in the topic. Possibly one of the most pertinent shifts in the past forty years in leadership theory has been the move from leaders to leadership. The father of modern leadership studies, with this shift in mind, is James McGregor Burns, noted for his 1979 book, *Leadership*, and for developing the term, *transformational leadership*.

The term transformational leadership was first coined by J.V. Downton in 1973 in *Rebel Leadership: Commitment and Charisma in a Revolutionary Process*.[144]   J. MacGregor Burns[145] first introduced the concepts of transformational and transactional leadership in his treatment of political leadership, but it is now used as well in organizational psychology. According to Burns, the difference between transformational and transactional leadership is what leaders and followers offer one another.

> Transformational leaders offer a purpose that transcends short-term goals and focuses on higher order intrinsic needs. This results in followers identifying with the needs of the leader. The four dimensions of transformational leadership are: Charisma or Idealized influence, Inspirational motivation, Intellectual stimulation, Individualized consideration and Individualized attention.[146]

Bernard Bass followed Burns' work developing it further.[147] He suggested that transformational leadership is the function of engaging people in a common enterprise, so that both, leaders and followers rise to higher levels of motivation and morality. He also contrasted transactional leaders (those that promise rewards to followers for performance) and transformational leaders.

Transactional leaders, says Bass, work within the situation; transformational leaders change the situation. Transactional leaders accept what can be talked about; transformational leaders change what can be talked about. Transactional leaders accept the rules and values; transformational leaders change them. Transactional leaders talk about payoffs; transformational leaders talk about goals. Transactional leaders bargain; transformational leaders symbolize. In short, says Bass, the transformational leader motivates us to do more than we expected to do, by raising our awareness of different values, by getting us to transcend our self-interests for the cause and by expanding our portfolio of needs and wants.[148]

Bakke Graduate University suggests that there are eight categories that identify transformational leaders: calling-based; incarnational; reflective; servanthood; contextual; prophetic; shalom; and global. Of all of these, an interesting body of research has been inaugurated on the area of Servant Leadership.

SERVANT LEADERSHIP

Researchers and leadership students[149] are comparing and contrasting Robert Greenleaf's seminal text[150] on servant leadership perspective with Burns transformational leadership perspective, positing that servant leaders are indeed transformational leaders. In addition, they are suggesting that transformational leadership "does not explain certain phenomena such as altruism to followers or humility ... leaving the door open for a new theoretical understanding..."[151]   Following this, they remind us that "where the purpose is leading, servant leaders seek to serve first as the primary means of leading ... and servant leadership stands alone in regard to this follower focus."[152]

Over the last twenty years, the construct of servant leadership (follower-oriented leadership) has developed, from the focus on inspirational and moral dimensions, to self-identity, capacity for reciprocity, relationship building, and focus on vision, credibility, trust and service.

Follower-oriented leadership theories are likely to continue to be refined as leadership research progresses in the 21st century. Although transformational leadership has dominated the research agenda, servant and self-sacrificial leadership theories have staked a claim on a portion of contemporary scholarly efforts.[153]

Of the theoretical discussion on servant leadership three have dominated the field: Spears (1998), Laub (1999), and Patterson (2003).[154] The goal here is not to describe in detail the developments in servant leadership theory, but to place some of the elements of transformational leadership as we understand them into the current academic discipline of leadership studies. Patterson presents servant leadership theory as an extension of transformational leadership theory. Patterson's observation is that transformational theory was not addressing the phenomena of love, humility, altruism and being visionary for followers. Because of this, Patterson's model of servant leadership includes the following dimensions as the essential characteristics of servant leadership: (a) agapao love, (b) humility, (c) altruism, (d) vision, (e) trust, (f) empowerment, and (g) service.

These characteristics are helpful in understanding the direction Neighborhood takes as it crafts its leader development. Important to note, however, while Patterson and BGU have a particular set of elements that define transformational leadership development, so do we.

AN OPEN DOOR

Indigenous leadership development in marginalized communities is often considered a risk taking venture. People have baggage, don't you know. They are undereducated, come from an immoral background, they aren't very "Christian." *They aren't ...*

they can't … they shouldn't. How do leaders emerge in an environment where so many people are on the long journey toward mental, spiritual, vocational and familial health? We've approached this problem (perspective) two different ways. The first is to accept that notion, but with this caveat: Which of us in leadership today wasn't a risk? And I say that from personal experience. I wasn't very Christian when I began as a leader. I came from an immoral home. I had lots of baggage, and only today am I completing my education. God looked around to see whose hand was in the air, and He noticed mine. That's what we do today, too. We take anyone, and I mean anyone, whose hand is in the air. Someone took a risk on me and we take risks everyday on others. Jorge also had his hand in the air. He confirms this process:

> *Whoever is available to be in the leadership, can take the role. If they are open to learn together, we will help them focus on what it's going to take. But they have to be willing, they have to want it. Here is the opportunity – to see what gifts they have for the ministry, and how we can help them see their gifts. We take a risk, letting them be part of the leadership. We know it's a risk, we know that our families struggle like crazy with issues, addictions, other things; we can, and do, fail. But we are willing to take that risk. Why are we willing? It is biblical. When Jesus called the disciples, Matthew, well, he was a tax collector, that's bad. Peter, he was a fisherman, that's a low skill job – And Paul when he describes Timothy, he says, 'I know you are young, but don't let anyone put you down'.*

Some of us are aware that our hand is in the air, I know I was. But sometimes our "desire" is something that has to be confirmed and drawn out by someone else to take that step into leadership.

Marcos remembers:

> *In 2006, I was off doing my own thing, in a season where I didn't know what I wanted to do, suffering with anxiety and depression. I had withdrawn from family and homeboys; I had a kid on the way. I was just released from the hospital and watching a documentary about Father Gregg and the homeboys. I didn't know him, but this show caught my attention. I was inspired by his story: A Father from the Catholic ministry who is reaching out to the homeboys, a guardian angel to them. I wanted to do something with my life, but didn't think that ministry was my desire. But I saw this man who has worked in different parts of the world, he could have been sent somewhere great. But he stayed in Boyle Heights. He not only knew this community, but developed relationships with genuine love and acceptance. Yes, the rest of the world, they have outcasts too, and their resources are limited also, but Father Gregg picked these outcasts. He loved them, gave them opportunities, regardless of appearance – was able to help them come to the Lord, a lot of those were veteran gang members. He was reaching out to rival gangs. I watched on T.V., these guys who were bald, a lot of tattoos, but something in them was peaceful, everyone around them admired them, there was genuine respect that they were not leading the youth to the gangs, to negativity. They were bringing these youngsters to the Lord. I hadn't prayed in a long time, and I prayed that night. I called Kit a couple days later, I told her I wanted to get involved. I met with her, Jorge, Billy … I wasn't expecting to do Kids Club that summer. But they invited me to come; they asked me if I wanted to be a leader at KC. I was nervous; I had unresolved issues with the Lord. In his own way,*

he was bringing me back to Neighborhood. I got enrolled in GED, I did tutoring classes, I did KC … through talking to Kit and Victor, that summer, I was baptized, I wanted to come back to our church, and I guess, I feel in my heart, it was the Lord calling me back, 'to come home'. Now I'm doing what I like to do, working with kids, doing just what those guys were doing on T.V. I found peace with myself, and as people recognize it, I can share it with them.

The other perspective is an asset-based approach. This community has all the potential in the world to lead itself. The leaders are here, possibly underdeveloped, but the creativity and innovation, the energy, the desire, the calling, it's all there. Harnessing it, investing in it and sustaining it is the big payoff. As our friend and co-laborer, Alan Andrews, likes to say, "Everyone gets to Play."[155] Panda reflects on this:

We find people with strong beliefs in God and have so much hope to change things, to help people. NM gave me (Panda) and my sister (Googoos) chances to be a part of the ministry. I thought it was weird when Heather wanted me to be a nurse during Kids Club. "Nurse Panda". I had never been labeled like that, I felt like I was important, I was needed. NM saw potential in us. In most other places, I don't think anybody, coming from where we came from, would see us with potential. We aren't supposed to be doing what we are doing, we're supposed to be on welfare, feeling sorry for ourselves. I think that is unique. I don't think people who come from where we are coming from should be working or going to college. But now I see it. I'm not just going to college and working, but I am building self-esteem, other people are listening to me and learning from me. I always thought, I'm too dumb, but now, I have seen in other people things that I have done that has changed their lives. With the parents, for example, at Katy's Kids, that's my strength. I could just open people up. I have more ability to get them to open up – they think I am one of them -- I am one of them. That's a big strength, I have been through it, I know how it is to be a mom with kids, they see me as someone they could confide in and talk to.

INDIGENOUS FOCUSED

Many leaders have been developed at Neighborhood; many from "outside" the neighborhood and many from "inside." We have learned over the years to be unapologetic about our preference. We are called to indigenous leadership development, to see those in the community have voice, power, influence, authority; we commit to intentionally develop those from the inside.

John Perkins has taught us much about developing leaders from the community. He says that the people with the pain are the ones that have the solution. During the years mentioned earlier, while we were trying to adjust to the vision of indigenous leader development in our church and moving in this same direction mission wide we invited Hispanic leaders from partner ministries to take on some key roles with us, i.e., the partnership with Young Life and inviting the pastor to preach at funerals or speak at church. While we did that, we also grabbed the ones growing up here and gave them tasks, even if they weren't always up to it, or prepared; a sort of on the job training approach. This is when we learned that everyone gets to play. Everyone gets to explore and experiment with what they bring to the table. No one is excluded if they are willing. Failure is a normal part of life. Take risks on people, give away responsibilities – my own fear of failure will become the final word if I don't. If I want to develop leaders in communities that have been marginalized, I have to remember that failure will be part of it.

Build an environment of grace that communicates patience, unconditional love and hope, and yet, still find ways to build into the work a quest for excellence. Live inside the tension of the graceful progress toward the goal and the desire to have leaders filled with capacity for the job at hand. If that isn't hard enough, have an open hand – some of your trained leaders will leave you. You have trained them, gladly, for someone else, for something else. Claudia has been invested in here. She is becoming an RN and will work in a hospital for the rest of her life, probably. She looks at her process of leadership development and comments on how it works:

> *I guess, what works is just to live together. Share life together. No matter how many times you fall into the same mistake, there is always that grace. And the support, whether it is just having someone to talk to, or having a need met, so I think in that sense, it teaches us -- why wouldn't we do the same for others, when we talk about leadership, that's what sticks out for me. So for example, right now, I am working here at Neighborhood part time, and I can see so much, as kids come in, I can see or reflect myself in them, and I am able to give them the encouragement, the same words that were given to me at one point. I can do for them, show them, because I live the life ... if you have already walked the walk, it is easier to put yourself in their shoes and relate to them. Sometimes I have interviews with these single moms, they become my first priority, I can show them where the training is, jobs, medical asst. programs – and I think when I find a good lead, "it would be so great if so and so could do this." I always carry them with me, in a sense.*

BEGIN WITH THE YOUTH

Indigenous leadership development begins with the youth at Neighborhood. It is an everyday, intentional, programmatic focus. Our youth begin hearing about "leadership" class in the eighth grade. This is a weekly component of our youth night. Ian describes:

> Everyone can be a leader, we are not cherry picking, not looking for the best and the brightest, this can be risky but usually holds wonderful surprises. If you are a youth minister, trained to do youth outreach, leadership development is usually about taking the youth through some sort of training to do the work of the traditional church in its youth department, or in outreach, games and entertainment. That's not our approach. One of the things we are experimenting with now, that is unique, we could call holistic discipleship. It isn't about spiritual disciplines per se. On its face, biblical discipleship has to call into question simply developing rigorous behaviors of prayer, scripture reading, etc. Clearly, that is part of what it means to be a disciple, but if you actually look at time in the day, percentages, what are you actually modeling, about what leaders are doing: How do we train the future leaders to go into their communities to bring change? Not everyone will be a spiritual worker or a traditional youth outreach minister; some are crafted to think about the business part of a community, some about public policy, etc. Because we are a holistic mission, we want them to think about which part of the community development work we offer, which part they are most interested in. Maybe they can choose multiple things they are interested in and they enjoy. We are getting beyond the stereotypical ideas of youth ministry, begging a holistic discipleship model of leadership development.

Our youth are role-models in the programs they grew up within. But as Ian describes, they are also recruited to serve in all eight departments of Neighborhood, workforce development, teen moms, education, businesses and bike shop. Some of these young leaders also participate at church, teaching Sunday school or part of the worship band. This was our seventeenth summer with interns running summer programs. Out of twenty-five, twenty-one came from this internal leadership program and focus.

The curriculum is and has been a combination of normal sorts of discipleship elements and community organizing training. Many of our youth and young adults now give leadership to our city's immigration reform efforts which is our major battle ground. There are social and physical barriers to leadership development with our undocumented youth, as illustrated in the *Dream Act*. For those of us working to inspire undocumented immigrant young people to believe that the mean streets of their communities don't have the final say, the message is, "believe in your inherent dignity and call of God; show you are overcomers." They and we must believe that there will be a solution for those that came over the border as small children. For these young people, the passage of the *Dream Act* would allow for a pathway to citizenship in exchange for military service or a college education. Heartbreak after heartbreak has occurred as issues of immigration are hotly contested and the Dream Act fails to become the law of the land. They are not waiting. They are fighting. Ed Pastor, our U.S. congressman has met with them. They traveled to Chicago to tell thousands at a CCDA conference about their aspirations as dreamers for a better future. They joined our community partners to focus on a voter registration initiative to make a dent in the over 300,000 Latinos in AZ who were eligible to vote who remained unregistered. In 2007, the last mayoral election, only seven percent Latino voters turned out at the polls, this summer the turnout was almost forty percent. You can imagine what hope that created in our young leaders. They can change things; they can affect the ways in which our community's voice is heard. Malissa has been watching this take place over her many years with us:

> *I think of Jose Luis, over and under him, he has been surrounded by these beliefs. As a community of people who have come around him and given him tools from the time he first grabbed ahold of his potential, he was invested in, he now has this opportunity to have his passion ignited to transform his community, his peers, and his family. He has many obstacles to stay that course, but he has a whole community around him that believes he can do it – though there are many messages that say to him you can't do it, you're not worthy, yet the mission of Neighborhood encourages him. He's informing students younger than him; they watch him in formal training, in mentoring relationships, in co-ministry kinds of things. His story has been repeated over and over again. "I believe in you, as an indigenous leader – you're the leaders this community needs." This is changing self and community perceptions. It is the fruit of much labor, and this fruit is beginning to surface in a more political sense (community wide). It is transforming the way in which the conversation is happening nationally, undocumented youth at CCDA in 2010 …while showcasing their story in other places, people being impacted like Ed Pastor, for one, so impressed by their preparation as young people, how they framed the issue. I thought, these kids are outstanding, they represent an entire generation, they are shaping culture, informing culture, they are leading the messaging that has gone out to many places. These young people are going to be relevant to a larger community for years to come.*

Our own American history will tell us the role youth play in leading change. We have been getting intimately reacquainted with the stories[156] of a previous generation of Civil Rights leaders (most of who are in their 70s now). They give us a glimpse of the potential futures these young activists might have. The lessons they are learning today will be retrieved and useful for the rest of their lives. Charles Marsh, in *Welcoming Justice* remarks that "the resurgence of faith- based activism and community organizing in recent decades is in some ways a rekindling of the Civil Rights movement's pursuit of redemptive community."[157]   Our young people, from our own beloved community, resemble those forerunners, in risk taking and seemingly fearlessness, in youthful idealism, hope that tomorrow is a better day and one day we will win, and of course, they lead out of their pain.

Maybe young leaders are the greatest sign that hope is on the horizon, many are acknowledging the uniqueness of this generation. A new generation of student leaders and activists gives us reason to hope that better days lie ahead. Young men and women inspired by the dream of the beloved community … they organize on behalf of undocumented immigrant workers and single mothers and abused children, form interracial and interfaith prayer groups, and develop networks of caring and compassion. Many young people are saying, as the SNCC leader Diane Nash said more than four decades ago, "Our goal is to rehabilitate, to heal, to tap the energies of the soul, rather than to gain power or assert control." This reminds me of the Chinese poem so many of us like to quote:

> Go to the people
> Live among them
> Learn from them
> Love them
> Start with what they know
> Build on what they have:
> But of the best leaders

When their task is done
The people will remark
"We have done it ourselves."

EMPOWERMENT

The previous discussion of leadership development from a servant leadership perspective can be wrongfully diagnosed as a disempowering approach. Servant leaders, when they "serve" the poor could create an image of those poor as unable to care for themselves. Our suggestion is that servant leaders are all of us, staff, community members, volunteers, young leaders and all of us are called to "serve" our community. That's where empowerment comes in. It charges the ALL of us to BE the change we desire.

While we're at it, the word "empowerment" can be disempowering. Bob Linthicum, in *Building a People of Power*,[158] responds to the question, "How can the church empower the poor?" by saying:

It's the wrong question because no one can empower another person. The only person who can empower someone is the person him or herself. The only group that can empower a community is the community itself. The task of the church is to join the empowerment of the community – to participate in it, to be an integral part of it, and perhaps even to help make it happen.[159]

What is the role of empowerment as it relates to leadership development, given the two previous disclaimers. What is empowerment? Our friend and fellow traveler Bob Lupton has an illustrative story he likes to tell in answer to this question:

Empowerment is a popular word these days. It may be a misnomer. People, like butterflies, have inbred capacity to emerge into creatures of unique beauty. But intervene in the chrysalis process while the caterpillar is undergoing the transformation and the process may be aborted. Assist the emerging butterfly as it struggles to break out of the cocoon and it may never develop the strength to fly. We may protect the cocoon from predators, even shield it from winter's hostile blast, but do more than create the conditions for timely emergence and we will cause damage. Butterflies, like people cannot be empowered. They will emerge toward their uniquely created potential, given a conducive environment.[160]

We tend to use the phrase "power transfer" as it relates to this process, some think that "mutual transformation" or "empowered by God" better sums it up. Regardless, what we are getting at when it comes to empowerment for emerging community leaders is the effort to see leaders grow to have an increased sense of their value, gifting and calling; to see their own communities changed, equipped with the knowledge that the power and authority reside inside themselves to get the job done. Susan describes a "power transfer" as she has seen it take place in her part of the mission:

> With Googoos, I have seen the potent healing agent of being given what sometimes we call a "power transfer". She has authority, she has leadership, she has a lot of responsibility, and it is given it to her with trust and confidence. Sure, I say, "I'm here, I'm behind you", and "yes you will make mistakes", but watching her grow into her own leadership capacities, as a human being, as a citizen, taking on more and more responsibilities with her whole life, getting off of aid, buying her own home is fun to watch and very exciting. Six years ago she didn't have any clue she could do this.

Though I believe we have had a penchant for giving power away, as Googoos' story illustrates, it wasn't until we began actively using the tools of community organizing that community leadership really accelerated. Saul Alinsky,[161] the father of community organizing, had several operating premises including: 1) Never do for others what they can do for themselves and, 2) There are two kinds of power: money/position and people. What poor people have are lots of people, and that's the basis of organizing.

Organizers know that people won't move toward change and do something about their problems without pain. This was our entrance into the empowerment, leader development tool of organizing. Our church and mission are filled with suffering fearful immigrants, whose lives were relegated to the shadows. This pain led many to trainings with empowerment tools -- fearful people regaining some power over their own lives. Alinsky was single-minded in his ideology and set the pace for all organizers to come. He taught that power is primary. "To know power and not fear it is essential to its constructive use and control."[162] The poor can be organized to take back what power has stolen, and in getting it themselves learn about their own power. Not too long ago, we had a Sunday at church where we focused on immigration issues. The sharers, who boldly told their stories, were immigrants. They have been telling their stories to politicians, pastors, and the media. Their training in organizing is equipping them to come out of the shadows and find their voice. If you asked them if they were powerful, I think many would say yes.

Community organizers remind us of a few Bible passages. One of their favorites is from Exodus 18:23-27. Moses was going to collapse if he didn't find a better way to lead the people. His father-in-law, Jethro, spelled out the better way. Find the leaders among you and empower them, give away some of your power, and set them over the situations that the people are bringing. By empowering others we are freed to do even more. Multiplication of leadership via leadership development is the key to greater community impact. Our people have God-given gifts and talents:

> *He is the one who gave these gifts to the church: the apostles, the prophets, the evangelists, and the pastors and teachers. Their responsibility is to equip God's people to do his work and build up the church, the body of Christ, until we come to such unity in our faith and knowledge of God's Son that we will be mature and full grown in the Lord, measuring up to the full stature of Christ (Eph 4:11-13).*

PROCESS

Having useful tools in your toolbox, like these we have mentioned, work to develop leaders and therefore leads one to … *teach a workshop.* All arrogance aside, having lived long enough to have attended many workshops by people with hefty toolboxes, there is more to leader development than good tools. Leaning into my age for a minute, I have learned that the right

way to tell the story about our development as leaders is to give God the credit. *He develops leaders.* I will testify to that. Unfortunately, I can also testify to the fact that many of the workshop presenters I have known along the way didn't make it. Some great conflict in their soul sabotaged their process and down went their ministry and their reputation. If we desire to develop kingdom minded leaders, the toolbox has to be in the hands of a different craftsman; this throws the ingredient of mystery into the mix. We humans are a work in progress; God's hand is in the mud.

There is a parable that Jesus taught about this mysterious work of God. "A farmer goes to sleep after scattering some seed in his field. He gets up and is busy doing the things he needs to do, and the seeds keep sprouting and growing, and he doesn't understand how. And then they grow into plants that produce grain, and the farmer harvests the crop (Mk 4:26-29)."

We were like the farmer. We got the ground ready. We threw out the seeds of an open door, servant leadership, and empowerment. Before we knew it, the seeds of leaders were sprouting and they kept growing, and, like the farmer, we decided that it must be God who grew the crop, because we didn't have a better explanation. Bobby Clinton[163] has spent a life-time studying[164] the process of leader development from the hands of God. His premise is that:

> God develops a leader over a lifetime. That development is a function of the use of events and people to impress leadership lessons upon a leader (processing), time, and leader response. Processing is central to the theory. All leaders can point to critical incidents in their lives where God taught them something very important.[165]

These critical incidents are many and varied. An alcoholic gets sober, a fearful adult faces their childhood demons, a closeted secret becomes exposed and healed, a religious person learns grace through brokenness, authority is trusted, a gross failure leads to opportunity ... there are so many it would take a library to contain them. These critical incidents have the potential to lead the spirit inside a developing leader to say "yes" to God. At risk of spiritualizing, there is no good commentary on this "yes". Simply put, the leader gives God permission to grow them up, no matter what the cost, no matter what it takes. "Yes God, your process is good."

Sarah adds some thoughts on this:

> *... it feels like a really slow and deep process in which NM builds indigenous leaders. We didn't have high capacity, obvious leaders at NM, so we intentionally kept at it. The per-*

sonal work being done takes longer, but that's the way to do it. As incarnational learners, we refer to what we know: this community has a lot of strengths, it is something to respect, and we recognize what is beautiful and strong about this place out of which the leaders come. We trust their process.

Jeremy describes how he understands this mystery:

As leaders here we learn to tell our stories, our whole stories. This leads to healing, but also leads to changing our communities out of love and compassion. The good and the bad, the grief and lament, all that is inside our story, all of this lead towards seeing the community through God's eyes and seeing ourselves the way God sees us.

As a leader herself, Sarah has done this hard work here at Neighborhood and learned to tell her story. She reminds us that it isn't just about the gifts and calling, the grief and lament, but "your family, roots, blood line, where you are raised, how you were growing up…." This process of knowing ourselves, receiving healing, experimenting with leadership, failing, learning, all of it, she says, "takes so much longer than we'd like and takes a lot of work. But we are seeing a whole new wave of growth, a lot of people stepping up into leadership here, and we haven't compromised our internal values to see it happen."

GRACE RULES – A PROCESS BY WHICH LEADERS GROW

A grace rule is the way grace rules. This rule describes a lavish gift from God as experienced in our community. By receiving it, grace rules – leading us further into love and action

God, by his grace, grows leaders. It is his work. We can structure classes or systems all we want, but the truth is, God grows leaders. It is his school we enroll in and his curriculum we're following. Furthering that metaphor, the Bible reminds us we have tests (temptations). Dr. Clinton, in using his unique leadership formation vocabulary identifies one of the processes of leader development – that of meeting tests and overcoming them. In his language, a test is called an "integrity check".

Two books look at the temptations of Christ as a framework for understanding leadership, Henri Nouwen in *In The Name of Jesus*[166] and also Kris Rocke and Joel Van Dyke, in their newly published *Geography of Grace*.[167] Emerging leaders meet tests, are proved by them, and continue to grow into godliness and influence. (I suppose the converse is: meet tests, fail them, and have to do them over again, and again.) The Bible gives us a glimpse of what this process looked like for Jesus. According to Rocke and Van Dyke, the temptations of Jesus are our story too. "Jesus carries all of humanity into this meeting or, to be more precise, he carries the fullness of humanity into his divine appointment with the tempter."[168] He was tempted in all things as we are (Heb 4:15). But do these temptations resonate with the process of the development of indigenous urban leaders? I think they do.

The temptation of turning stones into bread for our Lord, who traveled forty long days and nights without food, is imagined by Nouwen as the temptation to be relevant, and by Rocke/Van Dyke as the temptation to give into a scarcity mindset. What both authors recognize in this first temptation, is the devil trying to convince Jesus (us) that he has to meet his own needs, or to believe the public message, that more is better: more visibility, more popularity, more of what appears to make people fulfilled. "God is enough, man doesn't live by bread alone, but by every word that comes from the mouth of God," Jesus responds. How do leaders develop this quality? How do they learn that God is enough? Our leaders come from backgrounds where there wasn't enough; not enough love, not enough protection, not enough voice or power, not enough importance, not even enough food. Both Nouwen and Rocke respond that the leader's journey in their development is to discover, intimately and personally the deep, love of God who lavishly provides. "Jesus resists the myth of scarcity and declares God's word reliable in the face of deprivation. God is friend, not foe. God can be trusted. There is enough!"[169] Leaders grow by trusting God to meet their needs, emotional, physical, economic, educational, relational, spiritual, their whole needs.

In the second temptation, the devil takes Jesus to the top of the temple and says, "If you are the Son of God, throw yourself down." This temptation is to be a spectacular rescuer, as Nouwen judges it, or as Rocke/Van Dyke point out, this temptation for Jesus was to exert control over the oppressors of his people, to be a heroic rescuer.

"Why not put God's forgiveness to the test with an act of violence? Why not throw myself into the sacred center of my own house and deal with it on its own terms I will not only turn over the tables of injustice, I will tear the whole damn thing down to its foundations with my bare hands. Vengeance is mine!"[170]

Nouwen asks, "Where is the community of faith we belong to and surrender to? A community where vulnerability and shared life allow for truth-telling, birthing confession and forgiveness?" Where are the people I trust to walk into the fire with me? Who knows me, inside and out? How am I allowed to be a real and fragile person, instead of THE heroic rescuer? The leader is tempted to be the all and all. For people from wounded childhoods, from invisible communities and co- dependent homes, that feels good. But both authors mimic Jesus, "God will not be tested like this." His is not an example of the show-boat televangelist or the slash- and-burn, guns blazing revolutionary. He is the shepherd of the sheep, the humble and suffering servant, the merciful High-Priest, and He is the incarnate God. The developing urban leader will be tested to lead through learning to trust others, by being a part of a loving community that knows you inside and out and won't reject you or neglect you.

And in the last temptation, both our authors describe the temptation for power. Satan tempts Jesus with the kingship over all the kingdoms of the world, should he bow and worship him. Two kingdoms, two rulers, one the king of light, the other the ruler of darkness. And Satan offers Jesus the keys to the kingdom which will rightfully be his one day. But Jesus will not be tempted. Jesus' kingdom is an "upside-down kingdom" ruled by righteousness and justice. Its inhabitants live according to the kingdom's values and domain. Thus the rub! The temptation for Christian leaders, especially those we are focusing on, is to move from a rule of darkness where the corruption of power is compelling, to one expressed by the Beatitudes, one where the grieving, the poor, those persecuted for righteousness sake are blessed. "Choose, young leader, right out of a place of marginalization and powerlessness, choose more of the same!" Nothing is so enticing to developing leaders from oppressive communities than power, especially over those who have oppressed them. As Paulo Freire says in *Pedagogy of the Oppressed*, "...the oppressed, instead of striving for liberation, tend themselves to become oppressors, or sub oppressors. The very structure of their thought has been conditioned by the contradiction of the concrete, existential situation by which they were shaped." Their ideal is to be men; but for them to be men is to be oppressors."[171]

How do you turn down the temptation to play by the rules of this world order? How do you surrender to the rules of a different kingdom? How do you learn to trust

the rule of the kingdom of God? Howard Thurman, Civil Rights theologian and mystic, asked those same questions in an age where the temptation was to use power, the kind Satan wields, to meet power. He taught that we must trust the rules of the kingdom of God for a different kind of power:

What is the word of the religion of Jesus to those who stand with their backs against the wall? There must be the clearest possible understanding of the anatomy of the issues facing them. They must recognize fear, deception, hatred, each for what it is. Once having done this, they must learn how to destroy these or to render themselves immune to their domination. In so great an undertaking it will become increasingly clear that the contradictions of life are not ultimate. The disinherited will know for themselves that there is a Spirit at work in life and in the hearts of men which is committed to overcoming the world. For the privileged and underprivileged alike, if the individual puts at the disposal of the Spirit the needful dedication and discipline, he can live effectively in the chaos of the present the high destiny of a son of God.[172]

As leaders we will be tested (tempted). We will be tempted to choose to meet our own needs vs. trusting God who gives to us abundantly. We will be tempted to trust in our abilities, our capacity to be the spectacular rescuer vs. trusting our faith community, in all their wisdom, protection and even authority. And we will be tempted to trust in the way the power game is played in the world, using its rules to lord it over others, using intimidation, control, and manipulation vs. trusting in a different set of rules, those of the kingdom of God, where Jesus promises that we actually win in the end, whether we see it or not. Trust God from the bottom of your heart; don't try to figure out everything on your own.

Listen for God's voice in everything you do, everywhere you go; he's the one who will keep you on track. Don't assume that you know it all. Run to God! Run from evil! Your body will glow with health; your very bones will vibrate with life! Honor God with everything you own; give him the first and the best. Your barns will burst your wine vats will brim over. But don't, dear friend, resent God's discipline; don't sulk under his loving correction. It's the child he loves that God corrects; a father's delight is behind all this (Pr 3:5-12).

NOTES

143. Prayer has become public domain, but a copy can be found on the Chavez Foundation website: http://www.chavezfoundation.org/ (accessed May 18, 2012).
144. James Downton, *Rebel Leadership: Commitment and Charisma in the Revolutionary Process*, (Macmillan Pub Co., January 1973).
145. James MacGregor Burns, *Leadership*, (New York: Harper & Row, 1978).
146. Timothy A. Judge and Ronald F. Piccolo, "Transformational and Transactional Leadership: A Meta-Analytic Test of Their Relative Validity", University of Florida, *Journal of Applied Psychology*, 2004, Vol. 89, No. 5, 755–768.
147. Bernard M. Bass, *Leadership and Performance Beyond Expectations,* (New York: The Free Press, 1985), 191.
148. Leighton Ford, *Transforming Leadership, Jesus' Way of Creating Vision, Shaping Values and Empowering Change*, (Downers Grove: Intervarsity Press, 1991), 22.
149. A small stream of literature emphasizes the leader as servant, in addition: (Akuchie, 1995; Bordas, 1995; Brody, 1995; Buchen, 1998; Chamberlain, 1995; Frick, 1995; Gaston, 1987; Kelley, 1995; Kiechel, 1995; Kuhnert & Lewis, 1987; Lee & Zemke, 1995; Lloyd, 1996; Lopez 1995; McCollum, 1995; Mc Gee – Cooper & Trammell, 1995; Rasmussen, 1995; Rieser, 1995; Senge, 1995; Snodgrass, 1993; Spears, 1995, 1996; Tatum, 1995; Vanourek, 1995).
150. Robert K. Greenleaf, *Servant Leadership, A Journey into the Nature of Legitimate Power and Greatness*, (New York: Paulist Press, 1977).
151. Kathleen Patterson, "Servant Leadership – A Theoretical Model," Servant Leadership Roundtable, (October, 2003), 1.
152. Ibid., 10.
153. Jeffrey A. Matteson, "Servant versus Self-Sacrificial Leadership: A Behavioral Comparison of Two Follower-Oriented Leadership Theories," International Journal of Leadership Studies, Regent University, Justin A. Irving, Bethel University, (August 2005).
154. Laub, J. (1999). Assessing the servant organization: Development of the servant organizational leadership (SOLA) instrument. Dissertation Abstracts International, 60(02), 308. (UMI No. 9921922).
Laub, J. (2003). From paternalism to the servant organization: Expanding the Organizational Leadership Assessment (OLA) model. Proceedings of the Servant Leadership Research Roundtable. Retrieved July 15, 2004, from http://www.regent.edu/acad/cls/2003ServantLeadershipRoundtable/Laub.pdf
Laub, J. (2004). Defining Servant Leadership: A recommended typology for Servant Leadership studies. Proceedings of the Servant Leadership Research Roundtable. Retrieved October 5, 2004, from http://www.regent.edu/acad/sls/publications/journals_and_proceedings/proceedings/

servant_leadership_roundt able/pdf/laub-2004SL.pdf.

Patterson, K. (2003).Servant Leadership: A theoretical model. Dissertation Abstracts International, 64(02), 570. (UMI No. 3082719)

Patterson, K. A. (2004). Servant Leadership: A theoretical model. Proceedings of the American Society of Business and Behavioral Sciences, 11(1), 1109-1118.

Spears, L. (1995).Servant Leadership and the Greenleaf legacy. In L. Spears (Ed.), Reflections on Leadership: How Robert K. Greenleaf's Theory of Servant-Leadership Influenced Today's Top Management Thinkers (pp. 1-14). New York: John Wiley & Sons.

Spears, L. (1996). Reflections on Robert K. Greenleaf and servant leadership. The Leadership and Organization Development Journal, 17(7), 33-35.

Spears, L. C. (Ed.). (1998). Insights on leadership: Service, stewardship, spirit, and servant-leadership. New York: John Wiley & Sons.

155. Alan Andrews, "Everyone Gets to Play, Your Role in God's Kingdom," http://www.navpress.com/product/9781600064227/Everyone-Gets-to-Play-Alan-K-Andrews.

156. David Halberstam, *The Children*, (New York: Fawcett Books, 1998). I read the harrowing story of the young leaders from Nashville who found themselves propelled into the leadership of the civil rights movement. Though the names are different, and we don't have lunch counter problems, our youth are these youth, almost categorically. The Children, by David Halberstam, (New York: Fawcett Books. 1998).

157. Charles Marsh and John Perkins, 91.

158. Robert C. Linthicum, *Building a People of Power*, (Colorado Springs: Authentic Publishing, 2005).

159. Ibid., 273.

160. Mary Nelson, *Empowerment*, (Bloomington: iUniverse, 2010), 5.

161. Saul Alinsky, *Rules for Radicals*, (New York: Vintage Books, 1971).

162. Ibid., 52.

163. J. Robert Clinton, *The Making of a Leader*, (Colorado Springs: NavPress, 1988).

164. Clinton, Senior Professor of Leadership at Fuller Seminary, has codified an entire vocabulary and systematic thinking around God's process of leadership development. This paragraph helps in gathering some of his perspective on his research: "Leadership is a lifetime of lessons. It is not a set of do-it-yourself correspondence courses that can be worked through in a few months or years. In our attempt to 'think back on how [biblical and Christian leaders] lived and died', we will learn to analyze these lessons. Through this, we will accumulate data and process it by using a tool, the time-line. As we reflect on this data, we will see various patterns emerge that will indicate the many ways God developed and strengthened leaders in the past for their particular leadership roles. We can profit from both how God

developed them and what God taught them. As we apply these lessons to or lives, we will be imitation their faith." (Clinton: 1988, 40).

165. J. Robert Clinton, 25.
166. Henri Nouwen, *In The Name of Jesus*, (New York: The Crossroad Publishing Co., 1989).
167. Kris Rocke and Joel Van Dyke, *Geography of Grace*, (Tacoma: Street Psalms Press, 2012).
168. Rocke and Van Dyke, 107.
169. Ibid., 111.
170. Ibid., 114.
171. Paulo Freire, http://www.freire.org/paulo-freire/quotes-by-paulo-freire/ (accessed March 27, 2010).
172. Howard Thurman, *Jesus and the Disinherited*, (Boston: Beacon Press, 1976), 108.

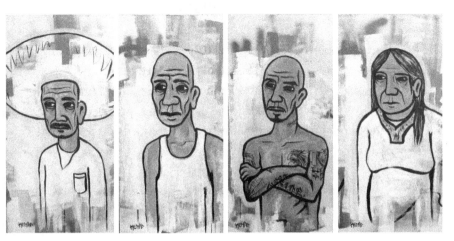

"Overlooking" series
Derrick Kempf

CHAPTER SEVEN

We are Called to
THE WORK OF JUSTICE

Core Value #6

Definition: Justice is consistent with the heart of God, leading to righteousness, the expression of God's love in society. Injustice is an affront to God and demands we press for a just social order. We believe that the Bible calls us to a preferential love for the poor and to pursue a lifestyle and stewardship consistent with justice.

"Injustice anywhere is a threat to justice everywhere."
– Martin Luther King, Jr.

Our son, Ian, leads our social justice work at Neighborhood. He is inclined to speak about the powers and principalities at work in our community that oppress those we love. So he teaches about community organizing, gives our youth tools to take their lives back and reminds all of us that Jesus walks with the powerless. Nothing has made us feel more powerless than the oppressive conditions that suffocate our immigrant friends. For going on ten years, things have gone from bad to worse. State and county leaders have set aside important matters and spent millions of dollars to make hunting immigrants their primary agenda. One day, about a year or so ago, federal dollars were spent to send eight hundred ICE agents into Arizona. With full swat gear and automatic weapons poised – these agents packed drove through our neighborhoods like an invading army. We had no idea until the end of the day what they were doing here. They were trying to shut down two van companies thought to be transporting immigrants from the border to other places in the country. The fear of our neighbors turned to hysteria, and our church opened a refuge all day for our friends who were sure the entire neighborhood was under siege.

Meanwhile, the war of attrition, as our public officials' state proudly, is in effect. If all resources are cut off, is the logic, immigrants will leave Arizona and go someplace else. They suggest they'll go back home, unaware, presumably, that most of those here have been here for decades, and call this home. And the wall along the border is built; a wall, not a fence, not a boundary, but a defensive barrier of iron and steel.

Our collective powerlessness had led us to Jesus, who teaches us not to be afraid, who reminds us he has overcome the world. A few years ago, faith leaders gathered to share stories of how all of us in our immigrant communities were faring. The term, "faith-rooted-organizing" had been floating around. It helps us better understand our unique organizing approach. As people of faith, we have a power, a supernatural power from on high. We were asked to remember another wall, the wall President Ronald Regan so famously challenged Soviet leader Mikhail Gorbachev to destroy –"Mr. Gorbachev tear down this wall!"

Did you know that for twenty years the German church on both sides of the wall had been praying, weekly, outside their church buildings on street corners? Every week faithfully they prayed asking God to destroy the wall. Every week multiple congregations came outside to a public place to pray. It was the church praying, like the horns of Jericho that brought that wall tumbling. So we started. Every week, in the hot, in the busyness, in the fear, in the sadness, we pray on our street corner for immigration reform. We pray for our friends who are detained, for laws to change, for the officials to be converted, for help for those we are overwhelmed about. We cry out. Our circle often has an icon or item we leave behind. We end each prayer time singing the same song, "The Lord hears the cry of the poor."

Miguel was picked up in an ICE raid. His children got wind of it and showed up crying at his place of business as they watched their father handcuffed and thrown into a vehicle. The days following were littered with getting a lawyer, the family trying to make decisions, hoping to get the message to Miguel not to sign anything, which is the first rule of thumb. The children, older and all born here, couldn't imagine going back to Mexico. What would they do, where should they go? How unsafe was it to remain here? Shockingly, Miguel signed something and was instantly deported to a southern state in Mexico, over a thousand miles from Phoenix. What now? We prayed. Everyone suffered. What would his wife do for work to make up for the salary lost by her husband?

A few weeks later, ICE showed up at her door. Though terrified she let them in. Instead of being there to arrest someone else, they asked for her husband. "Well, you deported him," she said. They were confused. The paper they had asked Miguel to sign was implicating his employer who had paid these workers to come over years earlier as his employees. Miguel would be a key witness – he was needed for their case. Travel fees were provided to bring him back to the border. ICE met him there with a work VISA in hand, a temporary social security card and escorted him back over the border and to his family.

LOVE COMPELS US

The social justice issue of our community and in our ministry is a broken immigration system that forces immigrant men, women and children into the shadows, separates families through deportation, and denies college access to young leaders who have grown up in the U.S. It has been a flagrant issue in Arizona since 2003; and has been the instrument in the hands of God to develop skills in us and in our organization to deal with the power structures that are oppressing our friends. We became community organizers; we moved from a strict focus on doing holistic ministry as an expression of our understanding of preaching a whole gospel and added public advocacy to our Christian work.

We engage in the work of social justice because we love our

neighbor, and we love our neighbor because we first loved God. Our justice work is a direct link to loving our neighbor. Though it might look like politics, it is really just love. Seeing the extension of love like this has opened us up to the Kingdom of God and its reign and rule.

> The doctrine of the Kingdom of God is meant to be the teleology of the entire faith because that is what Jesus himself taught! The Kingdom is both present and future, 'always coming, always pressing in on the present, always big with possibility, and always inviting immediate action (141).' It is a vision of 'humanity organized according to the will of God (142).' Thus it demands something of all of us. It demands that we press for a just social order. It demands that there be progress in the love of God and neighbor, not just with individual persons, but in the way we organize our common life together. This love finds its highest expression when its members begin to hold in common those things the super-personal forces of evil urge us to grasp and hoard, i.e. money, property, capital, personal rights, affluence, power, and control. This progressive reign of love should move each person toward the "other" in ever increasing unity.[173]

MLK, Jr. in his "I have a Dream" speech keeps reminding us that love can't wait. There is *the fierce urgency of Now*.[174] Immediate action, that's what is required so often with love, the act that can't stay suppressed because of the pain of the one loved. The house is burning down. Something must be done. The work of social justice at Neighborhood Ministries is the action of love inside the injustices affecting our community in real time. Jacques Ellul spoke to my generation and taught us that:

...there are moments when history is flexible, and that is when we must put ourselves inside to move the works. But when the atomic bomb is dropped, it is no longer the moment to attach a parachute to it. It's all over. I don't believe in a permanent determinism, in the inexorable course of nature. Fate operates when people give up; when the structures of and the relationships between groups, special interests, coalitions, and ideologies are not yet rigid; when new facts appear that change the rules of the game; then at these moments we can make decisions that direct history, but very quickly everything becomes rigid and mechanical, and then nothing more can be done. One of my greatest disappointments is the extreme incapacity of Christians to intervene when situations are fluid and their habit of passionately taking sides when it is too late for anything but fate to operate. They are pushing the wheel of a vehicle that is already rolling downhill by itself.[175]

DESCRIBE THE ONE YOU LOVE – IMAGO DEI AND HUMAN RIGHTS

I recall an incident when I was working in our local public school. I can still see clearly where I was standing. I was discussing a student with a teacher. I loved this particular kid; the teacher hated him. That was the moment I realized that our society could just throw a person away; that some human beings were considered disposable, expendable. How it must disgust God, our creator, that in our cultures and human societies we behave this way and find justification for it. "We must fully recognize that as any group of people is deemed disposable or expendable, any popularized American notion of 'liberty and justice for all' will remain nothing but a myth...a big lie."[176] Susan has also had one of these reckonings. She says:

I never knew there was so much injustice in America until I came here to NM. I used to believe that justice prevailed. I have watched such serious injustice done to people in our community by people in power, that I no longer believe it. It is a sad loss. I have watched it from a doctor's office, where a white family gets preference and our family is ignored, to seeing the way our families are treated in a broken immigration system. And lately our eyes have been opened to the way people are treated in the criminal justice system. I have said in the past, that social justice work gets our attention off of God, trying to put so much attention on the issues, but as we read The New Jim Crow, the first chapters were overwhelming, and then after reading more, I saw that everywhere I turn this is all happening around me. The very fact that I have some special standing, being white, offends me so much. I don't know what it all looks like, I don't have a vision for what can be fixed, but I have to be educated about it, I have to be willing to do some hard things that are outside my comfort zone, and to cry out to God for justice. What is needed is a changing of men and women's hearts from the inside out, a revelation. Just like it was for me. One thing, once you know, you can't pretend you don't know anymore. You see so many things. You can't go back to the way it was before, your eyes are opened.

There is a biblical and God-centered view of humanity that counteracts the disturbing human propensity to discard and make invisible "the other". It is the theology of Imago Dei, the stamp of the image of God on all human beings. Jurgen Moltmann, in *God for a Secular Society* grasped this:

> Theologically, the human being's likeness to God is not based on the qualities of human beings. It is grounded in their relationship to God. That relationship is a double one. It means God's relation to human beings and the re-

lation of human beings to God. Human beings' objective likeness to God subsists in God's relation to them. This is indestructible and can never be lost. Only God can end it. The dignity of each and every person is based on this objective likeness to God. God has a relationship to every embryo, every severely handicapped person, and every person suffering from one of the diseases of old age, and he is honored and glorified in them when their dignity is respected. This list can be expanded to all humanity... those in prison; those citizens of countries were we are engaged in military conflict, etc…. Without fear of God, God's image will not be respected in every human being and the reverence for life will be lost, pushed out by utilitarian criteria. But in the fear of God there is no life that is worthless and unfit to live.[177]

Our theological underpinnings protest all dehumanization. We are required by obedience to the Creator God, who made all human beings in his image, to embrace a common humanity. But, social forces being what they are, beginning sometimes at birth, assign one's identity formation. Instead of being of infinite worth, a person becomes part of the societal hierarchy, and based on a position in this hierarchy, can be launched into a process of dehumanization. In *Pedagogy of the Oppressed*, Paulo Freire calls dehumanization "a distortion of the vocation of becoming more fully human [and] the result of an unjust order that engenders violence in the oppressors, which in turn dehumanizes the oppressed."[178]

"We hold these truths to be self-evident," says the American Declaration of Independence, "that all men are created equal…." Every human being is a person endowed with inalienable human rights. We declare this, as Americans, but first and foremost, we must declare this as biblical (or Abrahamic) people. Again as Jurgen Moltmann so beautifully says:

> In the 'prophetic' religions, Judaism, Christianity and Islam, the liberty and equality of all human beings is derived from belief in creation … the fact that all human beings are made in the image of God is the foundation of human dignity. … In their relationship to the transcendent God, human beings become persons whose dignity must not be infringed. The institutions of law, government and economy must respect this personal dignity, which is the endowment of all human beings, if they claim to be 'humane institutions'.[179]

God desires that we afford all human beings dignity and equal respect or consideration; these are some of the ingredients of a Christian ethical ideal of the common good. We can't help but remember that the human beings who need this most are those whose basic rights are most imperiled. As the Bible says: "He pled the cause of the afflicted and needy; then it was well. Is not that what it means to know me? Declares the LORD (Jer 22:16)." Marcos educates us:

> *As someone who the church became the voice for, it feels joyful, less discouraging, knowing there are people [as much as minorities get racially profiled] – a community of Mexican Americans, whites, African Americans – who help out. It makes me feel loved and accepted, regardless of how authorities feel about us. Some minorities are uninformed, and because of their ignorance, they tend to get a bad end of stuff, they don't know their rights, they don't have someone to call. If they knew their rights, maybe not as an American citizen, but human rights, they'd know that they deserve dignity and respect. I see us as the church that is not silent, about unjustly*

racial profiling, which is very inhumane. When the church members become the voice for them, other ministries should follow our example. It just takes one to make a difference, as a community, as a ministry. What is happening in our city and state is inhumane and how can someone, (not my place to judge those other Christians), how can you say you are of God and you see things that are hurting people and don't speak up. But as members of Phoenix, the presence of the Lord is at work advocating for people. We have to remind our country that we are, after all, a nation under God indivisible with liberty and justice for all. That has to mean that if you're not an American, you can't be treated like an animal, when our nation was founded by immigrants.

What are the basic human rights that biblically ought to be afforded to undocumented immigrants, given that most have significant need, and many have particular vulnerabilities, e.g., women and children. People of God must respond with obedience to these decrees: offering hospitable treatment to those seeking work, supporting people fleeing harsh and even mortal consequences of staying in the homeland, nurturing children who are separated from their undocumented parents who are in detention facilities, and speaking out against threats of massive deportation. Panda adds:

I think that we should be fighting for the rights of people; it's wrong that people are accused of things that aren't even crimes. Being discriminated against, getting stones thrown at you for being Mexican is wrong. As a church that's our job, it's what God wants us to do. We are obligated to do something, to not just watch what is happening – the majority of us are Mexicans here – brown skinned – it just shows the love we have for God that our little church won't be si-

lent, we have a desire to do his will.

Recognition of the "stranger" or "alien" as neighbor attests to what the Universal Declaration of Human Rights calls a common "faith in fundamental human rights, in the dignity and worth of the human person."[180]   Under the International Bill of Rights, human persons are never divested of moral standing, and should never rhetorically be effaced as "illegal." Non- citizenship status does not equate with non-citizenship in the world community, in the Kingdom of God and in the church. Our immigrant friends carry a story that compels us to see, hear and act on their behalf, to redress the "oppression, intimidation, violence, and terrorism" that all too often induced them to migrate against their will.[181]   "Who is my neighbor," the lawyer asks Jesus. Today's immigrant (especially those that are undocumented) can easily be the one beaten on the road and also the one the religious walk on by. In solidarity with migrants, the disciple of Jesus could be heard to say, "What must I do to live"? "Turn to the world of the poor, of the half-dead stranger…," in the martyred Archbishop Romero's words, "becoming incarnate in their world, proclaiming the good news to them even to the point of sharing their fate.[182]

Marcos, Alex and Francisco, go back and forth about our need to be in solidarity with migrants. These are some of their thoughts:

I thought that the U.S. was the land of the free, but once you're here, nothing is free. The U.S. wants their crops picked. The immigrants that come here want to build houses, get a job, just to come and work; the U.S. wants the labor, but throws them back. To protect the immigrant is like protecting the poor. They are the poor. God is saying to these poor, 'come with me and I will take you to a better place.' They want to come here, work with the crops, and have a family. We all believe in one God, but this world is so cruel. It's like they are blocking God. One thing God has said, "Remember my people, the poor". And instead they are rejecting them. We should welcome them, they are our neighbors.

THEOLOGY, POWER AND COMMUNITY

We Christians, in order to embrace a complex conversation about power and community transformation, need to and usually do, construct new theologies. When we at Neighborhood entered the world of advocacy, we realized our tool box was pretty empty. Evangelicals aren't equipped with tools to engage in systems fighting. So we started learning. The tools that we were given enabled us to go further and farther with leadership development, than ever before. It was like a whole new world was opened to us. And we read books like *Transforming Power*[183] by Robert Linthicum. He became a sort of biblical coach alongside us as we proceeded into this new frontier. As evangelicals, we needed to know all this organizing, which we were becoming good at, was biblical. We had been outgrowing our old narrowness regarding change and the tools needed, anyway. Theologians and practitioners, who are committed to community transformation, are forced to address the divide between those targeting personal engagement, sin and repentance and those who change communities through systemic engagement, addressing systemic sin and demanding repentance. Linthicum focuses exclusively on changing evil systems and offers a method. He says "there has to be a better way"[184] recommending "the intentional use of power by God's people"[185] as the better way. The first part of his book is the full theological treatment of relational power and the second part is a primer on community organizing for those who have adopted the theological premise already stated. Power, as understood by Linthicum is for the elimination of poverty, and the establishment of a "shalom community" where justice reigns. Linthicum is attempting to equip the church in the use of power for community organizing in a way that influences values, systems and individuals.

The theological question here has to do with the biblical framework of systems. Linthicum suggests there are three: political, economic and religious. He begins with what the Bible has to say about systemic change, or "the world as God intended it to be". These can be found in Israel's "constitution," Deuteronomy, and also in the richest understanding of the word Shalom. The living it out is what Jesus meant by the kingdom of God. Approaching "the world as God intended it to be" by referencing these three, Deuteronomy, Shalom and the Kingdom of God and weaving them together, is beautiful and brilliant. The church is the current holder of the prophetic role calling the systems to accountability, to "how God intended it". This is really good kingdom theology.

Linthicum focus' on building relational power, it is the vehicle through which change takes place; building the right kind of relationships, and investing time and energy in them. The biblical examples here are Nehemiah, Jesus and Paul. They built a movement and changed the landscape of their day and the future by building relationships where together the vision of what it could be was agreed upon and drove their work. The challenge is to make relationships with people who have a "fire in their belly" who are hungry to see things transformed. Build relationships, not programs. "The way to enable people to 'do for themselves' is by enabling them to work together to empower each other, not by developing a program that only strengthens their dependency."[186] These biblical leaders, their theologies and their methodologies mentored and built some concrete practices. Linthicum's point is that these practices are the favored and tested practices of community organizers. In fact, Linthicum says that those who seek to bring transformation to their communities this way have become disciples of the power of a relational culture. Jeremy would say, these methodologies have mentored us as well:

Justice work in our community is one of the focal points -- because it has helped us – leadership development grows in leaps and bounds once we began doing justice work. It taps into the intuitive understanding of what communities need and want, and the intuitive understanding of what God wants and how He has created them; it helps to teach others about justice and reconciliation – a tool that binds the community together, because they share an understanding of what's wrong in the community. If we ignore that, it makes almost everything else we are trying to do, impossible, (how can you talk about the love of God and being created in his image, if you can't get a job). "We learn the value of working together through addressing the issues of what holds people back – instead of blaming them for what is wrong."

Does community organizing work? Of course it does, the tools are invaluable and have changed the way in which many have engaged their community's problems. Linthicum defends his thesis this way: "These are the principles and strategies that work. But are they truly biblical? Nowhere in Scripture will we find a text that reads, 'Thou shalt do community organizing.' But the principles of community organizing are woven through the warp and woof of Scripture as it presents a theology of relational power."[187] Claudia is not a theologian, but she knows what works:

Every time I think about justice, I think about immigration. God definitely works for justice. I have an upfront and personal story about that, justice was served, in my opinion, in my life. But of course, it's not just for me, I know that Neighborhood works toward making everybody valued and the individual is respected and seen as a whole person, the one that God created. It is seen in those trips to the capital and those trips to do voter registrations, vigils and the marches – getting involved – I think we are called to be Christ in your body; for me that means, sticking out for the people who are being persecuted and pushed around. It is exactly what Jesus came to do; he didn't come to judge, he came and was here, and stuck up for people who needed someone to comfort them. Representing Christ the way he would live, that's justice.

INDIVIDUAL VS. SUPRAINDIVIDUAL

Ian has become an educator and coach here at Neighborhood on these methodologies:

Our justice work keeps us from being from co-opted. It keeps us from being complicit, which the church often becomes, for its own survival. Justice allows us to think bigger, for the sake of the kid who I am already working with -- legislatures, civic leaders, city officials, make decisions that have real effect on other people's lives -- laws, policies, targeted practices ... all affecting the kid I work with. To the extent that we participate in the process of engaging those systems that affect my kid and introduce God's values into the situation, we will see social justice in our community. Justice also begs the reality that no one else will do this for us, when someone says, this isn't my issue, then "I'm" voting for the status quo, they will have to live with the consequences of their decision.

Historically, there has been a primary issue inside conservative Protestantism that keeps its adherents from being properly involved fighting injustice. It is the issue of the individual as the primary entity of concern. The embedded "rugged" individualism found in America, and in American Christianity (especially the Evangelical sort) is difficult to eliminate and complicates, significantly, a vibrant socio-political engagement. Sarah takes the long view:

> *I really am proud that Neighborhood spends so much time talking about justice. It feels tricky to be involved in issues of justice for a church, and the complexity of the politics, donors, words like that, when you publically start talking about something you care about. It is risking a lot, I know. I believe it is born out of the beloved community, where I agree that I am going to think and talk about this beloved community of mine. Yet it is global and bigger than this local community, too. My beloved community is these other human beings, and I must care about doing right by them, also, and also that laws do right by them. There must be respect for people who aren't given respect. This tricky road is not just about ministering to people who are distressed, but acknowledging how the national community does right by people. I have moved from caring about a person to caring about the national conversation.*

Injustices in our world today all have roots that lie inside systemic configurations, and therefore often require policy, law or political change. But the framework that most Christians carry solves all problems at the level of the individual and individual actions. Evangelical sociologists Michael O. Emerson and Christian Smith[188] have been revealing this problem for over a decade. Smith and Emerson refer to the white evangelical's cultural tool kit as containing three tools that make it almost impossible to look at the structural and embedded injustices in society. These are "accountable freewill individualism, relationalism (attaching central importance to interpersonal relationships), and antistructuralism (inability to perceive or unwillingness to accept social structure influences)."[189] These three organize evangelical's experiences and evaluate their reality.

Accountable freewill individualists exist independent of structure and institutions, and because of freewill are individually accountable for their own actions.[190] "The roots of this individualist tradition run deep, dating back to shortly after the sixteenth-century Reformation, extending to much of the Free Church tradition, flowering in America's frontier awakenings and revivals, and maturing in spiritual pietism and anti-Social Gospel fundamentalism."[191] There is distrust of public persons (non-Christians) and their moral guidelines and individuals (Christians) have the free will to make the choices they deem best. These evangelicals understand their roll in the public square through the modernist-fundamentalist schism even though this historical scenario doesn't necessarily claim dominance over evangelical engagement any longer. The assumed central theologies of sin and salvation which are leftover from the fundamentalist positions dominate.

Interestingly, though the issue of sin is so prominent for freewill individualists, it is sin in the narrowest understanding of it. If sin is simply personal wrong actions or individuals evil attitudes, then the sinful actions of groups and communities, to which we all belong and therefore all are complicit get dismissed, or worse these sins are none of our business. Tim Suttle writes to this point in *An Evangelical Social Gospel*. In this small book, he is rediscovering the theology of Walter Rauschenbusch the great social reformer. Suttle reflects on the "folk theologies of evangelicalism" (a very interesting terminology) including the theology of sin-as-one. Rauschenbusch took the consciousness of sin very seriously, so much so that he turned the critique on the defenders of evangelical folk theology of sin, noting how their overemphasis on personal sinfulness had left them completely blind to the ways in which they are culpable for the social sins which plague society. He wrote,

If the exponents of the old [read individualistic] theology

A COMMUNITY CALLED G.R.A.C.E.

have taught humanity an adequate consciousness of sin, how is it that they themselves have been blind and dumb on the master iniquities of human history? During all the ages while they were the theological keepers of the conscience of Christendom, the peasants in the country and the working class in the cities were being sucked dry by the parasitic classes of society, and war was damning poor humanity. Yet what traces are there in traditional theology that the minds of old-line theologians were awake to these magnificent manifestations of the wickedness of the human heart?[192]

To address this problem, the evangelical goes back to his toolbox and pulls out from it, the bedrock tool of relationalism. Relationalism (a strong emphasis on interpersonal relationships) "derives from the view that human nature is fallen and that salvation and Christian maturity can only come through a personal relationship with Christ."[193] "Evangelicals see themselves as uniquely possessing a distinctively effective means of social change; working through personal relationships to allow God to transform human hearts from the inside-out, so that all ensuing social change will be thorough and long-lasting."[194] In evangelical churches, the gospel message is about a sinner, who needs salvation, who can receive what they need by praying a prayer and asking the Savior to forgive them and who receives eternal life. This version of the gospel is only about the person and God, and carries few social implications.

What is heard is that Christianity is really just concerned with the souls of people and their spiritual needs. It doesn't concern itself with the well-being of the planet or even with justice. There is a subtle and sometimes not all too unsubtle message that, it's all going to burn anyway.

Unfortunately, this conflicts with a biblical understanding of God, a God who cares about all of life, who so loved the world and who requires we pray for "the kingdom to come on earth."

Tandem to this is rationalisms' form of "trickle down." Saved people, live differently, affect other people by evangelizing them, and they change, and then bad things that hurt other people are changed by Christians living good lives. Christian Smith, in another of his socio- treatments of evangelicalism, *American Evangelicalism*, calls this methodology of social change that happens from person to person, "the personal influence strategy." "As a subcultural tool for social change, the personal influence strategy constrains evangelicals' ability to understand how the social world actually works and limits their capacity to formulate appropriate and useful responses and solutions to social, economic, political and cultural problems."[195] He goes on to say that "this personal influence strategy exacts a cost. It tends to render evangelicals rather blind to the Supraindividual social structures, aggregate effects, power dynamics, and institutional systems which profoundly shape human consciousness, experience, and life- chances."[196] Ian sees this also:

> *Justice starts to address the issue of individual vs. corporate sins. Personal responsibility (which is an American value) says, 'if you make good decisions you will have good things that happen to you'. If you never address justice issues, the personal responsibility value is always brought up. It's "me and Jesus", familiar theological underpinnings aid in that value/viewpoint – we are forgiven for our personal sins, and not necessarily concerned with our corporate sins – we don't talk about the sins of the church, just personal salvation, and this is the biggest stumbling block. We have a responsibility to the community – but we lack understanding and imagination of the mystery of God. Because we have to have it all figured out – one of the best ways to do that is to individualize things – to compartmentalize everything.*

When evangelicals have a social world view that begins and ends with individuals and their decisions there is no room for a problem to be solved differently. For it must be acknowledged, it is not just people who sin, but systems that oppress, not just a good Christian who could make a difference, but a global church that together could represent the cause of Christ, and not just a street kid who drops out of school but a community that battles structural problems that have been broken for generations. This is very difficult for the average evangelical to hear. "Corporate sin is so disconnected from the reality of our typical American Christian life that we are shocked when it actually enters our world. Rather than confront sin, we begin to look for ways to categorize it as a theologically liberal agenda – thereby stripping corporate confession and repentance of its prophetic power." [197] This is the church experience which Isiah has known for his 65 years:

> *Neighborhood is dealing with the number one social issue in the country, immigration. And I think it should be, because of the hurt and pain coming out of this, especially for families, the separation of families. Unless things turn around, every Christian church will have to make hard decisions, it is something you can't assume is going away, in our city and state, even our country. The church will have to take a stand. It reminds me of slavery, the civil rights movement. Some will never get involved; I think that if we really look at God's word, the real conviction we have is to get involved, with the weak, the sojourner, the stranger, God requires it of us. It seems like, every issue like this that comes up, we never learn lessons, it is a repeat that has to start all over again, slavery, Native Americans, segregation, it is a repeat of the same thing. We have the history, but we don't use history*

to make these hard choices, or from God above, for the new generation to get involved. People have to rise up, to the urgency or the call.

The conclusion must be that our history of an individual-only-gospel is problematic for the fullest understanding of the ways in which Christians engage society on all issues pertaining to injustice, oppression and all forms of collective complicity against our neighbor. Building an apologetic for any Christian today who desires a biblical response to human suffering must encounter head on and become counterculture to the wedge of individualism.

CHANGING SYSTEMS

We get involved in social justice issues with biblical purpose and in some ways with ruthless faith, knowing that the implications of our involvement are designed to see bad things changed. Even Bono says, "The world is more malleable than you think. You can wrestle it from fools."[198] Changing the systems that are oppressing the people you love takes us beyond what we have been doing and are accustomed to. Ian is teaching our youth this principle:

> *I push a systemic perspective on problems, not telling the students that injustices are a result of their personal problems, and not challenging them to solve the problems personally. Instead we look at the root societal causes. It's important to flip the social message on its head with leaders. For example, "You've internalized the message that dads don't go to church on Sundays because people 'only come for stuff here' – is that the answer, really? The dads work all week, Sundays is the day off, Sunday may be set aside for mass at the Catholic Church, but rarely. I love to do that with leaders" How you are is OK, it isn't bad, do we have to create*

people who are little "messy"? We are not colonizing them; we are building the kingdom their way, based on their roots and their context. It might not facilitate our organizational growth, to develop community leaders, but we do it anyway.

Quoting the Reverend William Sloane Coffin, who was used to explaining this difference in "doing" to Christians, taught it this way: "Charity is a matter of personal attributes; justice a matter of public policy. Charity seeks to alleviate the effects of injustice; justice seeks to eliminate the causes of it. Charity in no way affects the status quo, while justice leads inevitably to political confrontation."[199] Dom Helder Camara, former Brazilian Archbishop, said, "When I give food to the poor, they call me a saint. When I ask why they are poor, they call me a Communist."[200] Dietrich Bonhoeffer said, "Bandaging the victims under the wheel is still important and necessary," I said, "but if we don't get at the root cause of those injuries—if we don't jam the spoke in the wheel that's creating victims—then people will continue to be injured."[201] These quotes highlight that engaging in justice work gets underneath something the status quo, or our religious structures and theological bents or maybe even evil doesn't want us to disturb. Malissa has heard these disturbances:

You can hear criticisms against the social gospel – even though justice is righteousness or right living – but justice is not the norm of where we are today. NM is a frontrunner in the faith community, standing among the poor, saying the poor have a voice, talent, dignity, are hugely important, fighting for them in all kinds of ways, expanding world views – fighting on the frontlines for our immigrant friends and the way they are being treated. And this is truly an injustice – since the beginning of our nation there has been exploitation of immigrant labor – what a disconnect! -- using immigrants to build the wealth of a nation and then labeling them criminal. NM has called it out early; it was unjust targeting children in prop 300 and unjust to demonize other human beings. This is today's issue of justice; we need to think about it in a sophisticated way. In the NM video, we are challenged to have "eyes to see—seeing things we have been trained not to see, seeing things we have been taught not to see."

PRINCIPALITIES AND POWERS

Thinking theologically and doing theology as it relates to injustice leads us into very difficult topics, that of evil, power and systemic corruption. This is the next necessary theology we must enter when trying to address necessary social and structural change. Remembering that evangelicals hold to change happening through conversion of individuals, evil is also seen through that same paradigm; evil is personal, and dealt with in the personal realm. But what about evil and Satan as they are manifested in the socio-political realm, both collectively and individually, in such evils as injustice, exploitation, oppression, materialism, war, ethnic hatred, persecution, destruction of humans and of creation? How can sin and the evil one be identified and fought in this realm? What if evil is both personal/demonic and also impersonal and embedded in systems and institutions? And what if both could equally be discussed through the lens of the Bible? Dietrich Bonheoffer wrote in 1932, "How can one close one's eyes at the fact that the demons themselves have taken over rule of the world, that it is the powers of darkness who have here made an awful conspiracy?"[202] The Bible says, "Our battle is not against flesh and blood but against the principalities and powers of this dark world." It is a reminder that there are people behind oppressive structures and those people are not the enemies, but the systems are.

What makes this so difficult to understand is our underdeveloped theological framework of evil and of the evil one, Satan. This statement by N.T. Wright helps:

> When we humans commit idolatry – worshiping that which is not God as if it were – we thereby give to other creatures and beings in the cosmos a power, a prestige, an authority over us which we, under God, were supposed to have over them. When you worship an idol, whatever it is, you abdicated something of your own proper human authority over the world and give it instead to that thing whatever it is. You call into being a negative force, an anti-God force which is opposed to creation because, being itself part of the transient world, it is bound to decay and die and will, if we're not careful, drag us down with it. That is why I think there is at least a grain of truth in the theory, made famous by Walter Wink,[203] that the inner or hidden forces latent within organizations, companies, societies, legislative bodies and even churches are the sum total of the spiritual energies which humans have put into them, abdicating their own responsibility and allowing the organization, whatever it is, to have it instead.[204]

But, what if in the fight, in the desire to defeat the enemy, we don't abdicate? And by "we" I mean the church. We don't defuse our God-given spiritual energies; don't relegate our God-given authority to principalities and powers bent toward injustice. What if, instead we strain toward the hope of the victory already won (Rom 5:1-5; 8:31-39), holding to the victory of Jesus Christ over all the powers of evil and darkness as "the central theme around which all the other varied meanings of the cross find their particular niche?"[205] And allow that victory to drive the activity of justice it promotes? That would be good news, good news indeed.

The primary weapon against the Powers has always been and will always remain the liberating message of Jesus. That small word or testimony is sufficient to bring down the whole army of Powers and Principalities. The Gospel is the most powerful antidote for domination that the world has ever known. It was that antidote that inspired the abolition of slavery, the women's movement, the non-violence movement, the civil rights movement, the human rights movement, the fall of Nazism, Fascism and Communism, the break-up of apartheid. [206]

And the anointed Church of Christ, living in the midst of, though set apart from the nations and the assorted principalities of the world, carries this powerful antidote.

The primary task of the Church with reference to the Powers and Principalities is to unmask their idolatrous pretensions, to identify their dehumanizing values, to strip from them the mantle and credibility and to set free their victims. This includes the testimony to the crucified - to the rulers and powers. It does not include a commission to create a new society; rather we are, in the midst of society, to call the Powers' bluff ... Central in calling the Powers' bluff, our offer of praise and worship to the one true God stands. Because in and through that praising of the one true God, the bluff of all idols is revealed. So as we fight the Powers, we shall ascribe to God glory and strength. [207]

COMMUNITY ORGANIZING AND POLITICS

Today has been our "fierce urgency of now." We jumped in and began to learn how to engage. Our lessons came from seasoned and tested community organizers. We learned the Iron Rule, *Never, ever, do for people what they can do for themselves.* And we began to learn the principles, the theologies and the methods of seeing our community address their complicated struggles through participatory politics, practicing the uses of power that are available to everyone in this democracy of "we, the people".

Christians have been involved in the political sphere for two millennium tackling social ills and systemic evil. Though some decades leave Christians alienated and detached, "Christian pessimism is historically unfounded. It is also theologically inept."[208] The reasons are myriad, that Christians got involved, but often it was because justice required that laws and society change for human beings were suffering. Though we can ask what the role of the church is in government and society, we can also ask what are the consequences of its absence?

> The Christian will never weary of insisting that the task of the state in God's creational and providential order is to promote justice and serve the common good. …The state often fails in its task of promoting justice … sometimes this happens because the state is in the grip of some ideology…. In such situations it is the calling of the Christian to denounce the ideologies, bring the injustice to light, name it for what it is, namely injustice, and insist that the state not shirk its task.[209]

Here are some theses concerning government that a broad range of Christians can agree upon:

> 1) Government is not a merely human creation, nor is it a work of the devil. Government is instituted by God as part of God's providential care for his human creatures.

> 2) The task assigned by God to government is twofold: to promote justice, both primary and corrective, and in its coordinating activities to enhance the common good.

3) Government, thus understood, belongs both to God's providential care for us as creatures and to God's providential care for us as fallen.

4) When government acts as it ought to act, it acts with genuine authority. That authority is to be understood as not merely human but as mediating Christ's authority.

5) The corollary of the exercise by government of genuine authority is that its subjects are obligated to obey that authority.

6) Among the things that governments are authorized to do is apply retributive punishment to wrongdoers – provided that the punishment is itself of a just sort.

7) Though government, along with such other social institutions as marriage, family, and economy, is instituted by God as part of his providential care for human beings as creatures and as fallen, government, along with these other institutions, is itself fallen. That is to say, government and other social institution never fully carry out the tasks assigned them by God.

8) Though not every failing on the part of government – or any other social institution – justifies disobedience, all too often governments do fail to such a degree that disobedience is required. The starkest example of such obligatory disobedience is those cases in which government demands that something other than God be worshiped.

9) The Christian may serve in the offices of government; in doing so, he is mediating the rule over the state of that

very same Christ who is the ruler of the church.

10) When the Christian occupies some governmental office, he or she must not be guided by customary practice but by the God-assignment task of government; to promote justice and the common good.

11) It is the duty of the Christian always to call his or her government to its proper task. Especially is this true for those of us who have some degree of voice in our governments.

12) Such calling of government to its proper task will ordinarily include proclamation. But whenever possible, it will also include the promotion of governmental structures that make it less likely that the government will fail in, or violate, its task.

13) Christians will honor and respect government; they will not talk and act as if government has no right to exist. And they will support government by paying taxes. They will not talk and act as if government, in assessing taxes, is forcefully taking from its subjects 'their money'. Financial support is owed government. [210]

One last comment from Ian:

The problems are so vast, they can take up all of our free time, and we can become removed from people in our community. How do we manage that tension? Do I still have poor people's phone numbers in my phone, while fighting these problems of injustice? Today I still feel OK that I can sleep at night, knowing that a good majority of my time, I am still planted in our community. Unfortunately people get removed. This isn't about some romantic notion of social justice and a few toke-nized leaders, who come canvas with us one day, talk about voting to their potential constituents, and never come again. The idealized narrative of changing the world must include how messy and slow and not glorious at all it really is. Tell the story of what fighting for justice really looks like.

GRACE RULES – PATIENCE

A grace rule is the way grace rules. This rule describes a lavish gift from God as experienced in our community. By receiving it, grace rules – leading us further into love and action

It helps, now and then, to step back and take a long view.

The kingdom is not only beyond our efforts,
it is even beyond our vision.

We accomplish in our lifetime only a tiny fraction of
the magnificent enterprise that is God's work.
Nothing we do is complete, which is a way of saying
that the kingdom always lies beyond us.
No statement says all that could be said.
No prayer fully expresses our faith.
No confession brings perfection.
No pastoral visit brings wholeness.
No program accomplishes the church's mission.
No set of goals and objectives includes everything.

This is what we are about.
We plant the seeds that one day will grow.

We water seeds already planted, knowing that they hold
future promise.

We lay foundations that will need further development.
We provide yeast that produces far beyond our capabilities.

We cannot do everything, and there is a sense of liberation in
realizing that. This enables us to do something,
and to do it very well. It may be incomplete, but it is a beginning, a step along the way,
an opportunity for the Lord's grace to enter and do the rest.

We may never see the end results, but that is the difference
between the master builder and the worker.

We are workers, not master builders; ministers, not messiahs.
We are prophets of a future not our own.

Amen.
–Archbishop Oscar Romero

NOTES

173. Tim Suttle, *An Evangelical Social Gospel*, (Eugene: Cascade Books, 2011), 87. The two quotes come from Walter Rauschenbusch, *A Theology for the Social Gospel*, (Louisville: John Knox, 1997).
174. Martin Luther King, Jr., "I Have a Dream," Speech http://www. americanrhetoric.com/speeches/mlkihaveadream.html (accessed March 22, 2012).
175. Jacques Ellul, trans. Lani Niles, *In Season Out of Season*, (San Francisco: Harper & Row, 1982), 106-7.
176. Antonia Darder, *Reinventing Paulo Freire, A Pedagogy of Love*, (Cambridge: Westview Press. 2002), 15.
177. Jurgen Moltmann, 84.
178. Paulo Freire, *Pedagogy of the Oppressed*, (New York: The Continuum Publishing Group. 1970, 2006), 44. 179 Jurgen Moltmann, 122.
179. Jurgen Moltmann, 122.
180. Preamble to Resolution 217 S (111), "Universal Declaration of Human Rights," adopted and proclaimed in the General Assembly of the United Nations, December 10, 1948. http://www.un.org/en/documents/udhr/. (accessed May 18, 2012).
181. John Paul II, Redemptor Hominis, 17 (1979). Cf. Drew Christiansen, "Movement, Asylum, Borders: Christian Perspectives," *International Migration Review* 30, no. 1 (Spring 1996): 7-17.
182. Archbishop Oscar Romero, *Voice of the Voiceless, The Four Pastoral Letters and Other Statements*, (New York: Orbis Books. 1985), 184.
183. Robert Linthicum, *Transforming Power*, (Downers Grove: InterVarsity Press, 2003).
184. Ibid. 81.
185. Ibid.
186. Ibid., 151.
187. Ibid., 161.
188. Michael O. Emerson and Christian Smith, *Divided by Faith* (N.Y.: Oxford Univ. Press, 2000).
189. Ibid., 76.
190. Ibid.
191. Ibid., 77.
192. Tim Suttle, *An Evangelical Social Gospel, Finding God's Story in the Midst of Extremes* (Eugene: Cascade Books, 2011), 55.
193. Emerson and Smith, 77.
194. Christian Smith, *American Evangelicalism*, (Chicago: Univ. of Chicago Press, 1998), 188.
195. Ibid.
196. Ibid, 202.
197. Soon-Chan Rah, *The Next Evangelicalism*, (Downers Grove: Intervarsity Press, 2009), 41.

198. University of Pennsylvania Commencement Address by Bono, co-founder of DATA (Debt AIDS Trade Africa), and lead singer of U2, May 17, 2004. http://u2_interviews.tripod.com/id166.html (accessed March 21, 2012).
199. William Sloane Coffin, *Credo*, (Louisville: John Knox Press, 2004), 62.
200. Dom Helder Camara, Brazilian archbishop, as quoted in *Peace Behind Bars : A Peacemaking Priest's Journal from Jail* (1995) by John Dear, p. 65; this is a translation of "Quando dou comida aos pobres chamam-me de santo. Quando pergunto por que eles são pobres chamam-me de comunista." Variant translations: "When I give food to the poor, they call me a saint. When I ask why they are poor, they call me a Communist". OR "When I give food to the poor, they call me a saint. When I ask why the poor have no food, they call me a Communist."
201. Dietrich Bonhoeffer, *Letters and Papers from Prison* (1943-1945, English publication 1967) (Minneapolis: Fortress Press, 1996).
202. Marva Dawn, "The Concept of the Principalities and Powers in the Works of Jacques Ellul. PhD", dissertation, University of Notre Dame, 1992, 12.
203. Walter Wink is the New Testament scholar whose stunning trilogy on the powers was seeded by William Stringfellow's work and who has since become the primary and practical North American spokesperson on the theology of the principalities and powers.
204. N.T. Wright, *Evil and the Justice of God*, (Downers Grove, IL: Intervarsity Press. 2006), 112.
205. Ibid., 114.
206. Knud Jørgensen, The Socio-Political Context: Powers and Principalities, http://www.lausanne.org/en/documents/all/nairobi-2000/196-socio-political-context.html.
207. Ibid.
208. John Stott, *Involvement: Being a Responsible Christian in a Non-Christian Society*, (Old Tappan, New Jersey: Fleming Revell Co. 1984), 98.
209. Sider and Knippers, 157.
210. Ibid., 160.

"Curiosity" Ana Moya

CHAPTER EIGHT

We Value
LEARNING

Core Value #7

Definition: Committed to "entering into" our community, we continually discover what we don't know and what we desire to learn. We are committed to remaining in a posture of learning, being among, not standing over, acknowledging change and transformation are a process and not often easily measured.

"Education either functions as an instrument which is used to facilitate integration of the younger generation into the logic of the present system and bring about conformity or it becomes the practice of freedom, the means by which men and women deal critically and creatively with reality and discover how to participate in the transformation of their world."
– Paulo Freire, *Pedagogy of the Oppressed*

We commit to becoming life-long learners, here at Neighborhood. It is a posture, to be sure, a humility we desire to acquire. But there is something under this commitment that is the prime machine, the motivator. It is a desire to discover what makes this community and its people tick. Our fascination and hunger come from our respect and love for Phoenix and its pain. These discoveries bond us further with the very specific place in our city we identify with and enlarge our understanding of the vocation we have chosen (or that has been chosen for us).

I'll open this core value with a story from the heartbeat of a learner, Samuel Clemens (Mark Twain). When he loved something, he became a diligent student of that thing. Imagine 21 year old Samuel Clemens about to step into the world of his greatest desire, becoming a Mississippi River boat pilot. He was to be mentored by Mr. Bixby, a captain who loved the river, piloting, and instructing the next generation of river learners.

Learning the River[211]

Presently he [Mr. Bixby] turned to me and said: "What's the name of the first point above New Orleans?"

I was gratified to be able to answer promptly, and I did. I said I didn't know.

"Don't know!"

His manner jolted me. I was down at the foot again, in a moment. But I had to say just what I had said before.

"Well, you're a smart one," said Mr. Bixby. "What's the name of the next point?"

Once more I didn't know.

"Well, this beats anything! Tell me the name of any point or place I told you." I studied awhile and decided that I couldn't.

"Look here! What do you start from, above Twelve Mile Point, to cross over?" "I–I–don't know."

"'You–you don't know,'" mimicking my drawling manner of speech. "What do you know?"

"I–I–Nothing, for certain."

Bixby was a small, nervous man, hot and quick-firing. He went off now, and said a number of severe things. Then:

"Look here, what do you suppose I told you the names of those points for?" I tremblingly considered a moment–then the devil of temptation provoked me to say: "Well–to–to–be entertaining, I thought."

This was a red flag to the bull. He raged and stormed so (he was crossing the river at the time) that I judged it made him blind, because he ran over the steering-oar of a trading- scow. Of course the traders sent up a volley of red-hot profanity. Never was a man so grateful as Mr. Bixby was, because he was brimful, and here were subjects who would talk back. He threw open a window, thrust his head out, and such an irruption followed as I had never heard before . . . . When he closed the window he was empty. Presently he said to me, in the gentlest way:

"My boy, you must get a little memorandum-book, and every time I tell you a thing, put it down right away. There's only one way to be a pilot, and that is to get this entire river by heart. You have to know it just like A-B-C."

The little memorandum-book which Sam Clemens bought, probably at the next daylight landing, still exists–the same that he says "fairly bristled with the names of towns, points, bars, islands, bends, reaches, etc."; but it made his heart ache to think he had only half the river set down, for, as the watches were four hours off and four hours on, there were the long gaps where he had slept.

It is not easy to make out the penciled notes today. The small, neat writing is faded, and many of them are in an abbreviation made only for himself. It is hard even to find these examples to quote:

MERIWETHER'S BEND
One-fourth less 3[3]–run shape of upper bar and go into the low place in the willows about 200 (ft.) lower down than last year.

OUTSIDE OF MONTEZUMA
Six or eight feet more water. Shape bar till high timber on towhead gets nearly even with low willows. Then hold a little open on right of low willows–run 'em close if you want to, but come out 200 yards when you get nearly to head of towhead.

The average mind would not hold a single one of these notes ten seconds, yet by the time he reached St. Louis he had set down pages that to-day make one's head weary even to contemplate. And those long four-hour gaps where he had been asleep–they are still there; and now, after nearly sixty years, the old heartache is still in them. He must have bought a new book for the next trip and laid this one away.

To the new "cub" it seemed a long way to St. Louis that first trip, but in the end it was rather grand to come steaming up to the big, busy city, with its thronging waterfront flanked with a solid mile of steamboats, and to nose one's way to a place in that stately line.

At St. Louis, Sam borrowed from his brother-in-law the one hundred dollars he had agreed to pay, and so closed

his contract with Bixby. A few days later his chief was engaged to go on a very grand boat indeed–a "sumptuous
temple," he tells us, all brass and inlay, with a pilot-house
so far above the water that he seemed perched on a moun-
tain. This part of learning the river was worth while; and
when he found that the regiment of natty servants respectfully "sir'd" him, his happiness was complete. But he was
in the depths again, presently, for when they started down
the river and he began to take account of his knowledge,
he found that he had none. Everything had changed–that
is, he was seeing it all from the other direction. What with
the four-hour gaps and this transformation, he was lost
completely.

How could the easy-going, dreamy, unpractical man
whom the world knew as Mark Twain ever have persisted
against discouragement like that to acquire the vast, the
absolute, limitless store of information necessary to Mississippi piloting? The answer is that he loved the river, the
picturesqueness and poetry of a steamboat, the ease and
glory of a pilot's life; and then, in spite of his own later
claims to the contrary, Samuel Clemens, boy and man, in
the work suited to his tastes and gifts, was the most in-
dustrious of persons. Work of the other sort he avoided,
overlooked, refused to recognize, but never any labor for
which he was qualified by his talents or training. Piloting
suited him exactly, and he proved an apt pupil.

Horace Bixby said to the writer of this memoir: "Sam was
always good-natured, and he had a natural taste for the
river. He had a fine memory and never forgot what I told
him."

LEARNING

Yet there must have been hard places all along, for to learn every crook and turn and stump and snag and bluff and bar and sounding of that twelve hundred miles of mighty, shifting water was a gigantic task. Mark Twain tells us how, when he was getting along pretty well, his chief one day turned on him suddenly with this "settler":

"What is the shape of Walnut Bend?"

He might as well have asked me my grandmother's opinion of protoplasm. I replied respectfully and said I didn't know it had any particular shape. My gun-powdery chief went off with a bang, of course, and then went on loading and firing until he was out of adjectives ....I waited. By and by he said:

"My boy, you've got to know the shape of the river perfectly. It is all that is left to steer by on a very dark night. Everything else is blotted out and gone. But mind you, it hasn't got the same shape in the night that it has in the daytime."

"How on earth am I going to learn it, then?"

"How do you follow a hall at home in the dark? Because you know the shape of it. You can't see it."

"Do you mean to say that I've got to know all the million trifling variations of shape in the banks of this interminable river as well as I know the shape of the front hall at home?"

"On my honor, you've got to know them better than any

191

man ever did know the shapes of the halls in his own house."

"I wish I was dead!"

....

We are Samuel Clemons, having been given the bow. Our Horace Bixby is Ray Bakke. He calls to us, and others in urban ministry, "Learn your city!" Do you know the streets, the lay of the land, the politics, and the details? As a young pastor, in the 1960's and uprooted from rural Washington State, Bakke, headed to inner city Chicago to begin what became a calling to the poor and urban cities. His central goal was to find a theology "as big as the city." Influenced by the explosive 1960's, including deep theological work, the pastorate, his congregation, and an emerging global reality which he was invited to experience and speak into, Bakke became Bixby for so many of us, showing us how to navigate the intricacies of our own cities.

This learning was captured in his seminal work, *A Theology as Big as The City*.[212] The enormous growth of large cities demands thoughtful urban ministry; the message remains timely. It is expected that 70 percent of the world population will be urban by 2050.[213] His charge to us was to develop a missiological, ecclesiastical, financial and theological framework to meet the future. The learning required to meet this challenge never ends. I'm about to round a fourth decade in this learning, and can testify that without a commitment to being a life-long learner; you will fail. Ron Sider, editor of *Toward an Evangelical Public Policy*, takes the challenge and makes it personal for our tradition:

Evangelicals do not have the kind of sustained, theologically grounded reflection on social and political issues that shapes some other Christian traditions. Partly because we lack this kind

of extended, careful reflection on politics, recent evangelical political engagement has too often been unbalanced, inconsistent, and
ineffective...We believe that as evangelicalism has matured it is increasingly committed to the regular, steady task of participating in
our nation's democratic political community.[214]

THE COMPLEXITIES

Though we are willing to be self-deprecating in this matter,
Jane Jacobs, renowned urban scholar and grass-roots activist, believes very few entities are fully educated about the complexities of
global urban development work. At the heart of her most famous
book, The Death and Life of Great American Cities, is a sustained
account of complex adaptive systems:

> "...Cities happen to be problems in organized complexi-
> ty... they present situations in which half a dozen or even
> several dozen are all varying simultaneously and in subtly
> interconnected ways..."

To cite from a recent biography: "...She found a natural
order beneath the seeming chaos of cities, one that she likened to.... delicate, teeming ecosystems. For Jacobs, cities
and economies alike are products of millions of individual
decisions and ideas that combine in cooperation to form
an 'organic whole'...."

What is the relevance for aid agencies? Current World
Bank estimates are that there are one billion extreme poor
in the world, of which more than 750 million live in urban
areas. This is based on a measure of people living on $2 per
day, and as Mike Davis, author of Planet of Slums, argues,
if you use other measures - for example, a proportion of
national median income – urban poverty is much bigger

than the World Bank measures.

Despite what might seem to be an astonishingly high proportion, research undertaken in 2006 by Lund University in Sweden shows that international organizations which focus on poverty have tended to place a very low priority to urban issues. Some researchers have put this down to a number of aid myths and a variety of institutional and historical factors, including:

1. the perception that 'urban poverty is not as bad as rural poverty' (Sanderson, 2002,
2. the institutional history of aid organizations, which is rooted in rural development,
3. the belief that urban areas are the responsibility of national and municipal governments,
4. the notion that project work is easier in rural areas due to simpler institutional and demographic structures, and
5. the lack of knowledge of the long-term impacts of projects in urban contexts combined with limited financial resources.[215]

We talk freely about the complexities, as if there is a list somewhere cataloging all the arenas of concern. In fact, the list doesn't exist. I could make our own, it could fill volumes. Mae Elise Cannon in *Social Justice Handbook*[216] isolated eighty-four issues facing justice in her "chicken soup" format. Take each issue she identified and remember that it will take someone a life-time to craft a healthy response, and each issue overlaps and has many ways they are inter- related to the other issues. Then combine the intricacies of the ways in which cities operate, the ways in which the church engages, non-profits and NGO's function, the complexities of working with people and cultures, the geo-political landscape, globalization, religious and ethnic conflict and don't forget the needful development of a missiological, ecclesiastical, financial and theological framework, as Bakke recommends. Hence, the challenge to become life-long learners. The number of issues and the complexities of each, demand it of us. Malissa learned to think about these things here at Neighborhood:

> *NM holistic approach has been important to my thinking problems in cities. NM learning has inspired my learning to stay in school – ironically, to pursue doctoral work. [in Chicago] It is the learning that has inspired me to try and grapple with the complex issues of the city. My mind is always thinking about structures, and systems and difficulties endemic to poverty. I see the hopelessness and despair; I am overwhelmed with the complexity. This has created a desire in me to not just stand with others in these things, but to enter into the complexity of this learning – using story telling, my story and others – whole people with whole stories. To share those stories with other people, opens them up to the realities of the problems showing them that it is not as simple as pulling up boot straps … if it was that simple they would all be taken care of by now.*

THE BIBLE AND AN ATTITUDE TOWARD LEARNING

I think we can trace our conviction to be life-long learners to our understanding of God's provision for His children (Eph 3:20; Mal 3:10-12). We believe that God makes it possible for us to become all He intends for us to be, personally, but also for this mission and our community (Phil 1:6). There is a part of us that is incomplete or underdeveloped which can be filled through education or learning and God desires that for us. Claudia can see this in her own life:

> Here at Neighborhood, I have learned how to be a parent, for starters. I was a sixteen year-old mom, woke up at twenty-one with three kids, and if there is definitely something I have learned, it was to be a mom. This place has been my resource to teach me. I'm not perfect by all means, definitely not perfect. And then, I have learned to look at someone and not just judgmentally, but to be compassionate, to believe in someone. I have learned to trust – definitely learned to trust, slowly, I have been learning how to trust men. I've learned not to be selfish, and not just be so consumed with what Claudia wants and her needs, but to look outside myself. You know, I have learned to value education. I dropped out when I was sixteen, because of the encouragement of the people from Neighborhood; I went back and got my GED. Now I am finishing a nursing degree, becoming an RN.

Because we believe this about learning, and its concrete applications to our lives, we promote education (formal learning) at Neighborhood Ministries. We have a pre-school that launches children into a future where the love of learning is nurtured. The children graduate from this classroom with eyes wide open. Our education department concerns itself with ALL the children of Neighborhood Ministries and desires a public education system that is relevant and alive. We are learning to become advocates and change agents inside that system by getting involved. Equally as important, we adults model a personal life-long commitment to learning by doing it. Many of us are pursuing more education inside our particular nuanced fields; I am one of many. Googoos talks about what it looked like for her to finish her GED:

Even though I wanted to give up, I didn't have enough faith and encouragement in myself, I couldn't. I couldn't let anybody down, everyone was cheering for me, and just saying you can do it, you can do it that gave me a sense of hope, and maybe I could do it. I wanted to be a role model for my son, and my brothers and sisters. Now they see in me, how I value learning. I tell others, 'If completing your education is in your heart, God will give you the desire of your heart; but it won't come easy. For me it wasn't easy at all.

Learning happens informally as well. Our staff (and sometimes our Board) reads together important books that inform our work theologically and practically. Susan acknowledges the help that comes from committing to learn together:

I was really blessed, when the intern training times opened up to those of us who weren't interns. Those book discussions have been really powerful in my own life. The discussions on race and power, for example, and realizing how much power I have simply from the color of my skin; and how awful that is and working hard to understand how that is true and how to change it. The books have been used by God in my life, in all of us, really, because different books have impacted us differently. It causes me to think in a different way, it has challenged me to rethink things I have learned, even from a biblical standpoint. So much of what we learn, in evangelical America is sort of standardized, nothing different is taught. I learned this from the book called, Reading the Bible with the Damned, reading the Bible from a different perspective. And then we did the whole CTM (Street Psalms) series, the opportunities to learn there are constant, over and over. These opportunities have changed my life,

with what was normal, my past cultural mindset, my evan-
gelical mindset, to let it be shaken and rocked, and be will-
ing to see God's truth from God's perspective, to embrace
an upside down kingdom, which proclaims good news from
below – I hope I can look at life through this point of view
from now on. I am always challenged. I am really grateful
that God still lets me learn, that I'm not too old to be shaken
out of old patterns.

In addition to our ongoing learning, we attend workshops and conferences and are periodically the persons presenting at these conferences. This co-sharing of sub-specializations has brought us into a variety of environments, Christian and secular, always reminding us of the starting point, to remain learners.

The Bible teaches us to love God with heart, soul and mind; our mind is a place to serve and honor Him. As it relates to the value of learning, we commit to becoming good and growing thinkers about our discipline of a multi-faceted holistic approach to Christian community development. This is an area of growing scholarship, most particularly theological. It also encompasses the undergirding research and best practice methodology as it relates to different expressions of love and service: affordable housing, homelessness, justice issues, church planning and multi-ethnic churches, the arts, alternative communities, health and mental health care, gentrification, leadership development, kids and youth programs, child advocacy, private pre-school, teen-mom program, business development, advocacy and politics and multiple elements of non-profit management.

Our discipline springs out of a theological core about how God has revealed Himself to us through Christ and the Bible. It's necessary, therefore, to remember that our learning has to include deeply investigated biblical studies. We pursue these excellent insights, because the Bible has a lot to say about what we do both directly and indirectly, so we search the Bible to become better urban ministers, and in so doing, find God further revealed. As Ray Bakke says about his formative years in ministry, it was the Bible he hoped would shed light on his transformational thinking.

> The Bible clearly describes a God who is completely interest and involved with both the structures and the individuals that compose society. In 1966 I began to read the Bible with urban eyes. I looked at the 1,250 uses of the word city in Scripture and developed case studies on cities and persons who lived in cities, while pastoring an inner city church. I likened it to Moses' experience of pastoring a largely unemployed community of mud-brick making migrants who lived in a bad neighborhood for forty years on 'food stamps' called manna.[217]

The point here is that the Bible wouldn't and couldn't ever discount our quest to become literate and smart as it relates to our work; a work, by the way, whose values emulate Jesus. Mark Noll, in Jesus Christ and the Life of the Mind, a scholar noted for his service to the discussion of a beautiful Christian mind says this:

> …for serious intellectual efforts, those who look to Christ as their prophet, priest, and king act most faithfully when they carry out those efforts with norms defined by Christ. The circularity of this reasoning when applied to Scripture is obvious, since the Bible tells us of Christ from whom we are to take our bearings when approaching Scripture. But in this case it is a propitious circularity.[218]

It would be a mistake to assume that we discount our academic allies who don't happen to be Christian or even religious. We don't. There is much to learn in our various disciplines, and when we find those that strengthen our cause, teach us how to think about a certain problem carefully or help us with a tool that works, we gladly welcome those. Our arms are wide and our welcome enthusiastic.

CHRISTIAN COMMUNITY DEVELOPMENT

Gladly, we have a landing place for a great deal of our learning. We participate in the world of Christian Community Development Association (CCDA) which has established a location for learners. Our gatherings put forward the finest thinkers we have in the multiple genres of faith-based work among the urban poor. There are churches and organizations at many levels of progress in their ministries who attend and hear the challenge to become a committed learner for the life-time of their work. Though there is never a perfect clearing house of information, this institution has a perfect mission for this purpose: "to inspire, train, and connect Christians who seek to bear witness to the Kingdom of God by reclaiming and restoring under- resourced communities."[219]   Christian community developers are being equipped to think, learn and innovate.

THE CITY AS CLASSROOM AND THE ADMISSION OF TENSIONS

Under our very feet is an instrument of instruction. Ray Bakke invites us to experience, the city as a living, breathing, and growing library of wisdom that functions in real time and is always accessible to those who are willing to sit at her feet and learn. This is because the city functions as both a magnet and a magnifier of culture. It is a magnet as people are drawn to cities for opportunity and refuge and a magnifier as the composite of all things global is marketed and exported from cities.[220]   Ian emphasizes:

... we have chosen to see our city as a classroom after this

fashion, and learn from Phoenix and many who have invested in her. Here are a few examples: our summer staff will interview the first African American City Council person of Phoenix, will visit a premier community garden, and get to know a former Arizona Republic *newspaper reporter who writes and thinks about community from a justice point of view that we need.*

But Bakke is also quick to remind us that as we enter in and sit at the feet of our city, to be ready for the "tensions." The very nature of urban ministry reveals the "both/and," the "either/or," the "yes/no" and the "give/take." These practical and theological paradoxes or two- truths can create some disorientation. Though the city is filled with the handprints of God, He seems to be speaking from both sides of His mouth. We agree that the longer you study your city and God's work therein, you must embrace the tensions. We look to Bakke who has identified ten:[221]

1. Creation and Redemption – "seeking both the spiritual transformation of persons and the social transformation of places"

2. Truth and Love – balancing the prophetic words of an Amos who in truth demands justice with the pastoral message of weeping Jeremiah

3. Individuality and Community – desiring but not exaggerating (preferring) either the rights of individuals or the community

4. Local and Global – the incarnation of Jesus affirms every local culture and community, while at the same time

the universal message of salvation is offered to every tribe and every tongue, most of whom are nonwhite and non-Western

5. Unity and Diversity – the tension between proclaiming unity in the body of Christ which is a particular passion of our Lord, while proclaiming diversity, acknowledging God-given unique qualities in culture, gifting, identities and generations

6. Power and Powerlessness – "We work to keep in balance two realities of Jesus' ministry – the voluntary setting aside of privilege and society's trappings while at the same time engaging in resource acquisition for the sake of advocacy and justice on behalf of the most vulnerable in society. The struggle here is to follow the humble Jesus while appropriating the Holy Spirit's power."

7. Certainty and Mystery – This is a New Age, where reason no longer reigns. But "when boundaries of reason and mystery are unclear or shifting, we seek the Holy Spirit's help to keep our core of basic theology connected to the historic orthodoxy of the church."

8. Commission and Commandment – loving God and Neighbor while preaching the good news of a Savior who came, died and rose for the forgiveness of sin

9. Past and Future – Acknowledging the lessons and continuity of where the church has been while wrestling with the prophetic work of a missional church that reforms the existing

10. Work and Rest – always looking for the rhythm God has built into life. "God worked, then rested. Jesus preached and healed, then retreated. I also must rest."

Here, at Neighborhood, we have found that the tensions we encounter routinely in our mission have been one way we choose to embrace the plan of God for us, as each side teaches us something important. Blaise Pascal wrote in his Pensées that "there are then a great number of truths, both of faith and morality, which seem contradictory, and which all hold together in a wonderful system."[222]

SYSTEMS THINKING

We continue to learn. Today, there is a new and uncomfortable frontier for today's Christian community developers who work among the poor; that of moving into a public arena to advocate for systemic changes. We are in motion to build a deeper, wider biblical apologetic that takes the previous work of community development to its logical next step.

In the same vein that the previous layer of work took place (albeit with a lot of learning) this social justice engagement has followed a similar pattern. Starting with obedience to the Scriptures, then getting involved and trying to figure out how to do it and live it. Social justice was the next logical step of the work of living, preaching and practicing a "whole" gospel. Could we prove to outsiders, that it was Jesus, the Bible, love in action, and not just politics?

This was necessary theological work, as engagement with systems, as naively intuitive as it may have seemed to us, doesn't look that simple to our friends, who comfortably sit outside our present danger. Walter Rauschenbusch, the forerunner of the social gospel movement created a parable he told often that describes the theological learning that has to take place:

A man was walking through the woods in springtime. The

air was thrilling and throbbing with the passion of little hearts, with the love wooing, the parent pride, the deadly fear of the birds. But the man never noticed that there was a bird in the woods. He was a botanist and was looking for plants. A man read through the New Testament. He felt no vibrations of social hope in the preaching of John the Baptist and in the shouts of the crowd when Jesus entered Jerusalem. Jesus knew human nature when he reiterated: 'He that hath ears to hear, let him hear.' We see in the Bible what we have been taught to see there. We drop out great sets of facts from our field of vision. We read other things into the Bible which are not there.[223]

Engaging the systems is something Ray Bakke says our biblical heroes were taught to do and this should give us courage as we navigate these unfriendly waters. He illustrates that leaders such as Moses, Daniel, Esther, Nehemiah and others who would eventually tackle the systemic issues of their day were prepared for their tasks by God Himself. "Moses, Joseph, Daniel, Nehemiah and others were able to sort through the public, ethical differences between co-belligerency and advocacy on issues and survive as capable leaders working for corrupt politicians. We who live and work in cities are not surprised by this. We know that every city-centered church needs political skills."[224]

We have been working alongside other evangelical ministries through CCDA who have had a similar practical and theological trajectory. As an association we teach to this topic, we call it advocacy. We teach that justice work goes hand in hand with our relational engagement with problems and our practice of providing holistic solutions. We teach that the systems that oppress the poor are broken and that we need to start at that place vs. managing the fall out of these injustices. Mary Nelson, a long-time CCDA board member, and instructor at many Christian community developer gatherings will often use this parable to help illustrate the point:

> A man went to the river one day and noticed that someone was drowning in the middle of it. He quickly swam out to save the drowning person. He brought the person to safety and attempted to catch his breath. A short while later, the man noticed another person drowning in the river. He mustered up all of his strength and dove back into the river water to save the second drowning victim. The second person was brought safely to shore. By this time, the man was exhausted and had a hard time breathing. Several minutes later, as he looked up, to his dismay, he noticed a third person floating down the river, crying for help. Once again, feeling he didn't have a choice, he dove into the water to save the third person. However, the man was so tired from having saved the first two victims that he wasn't able to continue swimming and he drowned.

> The man's response to the drowning people was one of compassion. His efforts were based on his love for them and his desire for them not to suffer. And his efforts made a huge difference to the first two people! The rescuer was certainly a compassionate man. However, if the man had driven up the road along the bend in the river, he would have noticed someone at a factory who was throwing people into the river. The abusive man was the source of the problem. If the compassionate man had intervened at the factory, that would have been an act of justice. [225]

The founder of CCDA, John Perkins, rarely teaches any Bible study without finding a way to direct the activity of the church and

Christian discipleship toward justice.

> A whole lot of our churches have decided to outsource justice. If the gospel of reconciliation is going to interrupt the brokenness in society, our churches are going to have to rethink their vocation. When I read the Bible, I always bring the problems of my community to God and ask when in history God's people have had to face a similar challenge. God is the same yesterday, today and forever. But God also chooses to walk with his people in history. That means we can't know the will of God for us today unless we're paying attention to what's happening and how God wants to work in this situation. As I look at our situation today and the problems we face, I hear God speaking to the church in the words that he spoke through his prophets after the exile. Coming out of our cultural captivity, I hear God saying that his is a time for rebuilding the church and remembering what it really means to be Christ's body in the world.[226]

I have mentioned in many of the other core values our learning inside the injustices of immigration and the questions pertaining to the progress of reform. Jeremy provides another example of a place in our mission where we are practicing that kind of learning, *Katy's Kids Preschool*:

> *How do we enhance the quality of care for children in Arizona? What a beautiful question. We at Katy's Kids Preschool like to quote an English poet, E. E. Cummings, who once wrote the beautiful answer is always preceded by the more beautiful question. This question has led to the development of an amazing program called T.E.A.C.H....*

As we engage a child's imagination and sense of wonder we see that they begin to ask beautiful questions like how and why things are the way they are. This is not only the foundation for our students learning process but for our staff as well. A partnership with T.E.A.C.H. was quite a natural blessing we did not see coming. They have allowed our staff to develop their lessons and educational philosophy while they continue to seek out the questions in their hearts.

Katy's Kids Preschool is rooted in the belief that early childhood and its development is a precious gift. Our school was founded on an understanding that education is either freeing or binding and learning is a life long process that everyone is on.

Though we are committed learners as it relates to dealing with unjust systems, outside the urban ministry sub-culture, there exists a Christian world still conjoined with an individualistic approach. Ron Sider in his article entitled, *"Evangelicals and Structural Injustice, Why Don't They Understand It and What Can Be Done?"* says:

Obviously, we need a great deal more sophisticated sociological analysis before we will know with any precision the full extent of this individualistic, one-person-at-a-time approach to solving societal problems. But we already have enough evidence to say with considerable certainty that white evangelicals have a one-sided, individualistic approach to societal transformation that does not understand the importance of structures and the reality of systemic evil. As a result, among other things, evangelicals still are more likely in their response to global poverty to respond to immediate disasters and also to the need for community development than they are to engage in changing economic structures to reduce poverty.[227]

Sider makes these further comments as he attempts to the answer the question poised by the article, *"Why Evangelicals Don't Understand Structural Injustice:"*

> 1. First, it may be that the fact that evangelicals frequently witness or hear about dramatic conversions that truly change broken people into transformed persons contributing to society leads evangelicals to emphasize the importance of personal conversion in a one-sided way. *(Please note: I think personal conversion is one important factor in societal transformation, but it needs to be accompanied by structural change.)* Smith borrows the phrase the "miracle-motif" from Woodbridge, Noll, and Hatch, to talk about this one- sidedly individualistic emphasis on conversion.[228] In this view, social problems would disappear if everyone were converted to personal faith in Christ. The solution to great economic inequality is "not a more equitable restructuring of income distribution, but for rich people to come to Christ and then practice voluntary generosity."[229]

> 2. Second, there is a very long history of individualism in evangelical thought and practice. It runs through the Protestant Reformation, Puritanism, the Free Church tradition, revivalism, pietism, and fundamentalism. Lacking Catholicism's emphasis on the community and the common good, evangelicals historically have been highly individualistic in their understanding of the church, conversion—indeed, almost every aspect of Christian faith.

3.Third, the pioneering spirit of the American frontier where the strong-willed, daring individual was the hero certainly shaped American evangelicalism as nineteenth century Baptist, Methodist, and other churches swept west across the continent along with the settlers. If the individual has the proper courage and persistence, one can solve one's own problems without governmental help.

4. Fourth, we ought at least to ask whether a certain kind of dispensational theology may contribute to evangelicalism's hyper-individualism. For those dispensationalists who link the anti-Christ with a powerful one-world government, every form of structural analysis of societal problems that would lead to structural changes implemented by government may lead to a fear that any substantial governmental intervention to solve social problems is just one step down a slippery slope toward the anti-Christ and one-world government.

5. Fifth, there is some evidence that political conservatism is linked to and is a strong predictor of individualistic explanations of economic equality between blacks and whites. In an article in the Journal of the Scientific Study of Religion, Hinojosa and Park show that those who are politically conservative are more likely to explain this inequality in terms of lack of motivation rather than lack of access to education and discrimination.[230] The fact that a majority of white evangelicals for several decades have been closely linked to political conservatives probably has contributed to their failure to understand the structural causes of poverty.

6. Sixth, I suspect that the fact that a Platonic spiritualism that emphasizes the soul over the body has exerted a powerful influence in the evangelical world has also contributed to our problem. Historically, evangelicals have talked about "saving souls," not saving the whole person the way Jesus did. If what really matters is the soul, then thinking about the way socio-economic, material structures and institutions shape people is hardly important.

7. Seventh, and closely related to the last point, evangelicals have largely defined the Gospel as the forgiveness of sins. Salvation means primarily asking God for forgiveness so that one can go to heaven when we die. I often say: if that is the entire Gospel is, then it is a one-way ticket to heaven and we can live like hell until we get there. Defining the Gospel primarily as forgiveness of sins rather than, with Jesus, the Gospel of the kingdom, greatly heightens both the individualistic emphasis and the preoccupation with the soul in a Platonic sense.[231]

8. Finally, the fact that evangelical theology has been weak at a number of points where a more fully biblical perspective would have corrected our hyper-individualism is also surely a significant factor. Many evangelicals have a dreadfully weak doctrine of creation; an almost non- existent understanding of either the prophets' or the New Testament understands of social sin;[232] and a weak grasp of the church as community.[233]

LEARNING FROM GOD AND OTHERS

If you are reading this chapter in order, then you may agree with me that we have talked quite a bit so far about learning from God and others. So, one more quick word about that here, to re-emphasize it. We must continue to be people who grow in Christ and who also contribute to each others growth, becoming disciples who follow Christ in all matters. As to remaining a spiritual learner, I like what Evelyn Underhill has to say on this. She is someone who I've been learning from:

> Now if you are to convey that spiritual certitude, it is plain that you must yourselves be spiritually alive. And to be spiritually alive means to be growing and changing; not to settle down among a series of systematized beliefs and duties, but to endure and go on enduring the strains, conflicts and difficulties incident to development. One chief object of personal religion is the promoting of that growth of the soul: the wise feeding and training of it. However busy we may be, however mature and efficient we may seem, that growth, if we are real Christians, must go on. Even the greatest spiritual teachers, such as St. Paul and St. Augustine, could never afford to relax the tension of their own spiritual lives; they never seem to stand still, are never afraid of conflict and change. Their souls too were growing entities, with a potential capacity for love, adoration and creative service: in other words, for holiness, the achievement of the stature of Christ. A saint is simply a human being whose soul has thus grown up to its full stature, by full and generous response to its environment, God. He has achieved a deeper, bigger life than the rest of us, a more wonderful contact with the mysteries of the Universe; a life of infinite possibility, the term of which he never feels that he has reached.[234]

And Jorge and Sarah make some good comments on continually learning from each other. Jorge sees this as the way most of us learn to see life.

> *It's kind of like giving back to the community – I don't mean like redistribution – I choose to stay in this community, when there is so much suffering and so much pain – because of the things I have learned. These are things I can give back to my community. I come from the people, but I am also learning from the people – not everyone is miserable, many of us are overcoming…often this is because we have chosen to learn from each other. The majority of the learning I have done has come from the people: this learning has taught me about myself. I am not the only person that suffers from certain issues; everyone has almost the same struggles that I have. I am not alone. It is like a co-op – Co-operative learning – some things I give away to others, some things they give to me. That's why I choose to be open about addictions – I can talk about what it means to come from an addictive family. I have learned how we can talk about these issues.*

Sarah has a slightly different take on this same idea. She says that her best learning came directly from living in the neighborhood.

> *I don't remember when that dawned on me, what it has done for me, that every encounter with a stranger becomes an opportunity to learn. I became a learner of that person, place, etc. It has really made my relationships with new people blossom – many that turn into deep relationships, because I came into it as a learner. They in turn learn from me. I especially notice it when some of these come from a background where people don't trust other people. Being at*

N. it has made me learn how to help people who don't trust. Today, [Sarah lives in Austin, Texas] I am around people and places that are like those at Neighborhood. And I tend to begin relationships by listening. I usually know pretty soon, I have so much more listening to do, more learning to do. Honestly, I know that this would not have happened if I hadn't been at N. This desire to learn, to understand, has impacted me more than other things. I have talked about it in all the core values so far, I think, it isn't about education, it is a conversation about listening and paying attention.

GRACE RULES – REST

A grace rule is the way grace rules. This rule describes a lavish gift from God as experienced in our community. By receiving it, grace rules – leading us further into love and action.

This grace rule of "rest" is very personal to me. That's because it addresses something I have been trying to learn for a long time. Though I could say this learning has brought me a good distance so far, I still feel like I am "learning" this grace rule. Many of us (Americans) don't receive the gift of rest very well. I am writing this during the great blessing of a first sabbatical in thirty years of ministry work. I have been aware from the day this sabbatical began, that this experience with rest would be unique and hopefully life altering. So here are a few thoughts, after years of attempting to understand and practice the rhythms of rest:

Burnout and the Relentlessness of Our Work

Most people assume that burnout is a fairly common problem of work like ours, and it should be addressed, and missions should be careful to watch for it, and help people avoid it, if that is possible. I couldn't help but think of this in light of a comment Panda made as I asked her about the core value of "learning". Panda said that here at Neighborhood, she has learned just about everything. Then she added: *"I was in jail at age nine, because I was removed from my home due to child abuse. All the church songs, all the lessons, I took them there with me. If it wasn't for our church, I would have probably hung myself, at nine years old."* The intensity of our stories, the depth of the pain, and the demand on the "shepherd" to care for the flock can break us down. How does God sustain us? What gifts does He give to enable us to do another day?

Receive a Day Off

God gives us a day off, every week. He gave it a nick-name so we would like it. He modeled a day off so we would believe we needed it. He placed it in his top ten things to do. "The point of the Sabbath is to honor our need for a sane rhythm of work and rest. It is to honor the body's need for rest, the spirit's need for replenishment and soul's need to delight itself in God for God's own sake. It begins with a willingness to acknowledge the limits of our humanness and take steps to live more graciously within the order of things."[235] Take a Sabbath day off, every week. Rest, it's on God.

Receive a Head-Message Break

What's equally as exhausting as the relentlessness of the work, are the messages that come into our heads and hearts everyday. Imagine getting a break from them. A.W. Tozer, in

The Pursuit of God, has a recommendation to free ourselves from this burden: "The heart's fierce effort to protect itself from every slight, to shield its touchy honor from the bad opinion of friend and enemy, will never let the mind have rest. Continue this fight through the years and the burden will become intolerable. Such a burden as this is not necessary to bear. Jesus calls us to His rest, and meekness is His method. The meek man cares not at all who is greater than he, for he has long ago decided that the esteem of the world is not worth the effort."[236]

Receive the Freedom from Anxiety

Some Bible commentators connect together the parable (story) of the sower (Lk 8:1-15) with Matthew 11:28-30. The sower, tirelessly spreading seed, will see some fruit born, but not all the places he has scattered seed. That's discouraging. We want ALL our seed to land on good soil. Jesus weighs in: "Come to me, all you who are weary and burdened, and I will give you rest. Take my yoke upon you and learn from me, for I am gentle and humble in heart, and you will find rest for your souls. For my yoke is easy and my burden is light." Googoos says this about the awful restlessness that comes from an anxious spirit and what she has learned to do about it:

> *I have learned to pray, pray, pray. I continue to learn to release all that is heavy on me to God. Believing that He can deal with whatever the problem, whatever the situation, he gots it! It reminds me of that song: 'He has the whole world in his hands.*

Rest, it is a free gift from God.

NOTES

211. Albert Bigelow Paine, *The Boys' Life of Mark Twain: The story of a man who made the world laugh and love him,* http://www.authorama.com/boys-life-of-mark-twain-14.html (accessed April 27, 2012).

212. Ray Bakke, *A Theology as Big as The City,* (Downers Grove: InterVarsity Press, 1997).

213. Population Reference Bureau, "Human Population: Urbanization," http://www.prb.org/Educators/TeachersGuides/HumanPopulation/Urbanization.aspx., (accessed March 31, 2012).
    The world has experienced unprecedented urban growth in recent decades. In 2008, for the first time, the world's population was evenly split between urban and rural areas. There were more than 400 cities over 1 million and 19 over 10 million. More developed nations were about 74 percent urban, while 44 percent of residents of less developed countries lived in urban areas. However, urbanization is occurring rapidly in many less developed countries. It is expected that 70 percent of the world population will be urban by 2050, and that most urban growth will occur in less developed countries. What is an urban area? An urban area may be defined by the number of residents, the population density, the percent of people not dependent upon agriculture, or the provision of such public utilities and services as electricity and education. Some countries define any place with a population of 2,500 or more as urban; others set a minimum of 20,000. There are no universal standards, and generally each country develops its own set of criteria for distinguishing urban areas. The United States uses a population density measure to define urban with a minimum population requirement of 2,500. The classification of metropolitan includes both urban areas as well as rural areas that are socially and economically integrated with a particular city.

214. Ronald Sider and Diane Knippers, ed., *Toward an Evangelical Social Policy,* (Grand Rapids: Baker Books, 2005), 9–10.

215. Ben Ramalingam, "Urbanization, Complexity and Poverty." *Aid on the Edge of Chaos: Exploring complexity & evolutionary sciences in foreign aid,* (2009) Blog. http://aidontheedge.info/2009/11/24/urbanisation-complexity-and-poverty-%E2%80%93-or-why-aid-agencies- should-be-reading-jane-jacobs/ (accessed: March 31, 2012).

216. Mae Elise Cannon, *Social Justice Handbook, Small Steps for a Better World,* (Downers Grove: InterVarsity Press, 2009).

217. Ray Bakke, 15.

218. Mark Noll, *Jesus Christ and the Life of the Mind,* (Grand Rapids: Eerdmans Publishing, 2011), Kindle Electronic Edition: Chapter 6, location 1394 of 2092.

219. Christian Community Development Association, "Mission Statement," http://ccda.org/about/vision- mission (accessed April 2, 2012).

220. Ray Bakke, 12.

221. Ibid., 204-205.
222. Klyne Snodgrass, *Between Two Truths, Living with Biblical Tensions*, (Eugene: Wipf & Stock, 1990), 15.
223. Paul Raushenbush, *My Faith May be Doomed to Failure.* Parable written by Walter Raushenbush: The following address titled My Faith May be Doomed to Failure was offered in October 2001 at the opening of the Walter Rauschenbusch Center for Spirituality and Service.
224. Ray Bakke, 49.
225. Mae Elise Cannon, *Social Justice Handbook, Small Steps for a Better World*, (Downers Grove: Intervarsity Press, 2009), 33.
226. Charles Marsh and John Perkins, *Welcoming Justice, God's Movement toward Beloved Community*, (Downers Grove: Intervarsity Press. 2009), 108, 109.
227. Ronald J. Sider, "Evangelicals and Structural Injustice, Why Don't They Understand It and What Can Be Done?", *Evangelicals For Social Action Publications*, 10/8/10, http://evangelicalsforsocialaction.org/document. doc?id=115 (accessed February 2012).
228. Christian Smith, *American Evangelicalism*, 190.
229. Ibid., 192.
230. Victor J. Hinojosa and Jerry Z. Park, "Religion and the Paradox of Racial Inequality Attitudes," *Journal of the Scientific Study of Religion*, 43:2 (2004), 229-238.
231. Ron Sider, *Good News and Good Works* (Baker, 1999), Chapters 3, 4, especially pp. 76-79.
232. Ron Sider, *Rich Christians in an Age of Hunger*, 5th ed., (Nashville: Thomas Nelson, 2005), Chapter 6.
233. Ron Sider, *Scandal of the Evangelical Conscience*, (Grand Rapids: Baker Books, 2005), Chapter 4.
234. Evelyn Underhill, *The House of the Soul and Concerning the Inner Life*, (Minneapolis: Winston/Seabury Press, 1929).
235. Ruth Haley Barton, *Sacred Rhythms, Arranging our Lives for Spiritual Transformation*, (Downers Grove: InterVarsity Press, 2006), 137.
236. A.W. Tozer, *The Pursuit of God*, (Harrisburg: Christian Publications, 1948), 112.

"Joy" Stephanie Farwig

CHAPTER NINE

We Value
RELATIONSHIPS

Core Value #8

Definition: We hold to the model that the best transference of love, hope and power is through relationships. The unconditional love of God compels us to a relentless pursuit of one another, where we chose to bear the pain each one carries as well as bring the good news of that unconditional love, practically and verbally.

The love for equals is a human thing –
of friend for friend, brother for brother.
It is to love what is loving and lovely. The world smiles.

The love for the less fortunate is a beautiful thing –
the love for those who suffer, for those who are poor,
the sick, the failures, the unlovely. This is compassion, and it
touches the heart of the world.

The love for the more fortunate is a rare thing –
to love those who succeed where we fail,
to rejoice without envy with those who rejoice,
the love of the poor for the rich, of the black man for the white
man. The world is always bewildered by its saints.

And then there is the love for the enemy –
love for the one who does not love you but mocks, threatens,
and inflicts pain. The tortured's love for the torturer.
This is God's love. It conquers the world.

— Frederick Buechner, *The Magnificent Defeat*[237]

As I sat down to write this chapter, I started scribbling memories and out flooded stories of *you*. After all these years, there are some stories that are stuck in me; meaningful in a way that probably says more about me than you. These stories memorialized a long wait, a terrible loss, a letting go, my mother's heart or the journey of a pastor. In many ways, there is no order here, and these stories don't represent them all. In fact, I could have gone on and on, and maybe will another day. But the ones that are here function to open up this chapter on relationships, small snapshots of some of the relationships I have that come from this cherished ground:

Boy
I can't remember who I was before you. Was I white? Was I rich? What you have done to me has altered my memory of me, and with that gave access to a Voice that called to a truer self. How can I thank you for this gift of entrance? You made a way for me, you have made it possible.

Angel
You were born in the afternoon. It was before cell phones. I heard about it, somehow. Your mom alone in the delivery room, naked and small, she wasn't ready for you. She gave you a name from the heavens and another one from the deep; it revealed the tear in her. And I stood outside the glass; she saw me as the wheelchair turned. And she was alone again, and so were you.

Nighttime
We laughed about the roaches and lice. Your mom put tissue in your ears at night so they wouldn't crawl in. A girl in your school tossed her hair and a bug spun off and landed in your soup. Disgusted you said "keep your bugs to yourself." She moved two seats down.

The Family
The house was filled with dangerous people, or so they would say when I got home. The crowd grew and I wondered if this visit mattered or would we all forget it soon enough. Questions flew through the air like pizza dough in the hands of a master. Mostly they wanted to know about judgment and the Second Coming. I was unprepared for this.

Stuffed Animals
That first Christmas Eve delivery happened when church was over. We should have been taking care of our young family with nostalgic devotion. But we packed the truck with the used bears and bunnies and stopped at your complex. You weren't home but the other doors flew open and little hands snatched all these small and large variegated animals. Nostalgia had a different interpretation that night.

Rescue
We sat on a brick ledge and you told me about the owl that follows people marked by the devil. You've seen it; it finds you in the dark, or like that time, in the day. I don't know how to help you. I think I see it too. What should we do?

Dunbar
I hate her. Her voice is shrill as she describes you. The words are ugly like sludge from a sewer. Why is she important, why does she get to vote? You are young and under her foot, and you can't multiply well enough to get up. We are both tortured by her.

COG
At your funeral everyone wore red t-shirts except for me, I wore a brown dress. He stood apart, blamed and identified. I stood inside, next to your family, lost and blinded. The preacher knew you

some, not like me, but you lived with him last. You lived with me first. Your bald head was carved with COG, I loved that you marked yourself with His name.

Prayer
The bedroom was splattered with El Diablo, a spray painted. They asked me to pray, to do the funeral. The empty apartment mirrored the void. We both felt it. I hoped he could find the words, he didn't. I decided he's probably not supposed to be a pastor. At least not for deaths due to insanity.

The Last One
No one could hear. The quinceañera music was too loud; You shouted your God questions into my ear, "what must I do to be saved?" You needed to know. I don't think you could hear my answers, but I know you heard my love. You trust me; I think it was because I was there for all their funerals. And I trust you.

Tia
The dark yard was jam-packed full of drunkenness. She needed some sleeping clothes and supplies for a few days; we tried to find a way to walk past you. But you grabbed me, shoving my face into your bosom and your sobbing threw me up and down inside a bear hug that wouldn't end. You asked me to forgive you seventy times seven and said to me "I asked you into my heart." That's OK, that you got it wrong. The Holy Ghost heard you loud and clear.

Three Days
Everything was colored by a frenzy of looking for you. The rumor was you did this terrible act, I wouldn't believe it. For three days, and all alone, I knocked on door after door in the neighborhood. They all knew, I don't remember if that mattered or not. Where were

you? I had to find you before they did. Were you hiding from me? Were you hiding from them? You turned yourself in. I lost my hope.

The Jesus Clock
You couldn't wait to pull open the breadbox bus's doors. You had to shove the Christmas present you bought for me into my hands. The brown paper bag that doubled as wrapping paper slipped off. You bought this with your own money from the street vendor. A red, heart shaped clock, with the crucified Jesus embossed next to a dark red rose. Your child face is forever available to me because of that night, though I know the adult you. I hold that face, still.

A RELATIONSHIP STORY

Victor was first kicked off our bus as a five year old, with his gargantuan, older brother, John, who at the time wore his hair long, testifying to the fact that they were full blooded Tohono O'odham. You're never allowed to kick a kid out forever in our ministry, but that bus driver didn't know this at the time. He was in the fourth grade when he reemerged, wilder than he could possibly have been on that bus as a small child. But, boy did I love them, both. John was mean. Already at age twelve he ruled the streets. Kids and adults alike were afraid of him. I just wanted him to know Jesus. We wooed them to our house. Those two and the pack they ran with. Whatever it took, we wanted them to experience our love for them, that they would find Jesus so compelling and attractive, they couldn't do anything but wish for Him to forgive their sins and give them resurrected life, of the Jubilee kind. Still to this day, we believe that the whole gospel is really good news to the poor.

Their dad was a violent alcoholic and their mother began her parenting when she was just thirteen. They had left the reservation in search of work and a better life. Being kicked around

is a good enough reason to hit the streets, and so Victor and

John lived outside their little apartment's front door. They knew where to get drugs at a young age. They knew everything, actually, everything putrid and wrong. They worshipped the local gang leaders and younger than most were jumped in.

I can still picture John at our first Kids Club. He was in my class. He would obey me most of the time, and as the two weeks wound down toward the end, listened to the Bible stories. I prayed earnestly that these stories would create a desire in him to be known by God and loved by him. The boys stayed late into the night when that club was over, helping clean our overworked campus, which only saw this kind of abuse once a year. They couldn't leave this love.

John was murdered barely a year and a half later. I could feel it coming ... so when he would call for a ride to pay the cable bill or I would see him in the neighborhood, I grabbed ahold of any chance to be with him. I usually used the ride to and from to talk to him about salvation and heaven and repentance. That is not my style, but I had a foreboding he was not long for this world. Whenever another loved one beats me to death, I picture that person waiting with the hordes of others who have gone before; I miss them already and hope to be with them one day. John is always in that pack, in my imagination.

I spent the next several years chasing after younger Victor, hoping I could do something about his destiny. Of course, I couldn't. He went in and out of juvenile jail, drugs, serious gang activity, horrible living. He had his son at fourteen, another baby born and died at age seventeen. He got tattoos for the deaths of all of his loved ones, and soon his neck and face were all marked up. He always came back to church and to our love, always. At seventeen he began the baby steps of walking with Christ. He gave his testimony publically by nineteen and began volunteering for us at that time, working with other little homies. He was preaching the gospel by age twenty-one and was a really good communicator. By twenty-four he pressured me into believing he was ready to be on our staff, something he longed to do for years. There were many beautiful things in this time; he has an ability to bring the word of God to life for others, and gave hope to some of his rescued old homeboys, who were miraculously finding new life in Christ also.

But, he hadn't finished looking for love and life in all the wrong places. In a full headlong plunge, he wholeheartedly gave himself back to the old filth he had climbed out of, years before. Finding himself back in jail, he cried out to the Lord, as he knows so well how to do. How many times can you be a prodigal son? He tries to name what's wrong, gets help, finds relief, and then surges backward. He is fragile, uncertain as to whether or not this new life in Christ thing can stick with him.

I am fragile too. He is the age of my son, and so I would say I have done about that many years with this young man. He has worn me out, loved me like a mom, been my pride and joy and made me want to blow my brains out all at the same time. I can't remember trusting him, yet I can spend hours talking to him as if all the things we know are the same. I am compelled by love to never, no never, give up on him, and yet for the first time, I have been tempted to do so. And that pain is what breaks my heart more than any other.

....

We value relationships. We go so far as saying that a relationship is the vehicle through which all these other good things, our ten core values, take place. We believe that change happens through relationships, rarely programs. We believe that hope is exchanged through relationships, hardly ever through a case plan. The things human beings need are experienced through relationships, rarely service delivery. The art of building healthy, supportive relationships will trump building successful programs every time, or maybe better stated, it is because of healthy relationships that we build successful programs.

Our mission statement begins this way: "to be the presence of Jesus Christ, sharing His life transforming hope, love and power." That's how it begins, *to be the presence*. Where? someone should ask. In the same space as someone else, should be the answer. Being the presence of Jesus suggests that He has full permission to be inside me, at work, inside our mission, at work. That his core values are ours – that we are obedient to the rules, which are all about love, all the time – that we give ourselves away, no strings attached to others. To be the presence of Jesus Christ means we have learned to be *present* inside a relationship and that, by the way, requires tremendous discipline.

Many of our friends have the kinds of problems that, in order to remain present, the desire *to fix them* is a temptation. The discipline of presence inside relationships where much of the time lives are messy and decisions being made are out of our control, can put us in a position of such uncomfortable weakness that in order to regain our equilibrium, we demand people change or we will have to get out of the relationship.

We are *in a hurry* for the relationship to make us feel good, as if that is the point. The value of relationships puts pressure on us to take the long view, to commit to loving someone for a life-time, to allow the relationship to birth things in us we desperately need, and to create space for the relationship to move us both to new and better places. All of this requires the disciplines of presence.

In ministry, we begin relationships with a lot of hopes but also *a lot of assumptions*. When ministering to the poor, many come into the relationship from a top down perspective. "These people have needs and I am supposed to meet those needs." We begin with an "us-them" category inside us. For each of us to become present inside a relationship, a true friendship must develop, where we genuinely agree how much we like each other.

Jeremy loves to teach this principle. He and his wife Jessica have been loving and liking a whole family of kids for over a decade. It began when Jeremy took Damian on as his mentee. This is a very long and large story, and won't get the space it deserves here, but I should tell you that because Jessica and Jeremy committed to figuring out how to stay in relationship with Damian and his siblings, many of us ended up adopting some of them. These twelve siblings were removed from their mom by the state of Arizona. Jeremy and Jessica adopted Ruby, we adopted Chella and Ximena, and Barry and Joanna adopted Emanuel and Adrienne.[238] Before the adoptions, Jeremy would go to pick up Damian, and would inevitably end up with a truck full of kids and a truck full of memories:

> *It was Christmas Eve, and my dad made all kinds of gourmet finger foods, things like that, and Chella said 'Shrimp! Where's the plate?' There were some small plates for hors d'oeuvres. She took one and loaded it up. 'Is there shrimp for anyone else?' I asked. Nope, it was all on her plate. ... One time I brought Damian home, it was late at night and one of the girls, she was about three at the time, was out on the playground alone digging in the sand by herself. ... Another time, we moved the family to a new apartment and about 8,000 roaches came out of the T.V. ... One of the kids had a birthday and there were some balloons, a cake and mom's boyfriend passed out in the front seat of the car. The child punched him and said, 'It's my birthday, wake up!' ... The first time when Ruby and Damian lived with us, and we sat down for dinner, we put the food in the middle of the table, and all the food is off the middle and onto Damian's plate. ... Those stories seem to stress how different our reality was from theirs, but the truth is, in hanging out with them,*

we realized that life is so much the same between us.

The following disciplines help us with presence, fixing, being in a hurry and the many and varied assumptions.

THE DISCIPLINE OF LOVE

Stephen Mott in *Biblical Ethics and Social Change,*[239] describes how relationships are developed on the bedrock of God's love. Relationships of the kind we want are those with ties to a supernatural love that in some ways defies explanation, it is a love that God pours into our hearts, a love that comes from God. "This is what real love is: It is not our love for God; it is God's love for us. He sent his Son to die in our place to take away our sins (1 Jn 4:10 NCV)." "We love because God loved us (1 Jn 4:19)." Love is a gift of God; it is in effect, an exchange of the love which we receive from God. We just pass it on to others. It is a gift of grace. The discipline of love is really just the desire to love. "Affliction produces endurance: and endurance produces character, and character produces hope. Now hope does not disappoint us because the love of God has been poured into our hearts through the Holy Spirit, whom God has given to us (Rom 5:3-5)." The Holy Spirit gives our desire power, making love of the kind we hope to exchange with one another possible. "I am giving you a new commandment, that you love one another; as I have loved you that you also love one another (Jn 13:34)."

Love is measured [in the scriptures] against the two strongest forces that we know: God's love for us in Christ and our own love for ourselves (Matt 22:39). Love seeks the good of the other person, of every person, looking to his or her well-being and not to our own self-benefit; this is the minimal statement of Christian love. But as grounded in God's sacrificial love and measured against the depth of our own self-seeking, love achieves its highest expression in self-sacrifice for the good of other persons. [240]

In light of this overwhelming evidence that God's love is operative in our relationships, these relationships are also modeled after God's friendship with us. Yes, God loves us and yes, He likes us. He wants us to love each other, but God also desires that we like each other. Christopher Heuertz and Christine Pohl in, *Friendship at the Margins,* have been working at understanding the ways in which we build friendships inside our community based on an understanding of our love exchange with God which often looks like a friendship.

Jesus offers us friendship, and that gift shapes a surprisingly subversive missional paradigm. A grateful response to God's gift of friendship involves offering that same gift to others – whether family or strangers, coworkers or children who live on the street. Offering and receiving friendship breaks down the barriers of 'us' and 'them' and opens up possibilities of healing and reconciliation. [241]

Susan describes her friendship with Maria:

Our friendship began on really rocky ground. Years ago, when CPS took Maria's babies, Amber and I were given custody for the time being. I would watch Maria's face, when she would come for a visit, she was afraid of me. I had power over her. We had the girls for six weeks, and then she got them back. I still saw the fear in her face; I still could take her children. What happened, by God's grace, He gave me the opportunity to tell her that I didn't want to take her children, that I wanted <u>her</u> to be a great mom. I wanted to be a pseudo grandma, but mostly I wanted to be her friend. Maria believed me, she trusted me to be in her life. Sometimes it is hard and painful, like our shared grief, both of us have lost our moms. And, sometimes it is light, she laughs *at my jokes. She taught me how to have a relationship across so many boundaries and differences, to find things that are common ground that we share; we love to eat together, we laugh, and she talks to me about deep important things to her. However, I don't think the relationship was built on common ground. It was built on risk. It set a precedent for me; it taught me how to enter into relationship in this community. To risk being vulnerable, to receive that in return.*

This love and like, which is based on and modeled after God's love and like of us is where we must begin relationships between all those in the mission. These relationships must be entered with an understanding that we are in this for the long-haul. Our goal is long-term relationships, birth to grave, multi-generational. Imagine all the life shared between loving partners with that as the standard, all the time invested, the beautiful memories, the heartbreak and the celebrations, the misunderstandings and the victories, the exposures on both sides of human error and presumption, the sacrifices, and the selfishness, the loyalty, the betrayal and the abandonment. Panda describes her relationship with Illa, who has become a surrogate mom to her over the years:

Illa and I have known each other for ten years. In the beginning, I thought, 'she's just going to be another white lady trying to change me, and be disappointed.' For a lot of years, that thought continued. 'She's just going to give up on me', I was always ready for her to walk out of my life and not care anymore. But she was consistent with us, my sisters and me, and our kids. She didn't just buy us stuff, she spent time with us. One of the things I remember had to do with one of her upcoming birthdays. "We have to give her something', maybe a card that says, 'I owe it all to you'. I feel like we've given her stuff she probably has given away to the Mercado. What can I give her? Then the thought came to me. You know, she is a teacher; we can give her an education (our education, my education). This was before I started my GED. No way, I'm too slow, too dumb. I really want to do this, and I really want Illa to be proud of me. My mom, she was never proud of me, she thought I wanted to be better than others. But Illa – even in my drug years, she never judged me – once I told her I was using, I can't believe she let us come to her house, during those years. She never left us. It is like a mother and daughter relationship. We can be on the phone all day. When she got her house broken into, I was thinking she is going to blame it on us – of course, it never crossed her mind – then with the bad economy we had to watch her lose her house, but her faith, handled this so amazingly. Well, I did give her that birthday gift – better than a card – to the one person who always stuck by me. When I got my GED I looked in the audience for her. There she was beaming, so proud of me. And for myself, I'm in it to win it – to go above and beyond. It helps my kids, which is what Illa wants for me, with them. The first day, when I went off to college, were they proud! They love that I'm working and going off to college, they help me around the house. They help me with everything; I know that this is to add to the possibilities for their life, making a higher bar. I just got my GED, which you could say is the easy way out; my kids are going to college!

THE DISCIPLINE OF FORGIVENESS AND NOT GIVING UP

Love—real, vulnerable, sacrificial and expensive—given freely away to others can result in some deep wounds. Miroslav Volf in, *Exclusion and Embrace,* lays out a detailed analysis on the way through the rough waters of pain in relationships.

> Forgiveness sums up much of the significance of the cross
> ... As Dietrich Bonhoeffer saw clearly, forgiveness itself is
> a form of suffering (Bonhoeffer 1963, 100); when I forgive
> I have not only suffered a violation but also suppressed the
> rightful claims of strict restitutive justice. Under the foot
> of the cross we learn, however, that in a world of irrevers-
> ible deeds and partisan judgments redemption from the
> passive suffering of victimization cannot happen without
> the active suffering of forgiveness. [242]

Pouring your life out onto someone else is risky business. It leaves you vulnerable to hurt and disappointment, with grief not too far behind. Ministry relationships can throw into the mix the hideous temptation to measure the relationship by so-called successes. And what if there doesn't seem to be any. Unhealthy finger-pointing "you" messages glob on: *You* aren't getting better. *Your* problems are huge and confusing. *You* abandoned or rejected me. *You're* a lot of work and most of the time I don't understand you. *You* don't believe in God and your life shows it. *You* betrayed me. We console ourselves by blaming the childhood stories of what happened to our friend when they were small. These stories are insane and demonic. Love requires that our hearts don't be- come hard, that we believe anew every day; though truth be told, that exact story has left me jaded. Love demands that we try again with the same person. Love waits ... love understands the jour- ney out ... love isn't required to publish a report of numbers and outcomes. Love exacts faithfulness instead of success. We have intentionally placed ourselves in direct solidarity with people who have been sorely sinned against, and then have turned around to hurt themselves and others. Forgiveness it is the only way to remain inside relationships where pain is a significant part of the narrative. Marcos talks about what it felt like to always be loved here, despite the hurt:

There has been love here for me throughout a big part of my life. You (Kit) were my leader, my teacher, my friend, my mentor, you have been there for me through happy times, through traumatic times; even though I went away for a long time, you never stopped loving me and been like another mother to me, not only been part of my life, but almost my entire family's life. Regardless of what I have done, or what I was accused of, I am thankful you were there for me as someone who really loved me and had my back, and I am very thankful for that.

"In his book *Is Human Forgiveness Possible?*, theologian John Patton examines the New Testament story (parable) in which Peter asks Jesus, 'Lord, when my brother wrongs me, how often must I forgive him? Seven times?' And Jesus answers: 'No, not seven times; I say seventy times seven times (Matt 18: 21-22).' Patton comments:

Peter's question seems to say, 'Please give me a rule so I don't have to keep dealing with this. How can I know when enough is enough? I want to know what to do instead of having to come to terms with the whole history of our relationship.' Jesus' response to the question says in effect, 'I am unwilling to give you a way out of a continuing relationship to your brother.'[243]

THE DISCIPLINE OF SEEING MYSELF IN YOU

"Love," says Mott, "is the fullest expression of God's grace. Both grace and love are expressed in actions that go far beyond the call of duty, but love ties the lover to the beloved with a greater bond of affection. Love's connection with grace is important for an understanding of its biblical meaning."[244] In light of the pain of loving, the grace of God reminds me of my own story. There are slight variations on the details of mine and the other stories here as it relates to, for example, childhood abuse and violence. We have that in common. But there is a gulf between us, revealed in the injustices of their culture and people that exacerbate personal violations and the privilege and opportunity my culture and people afforded me. These relationships have taught us how we learn to vulnerably tell our stories to each other: about injustice and how it affects relationships, about listening and discernment and how we learn to do it, and about lament and celebration as we figure out how to be on the journey together. Jeremy reflects on his relationship with Damian, again:

> *This whole 'seeing myself in you,' is really complex. When you care about someone and place yourself in their shoes, you can see reality in new ways – not sure you can actually break things down on how this works, but taking someone else's reality seriously, you have to bring into question what your reality was – your view has to expand to include both of them -- when something is not wrong, just different, their reality helps me to see things in a different light. I wish I could break down how that change happens, it is one of those mysteries of God I guess – something's just don't make logical sense. One thing I do know, that the pain in my life allowed me to enter a relationship with Damian and confirmed the understanding of what I believed: if I put value in my whole life, then he has value in his whole life.*

STORYTELLING

I don't know when it happened or how it started, but somewhere along the way, we started telling each other our stories. They brought us together, reminded us that we have hardly anything that technically separates us, and sometimes, despite our extraordinary differences, we really do believe we are really just the same. Same hopes, same desperations and fears, same desires and same insecurities, and often the same violations. And so we work out our stories in front of each other that the most basic questions of life which we share can be illuminated and confronted. Earnest Kurtz and Katherine Ketcham in, *The Spirituality of Imperfection,*[245] tell this great tale of our need for story:

> When the founder of Hasidic Judaism, the great Rabbi Israel Shem Tov, saw misfortune threatening the Jews, it was his custom to go into a certain part of the forest to meditate. There he would light a fire, say a special prayer, and the miracle would be accomplished and the misfortune averted.
>
> Later, when his disciple, the celebrated Maggid of Mezritch, had occasion, for the same reason, to intercede with heaven, he would go to the same place in the forest and say:
>
> 'Master of the Universe, listen! I do not know how to light the fire, but I am still able to say the prayer,' and again the miracle would be accomplished.
>
> Still later, Rabbi Moshe-leib of Sasov, in order to save his people once more, would go into the forest and say, 'I do not know how to light the fire. I do not know the prayer, but I know the place and this must be sufficient.' It was sufficient, and the miracle was accomplished.

Then it fell to Rabbi Israel of Rizhim to overcome misfortune. Sitting in his armchair, his head in his hands, he spoke to God: 'I am unable to light the fire, and I do not know the prayer, and I cannot even find the place in the forest. All I can do is to tell the story, and this must be sufficient.'

And it was sufficient.

For God made man because he loves stories.[246]

VULNERABILITY

Storytelling, if done well and truthfully, places us before each other with a naked candor that opens up spaces inside me/us that finally get an opportunity for light. There is so much we give up when we tell the truth of our stories to each other. We give up personal power and personal space. Sarah worked hard to build a relationship with a young man, who had a really hard time letting anyone into his life:

> I think more than anything, because of the work I had to do to be patient with another human being's process to become vulnerable, it could have become something I judged myself about and be so quick to recognize that I wasn't doing it right. But I chose not hating myself, realized it was OK to not do it the right way, let it break down pride issues for me, letting it be (take its time), and not over-owning how long it was going to take to build trust.

In urban communities, because there have been so many violations and traumas which happened at the core of the self, when the story gets told, as close to the violation and trauma as we can possibly get, the layers of protection that have been put in place to guard that core begin to be peeled away. There is great vulnerability in this act. Consistent with this, is when the so-called "mentor" or "leader" tells their story among community members, but does so authentically and truthfully, and exposes others to their frailties and weaknesses, and even dark side, there is great vulnerability in this act too. Jorge models vulnerability in our community, up front as the preacher, through personal illustrations, or one-on-one telling it like it is. He rarely covers up, but vulnerability, he will confess, has an underside, it is when those you have trusted with your story and shared life with, leave you.

> *This question about how relationships here have changed me is hard for me. Back in the day, [there were several people who] took care of the needs in our family and our problems. Only Kit is still here. …Today the role Wayne plays is another big role. The way I see it, Wayne, Alan, Jeff Boles, Albert – they're here. Will they stay? I am reminded of David and Jonathan – his promise to David that he would be loyal to him to death. How do we recover when people haven't been loyal to death – I am preaching this Sunday about Jesus coming into Jerusalem – one day, they cry out Hosanna, three days later, they cry out crucify him – I lose something when each of these people leave, but God has stayed with me, and he promises to never leave me. Matt. 28 says – I will go with you to the end of the world.*

What does vulnerability produce? It introduces us to a form of spirituality, a Christ- likeness that so many other activities just can't produce. Greg Paul works among the homeless in Toronto. In his book, *God in the Alley*,[247] he is confronted with the role mutual vulnerability plays in building relationships with his friends who live on the streets, where vulnerability can cost them their lives.

If it's hard to see the creative and liberating power of Jesus inherent in truly abandoning myself into God's hands, it's more challenging still to embrace the concept of vulnerability as a kind of power. Still, it's very clear that Jesus was never more Lord and Christ during his life than at the moment of his supreme vulnerability. That Jesus himself was very much aware of this is abundantly evident in his every recorded utterance from the cross – think of his promise to the dying thief, or his intercession for those who 'do not know what they are doing. Even the awesome power of the Resurrection is given its potency by the Cross that preceded it. Jesus's power to liberate me derives directly from his vulnerability on the cross. No death for him means no resurrection for me. [248]

For most people vulnerability is something that is hard to learn. Malissa tells her story about this:

Blanca and Mari were some of the first girls I met around 2000, in the 7th grade. I began mentoring them, and they began to mentor me. Mari, telling me the truth about her own life, helped me to become a more honest person. Blanca, sending me a handwritten letter in the mail, helped me just when I needed that encouragement. This was a gift to me, affirming my worth and my value. Over the years, they reaffirmed what I am called to do, they taught me how to be a better friend, with them I got to share pain and joy – we ended up bearing children around the same time, I helped them when they wanted to drop out of school, I was in their wedding, got to influence them on occasion with childrearing, they have become amazing women. They watched me struggle with rough seasons of marriage, watched me reconcile with my mom.

INJUSTICE AND LAMENT

These vulnerabilities in our storytelling often reveal the terrible things that have been done to us or remind us of the slaughter that has happened to the people we come from. Our storytelling brings us to a common grief, a personal and collective cry that can be heard to heaven, "Why did these things happen?" Bob Ekblad, in *Reading the Bible with the Damned,*[249] leads prisoners through the Bible who are beginning to disclose the deep closeted questions about a God who allowed terrible things to happen to them.

> As people enter into the language of the psalmist, the alienating distance and fear they once felt with God is gradually subverted by the psalmist's surprising honest and intimacy. The psalms articulate a wide range of uncensored sentiments and thinking before God…. When I read psalms of personal lament with despairing people who expect non comfort from the Bible, they are often shocked by the depths our of which the psalmist cries. How does the psalmist have the nerve to be that real before God? The rawness of emotion and reckless pleas and the graphic description of hardship make these prayers credible to those who are submerged in difficulties.[250]

As we listen to each other, and hear each one's ability to get close to their laments, to name the injustices that encircle their yesterdays and todays, we validate the real humanity we share. And somewhere in it all, Jesus is solidifying a body of Christ, who bears each others burdens. (Gal 6:2) Claudia's testimony is just that. As someone who bore the injustice of a childhood of abuse, she has experienced an encircling in her yesterdays and todays, from the body of Christ:

I have to speak about my relationships here as if they were one person; a whole group of people (though I want to talk about them as if they were 'one') who have loved me a certain way, and helped me with my life. ...This is a person (remember, she is a lot of people all rolled into one) who is very genuine. That is the main thing I love about her, how true, she doesn't hurt you, but is able to speak the truth in love, this person has been in my life for years, and has lived everything that has been hard for me, from confronting my background, to helping coach me as I discipline my own kids, I've learned from this person how to raise my kids, how to talk to them, how to be patient. I've found a friend in that person, and support, acceptance, but mainly it has been the love, the care that I missed as a child. This person has provided emotional, financial support and guidance – and compassion. A lot of the people that I have in my life now have filled that role of mother and father that I never had. Specifically, there is a couple that has known my children maybe seven or eight years, they look at them like their adopted grandchildren – they do the whole providing books, pencils, backpacks, clothes if they needed to, for their birthdays, they do all the things that grandparents do for them, definitely being God this way – I didn't have a relationship with my grandmother, I have certain memories, I didn't experience what it was like to have a grandparent love you and care for you. Because relationships are important to God, he makes it possible for people to just want to be with you, know you, just accepting us the way we are...

LISTENING AND DISCERNMENT

Often we will talk about our community of faith, using familial words, like "family" and "home". We do that to emphasize that the storytelling we have been doing has created a people who now belong together, for now we know too much. You are mine! Kurtz and Ketcham understand this:

> The word witness means 'one who knows the truth'. In an environment of storytelling and storylistening, where each person is at different times both teller and listener, the hearers do know 'the truth' – about the tellers – in a special way. For unlike seeing, where one can look away, listeners cannot 'hear away' but must listen. As the philosopher Hans-Georg Gadamer pointed out: 'Hearing implies already belonging together in such a manner that one is claimed by what is being said.'[251]

Listening is like a mirror. In the story we see the things we haven't the courage, the wisdom, the honesty to say ourselves, but should learn to do. One thing that sabotages relationships here at Neighborhood is in the inability of the "helper" usually, to come into the relationship where trust is beginning with their own self-awareness. Pride, self-deceit, hypocrisy, paternalism, latent prejudices, judgmentalism – all of that stands between us. How hard it is to know the truth about ourselves.

> Must we, then, forever grope blindly in the dark? What can we do, in order to be? Yet again, an ancient answer echoes across the centuries: *Listen! Listen to stories!* For what stories do, above all else, is hold up a mirror so that we can see ourselves. Stories are mirrors of human being, reflecting back our very essence. In a story, we come to know precisely the both/and, mixed-up-ed-ness of our very being. In the mirror of another's story, we can discover our tragedy and our comedy – and therefore our

very *human*-ness, the ambiguity and incongruity that lie at the core of the human condition.[252]

And as is true to the kingdom nature of all God births, this discipline of seeing myself in you which should feel heavy and dark, instead becomes an experience of liberation and joy. We use words like "breakthrough" having to do with insights we've gained, and "openness" for the space in our souls that feels less shut down or shut off.

CELEBRATION

What unites us in relationship with our God, with each other and with our selves is that in our storytelling – our weaknesses, our sin, our doubt, our messy spirituality, our brokenness – it is all exposed. I remember both encountering that word *brokenness* and the substance of it in my own life. It was like a new frontier I had entered, a discovered space; it contained a language and an opportunity. And I learned that Jesus is found in brokenness.

> This is the surprise of brokenness. The all-powerful Lord may seem distant and even frightening; the spotlessly perfect and unique Christ may seem unattainable. But I know what it's like to cry out in desperate prayer; I, too, seem to need to suffer in order to learn how to be the Father's obedient child – although, unlike the Son, it's generally my own sins that cause my suffering. It's the broken Jesus whom I can approach and even, in some small way, begin to emulate.[253]

And this is cause for celebration. I can know Jesus in deep intimacy, because I am no longer trying to hold it all together, or am no longer in charge. He has the answers for me, for my friends, for these poor I hang out with. He is Lord of us all, He is big, bigger than all we face, and that news is good for me to share, but more, for me to live. It is in these precious relationships here I get to learn that and experience all of this. "Blessed are you who are poor, for yours is the kingdom of God," and, "Blessed are the poor in spirit, theirs is [also] the kingdom of heaven (Lk 6:20, Mt 5:3)." Ian has learned this in relationship with the tenacious, hard-working immigrant women in our community.

> *Our moms in general have influenced me the most. I didn't really understand how strong our families were, until I saw how much they do in our neighborhood, without them we would be toast, a few of the dads, but the women do the real work. They have changed me, and have allowed me to see differently, Felipa, Elizabeth, Juana, Lupe, Lourdes, a lot more.*

GRACE RULES – TRUTH TELLING and STORIES

A grace rule is the way grace rules. This rule describes a lavish gift from God as experienced in our community. By receiving it, grace rules – leading us further into love and action.

We have been trying to grab a hold of a by-line (tag-line) at Neighborhood that captures our mission and values. We have chosen: REAL LIFE – REAL FAITH. What this is trying to say is obvious, we hope. We are committed to know and embrace the "real" world, not a better one than the real one (denial) or a darker one than the real one (despair); one where our faith in the Living Lord helps us to live inside the truth of our world. "As Christian people, we form our community consistent with our conviction that the story of Christ is a truthful account of our existence. For as H.R. Niebuhr argued, only when we know 'what is going on', do we know 'what we should do'. And Christians believe that we learn most decisively 'what is going on' in [through] the cross and resurrection of Christ."[254]
This idea informs our practice of truth-telling as we gift our stories to each other. Inside the hope of the gospel, we find the courage to tell each other our stories. We can handle the truth, because we find hope and courage in the cross that bears this extant reality. And we can tell each other the truth of our stories because of the grace we each have received, no one better, and no one worse. It becomes our shared place of humanity, real life, real faith.

> Listening to stories and telling them helped our ancestors to live humanly – to be human. But somewhere along the way our ability to tell (and to listen to) stories was lost. As

life speeded up, as the possibility of both communication and annihilation became every more instantaneous, people came to have less tolerance for that which comes only over time. The demand for perfection and the craving for ever more control over a world that paradoxically seemed ever more out of control eventually bred impatience with story. As time went by, the art of story telling fell by the wayside, and those who went before us gradually lost part of what had been the human heritage – the ability to ask the most basic question, the spiritual questions. We're interested in the news of the day and the problems of the hour. Thus distracted, we no longer listen to those who speak of the eternal values that have to do with the centering of our lives.[255]

Stanley Hauerwas provides a prayer toward this grace filled truth-telling:

Dear God, we often ask you to invade our lives, to plumb the secrets of our hearts unknown even to ourselves. But in fact we do not desire that. What we really want to scream, if only to ourselves is 'Do not reveal to us who we are!' We think we are better people if you leave us to our illusions. Yes, we know another word for a life of illusion is *hell*. But we are surrounded by many caught up in such a hell – people too deficient of soul even to be capable of lying, but only of self-deceit. Dear God, we ask your mercy on all those so caught, particularly if we are among them. The loneliness of such a life is terrifying. Remind us, compel us to be truthful, painful as that is. For without the truth, without you, we die. Save us from the pleasantness which too often is but a name for ambition. Save us from the temptation to say to another what we think she wants to hear rather than what we both need to hear. The regimen of living your truth is hard, but help us remember that any love but truthful love is cursed. The lie wrapped in love is just another word for violence. For God's sake, for the world's sake, give us the courage and the love to speak truthfully, so that we might be at peace with one another and with you. Amen.[256]

NOTES

237. Frederick Buechner, *The Magnificent Defeat*, (New York: HarperSanFrancisco, 1966), 105.
238. The four older siblings were in our homes for a period of time, and are now independent adults; the oldest daughter's babies were adopted by one of the Mom's Place volunteers and another family in our church.
239. Stephen Mott, *Biblical Ethics and Social Change*, (Oxford: University Press, 1982).
240. Ibid., Kindle Electronic Edition, Chapter 3, location 588 of 3525.
241. Christopher L. Heuertz and Christine D. Pohl, *Friendship at the Margins, Discovering Mutuality in Service and Mission,* (Downers Grove: InterVarsity Press, 2010), 30.
242. Miroslav Volf, 124.
243. Ernest Kurtz and Katherine Ketcham, *The Spirituality of Imperfection, Storytelling and the Journey to Wholeness*, (New York: Bantam Books, 1994).
244. Mott, Kindle Electronic Edition, Chapter 3, location 540 of 3525.
245. Ernest Kurtz and Katherine Ketcham, *The Spirituality of Imperfection, Storytelling and the Journey to Wholeness*, (New York: Bantam Books, 1994).
246. Ibid., 8.
247. Greg Paul, *God in the Alley, Being and Seeing Jesus in a Broken World*, (Colorado Springs: Shaw Books, 2004).
248. Ibid., 65.
249. Bob Ekblad, *Reading the Bible with the Damned*, (Louisville: Westminster John Knox Press, 2005).
250. Ibid., 129.
251. Kurtz and Ketcham, 239. (quoting From Gadamer, *Truth and Method*, pp. 419-20.)
252. Ibid., 63-64.
253. Greg Paul, 110.
254. Stanley Hauerwas, *A Community of Character*, (Notre Dame: University of Notre Dame Press, 1981), 10.
255. Kurtz and Ketcham, 8.
256. Stanley Hauerwas, *Prayers Plainly Spoken*, (Downers Grove: InterVarsity Press, 1999), 39.

"Liminal Ground" Craig Goodworth

CHAPTER TEN

We Value
COMMUNITY

Core Value #9

Definition: Community as we know it has two parts, the first is best expressed as diverse people who work together for the common good, caring for the sacred space that is their God appointed neighborhood. Community is also expressed as the solidarity that members experience with one another as they seek to serve, advocate and align themselves with each other in their communal space.

Community is a by-product of commitment and struggle. It comes when we step forward to right some wrong, to heal some hurt, to give some service. Then we discover each other as allies in resisting the diminishments of life. It is no accident that the most impressive sense of community is found among people in the midst of such joyful travail: among minority groups seeking identity and justice, among women seeking liberation into fully humane roles, among all who have said No to tyranny with the concrete affirmation of their lives.[257]

– Parker Palmer

At Neighborhood, when we say the word *community* we mean two things. One has to do with the physical place of the community we live in. That is a sacred space for us. It has physically been marked off by God for us to care about, the people in it, the health of all of its activities from schools to businesses (the institutions), the presence of evil and things that would fall into the category of principalities and powers (from drug dealers to political efforts that oppress) and the many friends who are also trying to make our community a better place.

The words that come to mind when I hear the value of "community "are: HOLY GROUND. God has given us a state, a city and a neighborhood. We choose to know and invest in the people there, yes. They become our community, yes. But community also begs, for us, notions of place and geography. The literal land where we are placed becomes sacred. The neighborhood as holy ground. We refuse to abandon or neglect this place as that would be to neglect that which God, himself, cares deeply about. Roman Catholic and other denominational notions of "parish" are helpful constructs for us as we sort out the practical implications of this theology of place. Beginning to define and adopt a particular locale is a deeper and more important exercise for us than simply describing our 'service boundary;' this process is instead, for us, discerning the physical space and place that God wants us to care for, adopt, plant roots, invest in, cultivate, protect and defend. The people who live lives there become enormously valuable and precious for us; those we know and those we have yet to meet. The politics of the place become increasingly important as the impact of decisions are felt with growing acuteness and ever deepening awareness. The economy of the place is now ours to invest in and add to; the schools there educate our children who represent our potential and future. We end up seeing everyone and everything as precious and full of capacity because despair is no longer an option and everyone has something to contribute. Despair is not an option because we have nowhere else to go and when you have nowhere else to go, you must choose to hope. All of the life in the place, in all of its dimensions, becomes enormously valuable to us, spiritually. God has given us the things in our place to steward, protect, and cultivate. Our obedience to God necessitates a commitment to our place. – Ian Danley

The second way we define community relates to the commitment we make to one another to do life together. This is a broader category than what we defined to be "The Beloved Community" earlier, and includes everyone who calls Neighborhood home for any reason at all, including our partners who feel like surrogate family.

> *The word that comes to mind when I hear the value of "community "is: MODELING – At Neighborhood I have seen these things modeled in our community, genuine love, as for a family, vulnerability with each other, unconditional love, I have seen that over and over, not just with the kids or with the staff, but also the family members in the neighborhood.*
> *– Isiah Oakes*

There are a few texts that inform our understanding of community. They have relied on the Bible, socio-political literature, history and/or author's experience to craft a working definition:

1) Walter Fluker on Howard Thurman and Martin Luther King's combined understanding of community: "The idea that the word community denotes some determinate object, a particular type of social life and experience, e.g., a sense of belonging, a sense of place, a sense of identity, or shared values. Such a common sense view of language, however, fails to address the problem of multi-dimensional levels and varieties of experiences covered in the broad terminology of community. In this sense, community, like love, covers a multitude of definitional and methodological sins."[258]

2) Stanley Hauerwas on Christian communities that are capable of hearing the story of God and living in a manner that is faithful to that story: "Communities formed by a truthful narrative must provide the skills to transform fate into destiny so that the

unexpected, especially as it comes in the form of strangers, can be welcomed as gift."[259]

3) Stanley J. Grenz on a theology of community: "...Our theological reflections around the concept of community are understood as the goal of God's program for creation. God is at work in our world, we declare. And God's purpose in this activity is the establishment of community – a reconciled people who enjoy fellowship with him, with one another, and ultimately with all creation."[260]

4) Jean Vanier quoting David Clark (*Yes to Life*, 1987) on community: "Without a strong sense of community human beings will wilt and begin to die. Community is the foundation of human society, the zenith of interdependence, the epitome of wholeness; in fact, the end of our journeying."[261]

5) John Fuder and Noel Castellans, editors, take on the topic of community, as Christian Community Developers: There is a biblical basis for community analysis, boldly suggesting a theology of research using the book of Nehemiah. "When Nehemiah gets the news about the state of disrepair of Jerusalem, he goes out and conducts research, thoroughly 'inspecting the walls' (Neh 2:13-15). He then builds community (remainder of chapter 2), assembles a team around a common vision (chapter 3), and gets to work despite persistent opposition (chapters 4-6), until the job is done and the celebration begins (chapters 7-8)."[262]

COMMUNITY – THE SACRED SPACE

The word that comes to mind when I hear the value of "community" is: RELATIONSHIP – we're not just saying it but doing it – standing together, whatever the situation may be, or the cost may be, standing together as a family, as a people, so much more than individually, the whole community. Through communication, through understanding, through relationship, we develop love for one another, where there is love there is hope, where there is hope there is miracles. – Marcos Marquez

There is an unusual and possibly supernatural aspect to loving ones community. I have on occasion likened it to being a gang-member, who loyally wears the street name or number on his arms or neck, and when lost and having nothing to live for, will even die for that street. Our loyalty is less dark, and certainly not visionless, but bears a similar commitment to the place we live. And thanks to God, our desire is not to violently protect the space, but to see it thrive and all manner of beauty to be born within. This belonging and commitment harkens back to an old understanding of parish ministry. The whole community, space and people, are of concern to the parish priests. Archbishop William Temple famously said, "The Church is the only society in the world which exists for the sake of those who are not members of it."[263] We are people who live "outside the walls" so to speak and spend devoted time living alongside each other. We have come to love and know our community, and are committed to learn its story. Similar to the parish concept, NM thinks about community in two ways: the physical place we live in and how we live life together.

A COMMUNITY THAT DOES LIFE TOGETHER

The word that comes to mind when I hear the value of community: TRUST – We trust each other; we visit each other and sit with each other; we do life together and that really means being open about the reality we are living and offering each other the support to make decisions. We pick up each others kids for all kinds of reasons; we buy groceries for each other; we celebrate together; we cry together; and we

learn from each other.
– Claudia Sanchez

We live alongside a watching community, embedded among them for the purposes of love. We are not settled here in community with these particular people by accident as this poem by Walter Brueggemann called, "Can We Risk It?", reminds us.

> We have been sent dangerously by God's address – called by name, entrusted with risky words, and empowered with authority. We are to tell the truth openly, work for justice, and stand in solidarity with our neighbors. The cost is high, but the purposes are those of the Holy God.[264]

SOLIDARITY

The word that comes to mind when I hear the value of community is: UNITY – Together we're stronger, "wholer", truer; together we are the incarnation; together we love; together we move forward; together we live and love; together we're real; together we have faith . – Jeremy Wood

As a community, we experience an intimacy in doing life with one another that is difficult to put into a framework that others can understand. I am often asked by people who have never been to our campus if we all live together. It must sound that way sometimes when we talk. We use the words *family, togetherness, coming alongside, sharing the load* and of course *solidarity* freely, but it is also how we live. When we hear that someone in the neighborhood has been shot, we investigate; and lately have begun using a liturgy called "The Moment of Blessing," to acknowledge the life and provide a reclamation of that bloody land, (believing that "precious is their blood in His sight" Prov 72:14). Most of our kids programs draw a significant number of children from our direct community, a few hundred. As they grow in our programs and become more and more engaged, a young person can do many different activities with us through the weeks and years, and literally grow up here. We have businesses and an in-kind barter system that economically sustains over a hundred households. And we battle on the front lines with our friends for immigration reform. The site work on our campus is coming to completion this year and will be designed around a traditional Latin American plaza in the center of the four acres for the purpose of community gathering. Also, soon to be completed is the acquisition of some slum housing which sit directly next door. These houses are for our community, not just members of Neighborhood Ministries. (We don't have a membership).

LOVE AND MISSION

> *The word that comes to mind when I hear the value of community is: FAMILY – I used to love our old church name, "Open Door," because it means anybody could come, anybody. I love being part of our community, getting to know new people. To introduce them to our church, I know it isn't like any other ordinary place, like our Katy's Kids preschool; it's not like a regular Headstart. Our community is all of us. It's not just for you. We are a whole unit, with the 'w', wholistic, we are family, that's the only word that comes to me, family. – Panda Corral and Sister Googoos Medrano*

We are family members and co-dwellers in this shared life. But we are also the called- out ones, the ekklesia, which is Greek for church. Called to go out, called to be in the community, to love, to be about the common good, to incarnate and preach the gospel of Jesus Christ. I really like the way Tim Suttle, who is uncovering an evangelical social gospel, describes called-out-ones.

Every week God breathes his church into his lungs. It's a cosmic inhalation that draws the church together every seven days. What happens when the church gathers is of great importance. The people of God gather, first and foremost, around the story of God – the Scriptures – and they tell and retell the story in the most creative and imaginative ways possible. Over time they begin to see themselves as living in that story – not the story of our culture, but the story of God – it comes to define them as a people more than any other rival story. Then God exhales. He blows us out of his lungs and into the world. As little transformed agents of redemption we are sent out into the places we always go. We go there as salt and light. We go there as people who do not walk by sight but by faith. We are transformed vessels of God's redemption sent to season all of creation. We image God. So, when people look at us they actually see past us, and get a good look at God. We become caught up in the love of God and become transformed into the kind of people who go out into the world as salt and light and actually image God to all creation because we're image-bearing people.[265]

TRUTH AND THE COMMON GOOD

> *The word that comes to mind when I hear the core value of community is: BELONGING – We belong to each other, we celebrate, we make phone calls in the middle of the night, we have fun together, we challenge each other to be more honest, and we want to see each one fulfill their potential. We belong together, a diverse group of people, a huge extended family of belonging. – Malissa Geer*

We understand that because the love of God has been poured into us [for our community] and compels us to share it, in deeds, yes, but also in words, words that bring salvation, hope and reconciliation (2 Cor 5:11-21).

Miroslav Volf, in *A Public Faith,*[266] calls these words of truth, wisdom. "Christians have traditionally understood their faith not as a religious add-on to life but as itself constituting an integrated way of life. Correspondingly, Christian wisdom in one sense is that faith itself – an overarching interpretation of reality, a set of convictions, attitudes, and practices that direct people in living their lives well."[267] He has some suggestions on how we share the wisdom of Christ with our neighbors. First, we remember we come purely as witnesses to a self-giving God, beggars showing other beggars where the food is. Second, we are not merchants who sell. God isn't a commodity, we are not in some kind of corporate competition and after all, the wisdom we offer is free (Isa 55:1). Third, our witness should be confirmed by our actions. The wisdom we are describing is best revealed through this wisdom lived. St. Francis is legendarily known to have said, "Preach the gospel at all times and when necessary use words."[268] "Fourth, Christ's wisdom points to Christ, the witness is not 'open minded' where any wisdom will do, the witness is a true witness to what has occurred outside oneself to Christ and the wisdom he was and continues to be."[269] Fifth, Christians should honor and respect all hearers, their traditions, their ability to integrate any nuggets of wisdom with gentleness and reverence (1 Pet 3:15,16). Always recognizing that the wisdom we share requires eyes to see and ears to hear (Ezek 12:1-2). "Wisdom may not appear wise at first"[270] And lastly, wisdom is an exchange. We have much to offer our community as it relates to the love and wisdom of God, but our community has much to offer us, as it relates to wisdom. Our job is to be open, discerning and accepting of this co-reciprocation of these precious gifts. The wisdom of God, of which the scriptures are filled, of which the Holy Spirit ignites for our remembrance and for our self-giving is for the blessing and benefit of those God has given us to love, which is our community. "A vision of human flourishing – and resources to realize it – is the most important contribution of the Christian faith to the common good."[271]

TOP TEN WAYS WE HAVE LEARNED TO "SEE" OUR COMMUNITY

The word that comes to mind when I hear the value of community is: FRIENDSHIP – As a family we are walking alongside each other, doing life together, the best friendships and the deepest relationships, its stumbling together, but picking each other up and holding each other up. It's crying together and laughing together. –Susan Leon

Our community is invisible to a lot of people. One glaring example recently revealed this. Our city is moving into the twenty-first century with a new form of public transportation, a train called The Light Rail. The next phase of railway to be added in the coming decade is planned to run through our neighborhood. Engineers and planners mapped a route right through a part of our community that would be disastrous. They thought no one would notice. We noticed. How do people learn to see things that are invisible to others? There is a progression in seeing. The following are some of our ideas on how we learn to see our community:

1) Practice seeing – We know our community is invisible to others; it is the way of poverty. There are lots of reasons outsiders don't want to see our community: it has been stereotyped to be dangerous; it has blight; the perceived pain is hard to face. We argue that, seeing is a spiritual discipline, it can be cultivated, even though it doesn't come naturally. Kris Rocke, in *Geography of Grace*, reflects on developing sight from Robert Barron's *And Now I See: A Theology of Transformation*:

Christianity is, above all, a way of seeing. Everything else in Christian life flows from and circles around the transformation of vision. Christians see differently, and that is why their prayer, their worship, their action, their whole way of being in the world, has a distinctive accent and flavor.[272]

2) Live here and have trusted relationships – Over the years, more and more of us have moved into the neighborhood, and progressively, original residents are moving back in, instead of moving out to the suburbs. In doing life with our friends, the realities of our community struggles are exposed. Love opens our eyes and, once our eyes are opened, it is impossible to close them again.

3) Come as a listener273 – Surprisingly, it is still necessary to help people enter a community with respect. The community can and ought to be our educator about itself. All desire to fix, all efforts to reform and all intention to bring something in that has previously been determined the community needs, before asking good questions, is called paternalism and should be discouraged.

4) Prayer walk – God is in love with our community. Imagine seeing through His eyes. The concept of prayer walking is actually very simple but can be life changing. Walking around the community and praying for what you see and what the Lord brings to mind, alerts the heart and mind about the hidden oasis' of beauty and situations that break the heart of God.

5) Asset Map – Up until recently the favorite approach to evaluating problematic communities has been using a needs assessment model, where program development comes from the deficiencies and problems discovered. For most of us, this needs approach reinforced the already entrenched mental images most have of so-called "needy" neighborhoods: crime, violence, joblessness, welfare dependency, gangs, drugs, homelessness, vacant and abandoned land, boarded-up buildings. And though they tell some of the story, they are by no means the whole story. As

specialists in far away think tanks and social laboratories study the problems and come up with solutions to the neighborhoods as outsiders, the community takes on the self understandings of the service providers and begins to view themselves as clients. As a rule, from universities to the media, the primary way in which poor communities are viewed is through the grid of the deficiency model. In contrast, wherever effective community development efforts have been discovered, those efforts were based upon an understanding of the community's assets, capacities and abilities. Come and see the assets.

6) Network and make alliances – Community developers and community organizers recognize that the work of rebuilding communities is relationship business. Building and rebuilding relationships between local residents, associations and institutions is a good way to learn to see.

7) Evaluate, study and explore – Nothing is static; our community is always changing. We must be committed to relevant research and ongoing innovation to participate with the community around its concerns. Often the local university or city has some level of research they are doing in our community in an effort to *see* themselves or to help someone else *see*.

8) Get involved in community affairs – Community organizing is about engaging disadvantaged communities in order to help them achieve power. It begins with an anger that comes from seeing.

> ...an anger that seethes at the injustices of life and transforms itself into a compassion for those hurt by life. It is an anger rooted in direct experience and held in collective memory. It is the kind of anger that can energize a democracy – because it can lead to the first step in changing politics.[274]

9) Locate and learn from historic mentors – If we have eyes to see, and determination to seek them out, the educators of how our community was formed can be found. We can ask them an infinite amount of questions: how our community has changed, what icons and symbols remain of a time gone by, residents who have made significant contributions, ethnic histories and even spiritual mapping.

10) Go door to door – There is nothing like knocking on someone's door and beginning a relationship that opens the eyes to see who and what is all around us. We go door to door for, voter registration, community listening projects, asset mapping, program for church, surveys, census work, etc. Every time the project is completed, we see our community better, deeper.

Seeing is a spiritual discipline, and as it is activated it opens up the heart and mind to stories that are hidden, and hardly known. It has been helpful to us, as a ministry, to learn the back story of what we are seeing. Our community has a back story.

HISTORY – ARIZONA AND IT'S STORY

It's impossible to tell our Neighborhood Ministries' community's story, without telling the story of Arizona, where our story takes place. There are many ways to tell the story of Arizona: we can talk about it's beauty, pointing to the majesty of the Grand Canyon; we can survey the Arizona that provides scientists, anthropologists and archeologists their dream location to study ancient tribal peoples, meteors, dinosaurs and even volcanos. OR we can talk about our racial and social justice history; it is a lens that is rarely used to see our state and city.

I believe that Arizona has been the state of "SB1070"[275] since its inception. In other words, the acts involved and the mindset needed to pull off an SB1070 is inherent somewhere deep inside our state and its history. Could it be that we are living our unredeemed, discompassionate identity over and over again? Could it be that for such a time as this, we and our cohorts might see transformation in that self-identification, and that this engagement with the "principalities and powers" is for that end? This remains a reflection; meanwhile let's take a look at some Arizona highlights through the lens of social justice and human rights.

Arizona is the 48th state, becoming so in 1912, ten years after its first application for statehood was denied, thought by some historians to be because Arizona was too "Mexican."[276] In 1917, the United States entered into World War I, thus beginning a boom in the economy of Arizona. After suffering through the Great Depression, the implementation of the New Deal and another economic boom after World War II Arizona was brought into a state of stability. During this timeframe, industries such as cotton, copper, farming, and mining began to flourish in the state. The military began using Phoenix and Tucson for military bases and academies, with the army becoming the community's largest source of revenue. During the war, people also began to move to Arizona from other regions of the country because of its inland position and protection from aerial attacks. In 1946, Arizona began to enforce right-to-work laws, which allowed workers to decide whether or not to join or financially support a union. The dual-wage system, in which Mexicans made $1.15 less per shift, was abandoned. In 1948, the high tech industry began in Arizona, with Motorola building one of the first plants in Phoenix. 1948 also saw American Indians gaining the right to vote, after having been disqualified for twenty years for being "wards of the state."

Phoenix

Unlike the older cities in our nation, Phoenix doesn't have much of a history.[277] Phoenix was never a center of innovation, corporate power, never had a rich culture or a quilt of ethnicities with deep bonds to neighborhoods. And yet, like the older cities, Phoenix has quickly become a place of terrific racial politics. Modern Phoenix was conceived as a city for white people. It kept its barrios and black neighborhoods in the shadows, and the Anglo population was always the super-majority. Phoenix was surrounded by so-called "boomburbs," that supported low-wage jobs, fueled an economy that cratered into house-building, and featured an insatiable demand for immigrant labor.

Phoenix was never built as an entry-point into the American Dream. The economy is narrow, capital flows even more so. It has disproportionately attracted low-skilled immigrants from Mexico. Nearly 29 percent of city residents were foreign born in 2009 up from 19.5 percent in the city in 2000. Even in the best of circumstances, the old ladders — the factory jobs that allowed immigrants in the late 19th and early 20th century to rise — are gone. The barriers to reaching prosperity in an advanced 21st century economy for these individuals are nearly insurmountable. In a world where mastery of English is the ticket to advancement, 38.2 percent of Phoenicians speak a language other than English at home. To make the human capital crisis worse, Arizona policies are hostile to funding the education and infrastructure that would provide economic mobility. Instead, Hispanics are "the enemy to be feared" to the political establishment, while simultaneously an easily exploitable workforce. Hispanic voter participation has been shockingly low, thus, no leveraging of numbers into political power. Phoenix, with its miles of older tract houses turning into linear slums, with its aging infrastructure, is increasingly the place for the working poor. Phoenix's central core did not revive outside of some major public projects. Instead, the footprint of the poor Hispanic population grew. The core was unable to draw substantial private investment and lost private- sector jobs. Neighborhoods such as Garfield, Oakland and St. Matthews have remained ungentrified.[278]

COMMUNITY

Segregated City

The city of Phoenix became physically segregated at its inception with South Phoenix comprised of many cultures and distinct districts separated as all cities do with a physical landmark, here it was the Southern Pacific railroad tracks. Eventually it was the Salt River that defined white from color. Only today is this slightly changing.

Phoenix's relatively small Mexican-American and African-American populations were historically located south of the tracks. Schools were segregated and inferior. Poverty and injustice were severe and corruption by city officials was legendary, at least through the 1940s. Most property ownership was controlled by deed covenants that largely excluded minorities but land ownership was more possible south of the river. Minorities were also heavily employed as agricultural labor. It is common knowledge in Arizona, as in the whole of the Southwest; farmworkers have been victimized by agricultural businesses that valued the produce more than the lives that harvested it.[279]

Native Americans

As the state with the most land mass dedicated to Native American nations, Arizona's twenty-one federally recognized tribes were given the most desolate and inhospitable places for reservations. Much has been written about Native peoples in the Americas. The intent of this paper's vignette is to use one incident to describe hundreds of years of Native injustices in Arizona. Much longer treatments are necessary to fully grasp this part of our history.[280]

The Navajo nation has its own "Trail of Tears" story; it is called *The Long Walk*. In the 1860s, more than 10,000 Navajos and Mescalero Apaches were forcibly marched to a desolate reservation in eastern New Mexico called Bosque Redondo. The Long Walk was

largely ignored by a nation embroiled in the Civil War. Beginning
in 1863, Gen. James Henry Carleton, commander of New Mexico
Territory, decided to solve, once and for all, the "Navajo Problem."
Ragged queues of defeated Navajos left in batches from Ft. Defi-
ance, Arizona. Men, women, children and the elderly walked 450
miles, in frigid winter and baking summer. Some drowned crossing the Rio Grande. Stragglers were shot and left behind. Their
destination was Fort Sumner. The Navajo, and a smaller number
of Apache, lived in crude shelters improvised from branches and
tattered canvas. Pneumonia, dysentery, smallpox, exposure and
hunger devastated their numbers. Nearly one-third of those interned there died, held captive by the U.S. Army.[281]

Mexicans

Arizona has a long history of discrimination, xenophobia and
scapegoating as it relates to Mexicans, both American citizens and
immigrants. Mexicans have been blamed for the states political and
financial problems for at least a century. In the middle of World
War I, employers used fears of socialism as an excuse to fire Mexican
workers, even as agricultural employers cited wartime labor short-
ages to justify hiring more. During the Great Depression, when
Mexicans were seen as competition for jobs and burdens to public
welfare, Arizonans used racist threats and scare tactics to pressure
Mexicans to return to Mexico. Fears of invasion by an Axis "Fifth
Column" preoccupied Arizonans during World War II, so Mexicans
had to register with local officials and state their loyalties. Similarly,
during the Cold War, the McCarran-Walter Act justified deportation
of suspected subversives, creating yet another pretext for discrimination against Mexicans in the name of political necessity. Further
Cold War-era demonization came in the form of Operation Wet-
back, a government tactic used to deport a million Mexicans during
the mid-1950s. More recently, economic hardship during the 1970s

made Mexican immigrants convenient targets of violence. In the 1976 Hanigan incident, white ranchers were accused of kidnapping, robbing and torturing Mexican immigrant workers. As Congress debated the Immigration Reform and Control Act of 1986, Arizonans again ratcheted up threats against Mexican immigrants. Operation Gatekeeper and California's Proposition 187, which aimed to crack down on undocumented immigrants, characterized anti-Mexican sentiment of the 1990s:

> The attitudes and the actions of the dominant Anglos in Phoenix and other urban centers directly influenced the ethnic emergence of the Mexican minority. Ethnic consciousness was motivated by economic, political, and cultural exclusion from the mainstream. Ethnic prejudice, stratification, segmentation, and exploitation isolated Mexicans as a subgroup. Barrio residents faced poverty and despair. The historical dynamics of segregation caused problems, especially geographic isolation from mainstream society and institutions. Despite problems, however, Mexicans and Mexican Americans not only survived but forged their own viable communities.[282]

Japanese

The most successful Arizona farmers were the Japanese, who arrived early in the twentieth century and were able to purchase farms in the 1930s, after Arizona's anti-"Yellow Peril" law was found unconstitutional. The Japanese were among the most innovative growers, raising a variety of crops. This also raised much jealousy among Anglo farmers, who were happy to see them interned during World War II. The War Relocation Authority (WRA) was the U.S. civilian agency responsible for the relocation and detention of Japanese Americans. The WRA opened ten facilities in seven states, and transferred over 100,000 people to these. Two of the largest were in Arizona, again, in terrifically hot and desolate land.

African-Americans

Black history in Arizona is a minor part of Arizona's story until around 1920, when migration increased due to the pull of the cotton industry and western freedom, for those southerners fleeing the oppressive Jim Crow Laws. But by 1926, Arizona had its own segregationist laws on the books for schools and marriages, and the Ku Klux Clan had its own chapters throughout the state. Real estate in those days in my neighborhood came with a whites- only clause we have learned. Interestingly, many of the migrants during the 1950s through the 1970s came from places where Civil Rights work and victories were being championed resulting in many local activists. Their work led to the desegregation of schools in 1953, one year before Brown vs. The Board of Education decision in 1954. Though this gain and a few others gave hope and courage to the African-American community in Arizona, white supremacy and racial inequalities still ruled the day. In 1988 Evan Mecham, then Governor of Arizona, was impeached. One reason for his lack of popularity was his cancellation of a paid Martin Luther King, Jr. Day holiday for state employees. The holiday had been first proposed in 1972 by former state senator Cloves Campbell, a well known African-American public official. The bill experienced a series of failures in the legislature. Eventually pressure came upon Arizona. It lost its chance to host the Super Bowl costing the state tourism and other benefits that naturally come from these events. In 1992, in the face of a tourist boycott and losing the chance to host Super Bowl XXVII, 61 percent of Arizonan voters publicly approved the payment of state workers on a Martin Luther King Day/Civil Rights Day holiday. It was the 49th state in the United States to approve the holiday.

CONCLUSION

These important history lessons remind us that our community has been a place of significant struggle, maybe since its very beginning. But that produces the kind of community we are talking about in this chapter, one of solidarity and common heartedness. As the quote in the beginning of this chapter so aptly reminds us, the kind of community we are seeking and we desire can be found right here, because of our struggle.

Community is a by-product of commitment and struggle. It comes when we step forward to right some wrong, to heal some hurt, to give some service. Then we discover each other as allies in resisting the diminishments of life. It is no accident that the most impressive sense of community is found among people in the midst of such joyful travail: among minority groups seeking identity and justice, among women seeking liberation into fully humane roles, among all who have said No to tyranny with the concrete affirmation of their lives. – Parker Palmer

GRACE RULES – GRACE POOLS IN LOW PLACES

A grace rule is the way grace rules. This rule describes a
lavish gift from God as experienced in our community.
By receiving it, grace rules – leading us further
into love and action.

Our friends from the Street Psalms Community have
been theologizing for over twenty years around this premise,
that "grace is like water – it flows downhill and pools up in the
lowest places."[283]   The premise is that God shows up in ways
so profoundly unlike what humans expect, in unlikely places
with love so extravagant that the darker the reality, the more
we are certain his presence is greater still. Consider this poem
by Denise Levertov that looks to discover that very thing.

City Psalm

The killings continue, each second pain
and misfortune extend themselves
in the genetic chain, injustice is done knowingly, and the air
bears the dust of decayed hopes,
yet breathing those fumes, walking the thronged
pavements among crippled lives, jackhammers
raging, a parking lot painfully agleam
in the May sun, I have seen not
behind but within, within the dull grief, blown grit,
hideous concrete facades, another grief, a gleam as of dew,
an abode of mercy,
have heard not behind but within noise
a humming that drifted into a quiet smile.

Nothing was changed, all was revealed otherwise;
not that horror was not, not that killings did not continue,
but that as if transparent all disclosed
an otherness that was blessed, that was bliss.
I saw Paradise in the dust of the street.

NOTES

257. Parker Palmer, "A Place Called Community," *Christian Century*, 3/16/1977, 252. http://www.religion- online.org/showarticle.asp?title=1143 (accessed May 1, 2012). Dr. Palmer is dean of studies at Pendle Hill, a Quaker living-learning community near Philadelphia.
258. Walter E. Fluker, *They Looked for a City, A Comparative Analysis of the Ideal of Community in the Thought of Howard Thurman and Martin Luther King, Jr.*, (Lanham: University Press of America, 1989), xi.
259. Stanley Hauerwas, *A Community of Character, toward a constructive Christian social ethic*, (Notre Dame: University of Notre Dame Press: 1981), 10.
260. Stanley J. Grenz, *Created for Community*, (Grand Rapids: Baker Books, 1998), 23.
261. Jean Vanier, *Community and Growth*, (New York: Paulist Press, 1989), 3.
262. John Fuder and Noel Castellanos, *A Heart for the Community*, (Chicago: Moody Publishers, 2009), 72.
263. Archbishop of Canterbury William Temple, *Feasting on the Word*, (Year A, Volume 1), 336.
264. Walter Brueggemann, *Prayers for a Privileged People*, (Nashville: Abingdon Press, 2008), 111.
265. Tim Suttle, *An Evangelical Social Gospel*, (Eugene: Cascade Books, 2011), 94, 95.
266. Miroslav Volf, *A Public Faith, How Followers of Christ Should Serve the Common Good*, (Grand Rapids: Brazos Press, 2011).
267. Ibid., 101.
268. Public Domain.
269. Miroslav Volf, A Public Faith, 109.
270. Ibid., 110.
271. Ibid., 63.
272. Kris Rocke and Joel Van Dyke, *Geography of Grace*, (Tacoma: Street Psalms Community, 2012), 256.
273. Listening to the Community – one of CCDA's Eight Key Components: Often communities are developed by people outside of the community

that bring in resources without taking into account the community itself. Christian Community Development is committed to listening to the community residents, and hearing their dreams, ideas and thoughts. This is often referred to as the "felt need" concept. Listening is most important, as the people of the community are the vested treasures of the future. It is important not to focus on the weaknesses or needs of a community. Again, the felt need concept, as referred to earlier, helps us as community developers to focus on the desires of the community residents. The priority is the thoughts and dreams of the community itself. What the people themselves believe should be the focus. Asset-based community development focuses on the assets of a community and building upon them. When fused together through Christian Community Development, they can have extremely positive results. Every community has assets, but often these are neglected. When a ministry utilizes Asset-Based Community Development (ABCD), it names all of the assets in the community that helps the community see its many positive characteristics. It is through these assets that people develop their community. Christian Community Development realistically points out, through community meetings and efforts, some of the areas that people in the community would like to see improved. The areas to be focused upon are not looked at from some outside group or some demographic study that is laid upon the community. Instead, it is the community members themselves that decide what area they would like to improve. After a community has decided where they want to focus some of their attention, it is then directed to the means with which they themselves can bring this about. What qualities, talents, and abilities does the community have that can help solve these problems? The focus is on the community members seeing themselves as the solution to the problem, not some government program or outside group that is going to be their salvation. It is essential for community leaders to help the community focus on maximizing their strengths and abilities to make a difference for their community. The philosophy of Christian Community Development believes that the people with the problem have the best solutions and opportunities to solve those problems. Christian Community Development affirms the dignity of individuals and encourages the engagement of the community to use their own resources and assets to bring about sustainable change.

274. Mary Beth Rogers, *Cold Anger, A Story of Faith and Power Politics*, (Denton: University of North Texas Press, 1990), 9.
275. Through SB 1070, the world became alerted to the state of affairs in Arizona as it relates to immigration issues. The law, which proponents and critics alike said was the broadest and strictest immigration measure in generations. It made the failure to carry immigration documents a crime and gave the police broad power to detain anyone suspected of being in the country illegally. Opponents have called it an open invitation

for harassment and discrimination against Hispanics regardless of their citizenship status.

276. Sal Acosta, *Hispanics in Arizona: The History Continues*, University of Arizona, http://www.azlibrary.gov/convocations/images/pdf/acosta2.pdf, 1. (accessed August 10, 2011).

277. Jon Talton wrote for *The Arizona Republic* for years and is now retired. He writes a blog about the kind of state Arizona has been and is becoming; underlying his writing and reflection is a desire for a more compassionate Arizona His voice is reflective of the picture I paint of the city and our state, as well as directly referencing his historical research. http://roguecolumnist.typepad.com/rogue_columnist/2009/06/phoenix-101-the-old-city.html.

278. Our ministry takes place in these three neighborhoods, and The Neighborhood Center is in the St. Matthews neighborhood.

279. The United Farm Workers (UFW) have been tirelessly fighting on behalf of farm workers who died from not receiving enough breaks in the shade or water during the workday or were subjected to sexual harassment, pesticide exposure or a number of other preventable deaths, injuries or injustices.

280. This book list is one of the most contemporary and extensive I've been able to find: http://www.firstpeoplesnewdirections.org/books.php, (accessed Sept. 2011).

281. Geraldo L. Cadava, http://azstarnet.com/news/opinion/arizona-has-a-long-shameful-history-of- demonizing-mexican-migrants/article_9ce82df4-1b82-5bb8-9d2b-005c301457b0.html#ixzz1msAbxxn6 (accessed Sept. 2011).

282. Bradford Luckingham, *Minorities in Phoenix, A Profile of Mexican American, Chinese American, and African-American Communities*, 1860-1992, (Tucson: The University of Arizona Press, 1994), 192.

283. Rocke and Van Dyke, 16.

"Working Together" Marco Perez

CHAPTER ELEVEN

We Value
PARTNERSHIPS

Core Value #10

Definition: We acknowledge that the complex work of Christian Community Development cannot be done single-handedly. We enter into and create partnerships and collaborations with individuals, businesses, non-profits, churches, para-churches, social service entities, government, education ... all of whom have an interest as we do in seeing forgotten communities reimagined and restored.

> Two in a bed warm each other.
> Alone, you shiver all night. By yourself you're unprotected.
> With a friend you can face the worst.
> Can you round up a third?
> A three-stranded rope isn't easily snapped.
> – Ecclesiastes 4:11-13 (The Message)

I had barely begun this calling when I experienced this funny, lovely story. I was twenty-one and had just graduated from college. I came home, by God's direction, to dreaded Scottsdale. It was dreaded because it was not the place of my heart. Scottsdale was where I was coming from, not where I was going back to. But, it was where I was supposed to be for the time being and so I took the first job that was in front of me, a dorm counselor at a boarding school for the discarded children of the richest of the rich. I said in my interview, "I'm called to the poor, I don't belong here. Even though this is the very neighborhood I come from, this is not where I intend on living the rest of my life." They hired me anyway, telling me these children were poorer than I realized. Settling in, I walked down the street and introduced myself to the neighborhood church, Scottsdale Bible Church (SBC). "Hello," I said. "I just got a job at Judson School, down the street, and will be living there with twenty-one junior high girls. I intend to love them and teach them about God and will need somewhere for them to go to church. Can I bring them here?" "Just a minute," the secretary said, obviously uncomfortable, and left to find someone more suited to deal with me. Out came Tim Kimmel, the youth pastor at the time, who welcomed me back into his office. (Interestingly, thirty-six years later, my son, Ian, married Tim's daughter, Shiloh.) I spilled out my heart, for these Judson rich kids who I hoped would be loved and cared for, my desire to not be here in Scottsdale for long, and then of course, how I wanted him and his church to help me. He happily welcomed me into the fold; I did bring girls to church, actually to all the services, every week. Because I was in church there so often, I began working with their youth, and eventually, was offered a job. One Sunday evening service, I was daydreaming and a vision from God settled on my mind and heart. It was very clear. I saw and heard from God who told me, "This church will help you one day, in a neighborhood far from here. This church will be a partner to you and your work." Tears came; I brushed them away and instantly reordered myself to my surroundings and the host of abused and sullen twelve and thirteen year olds sitting next to me. I held that moment of the future in my heart, for awhile anyway.

I left that church to marry Wayne. Open Door Fellowship, our church at the time, had relocated to the neighborhood where my ministry would develop. When Neighborhood Ministries was about five or six years old, I received a call from SBC's missions pastor, Walt Edman. He had become familiar with the early efforts of our outreach from some church members. He asked if we would absorb their mission's candidates, giving them a cross-cultural opportunity before they went overseas. We agreed, and so it began. Prior to his phone call, I had drawn the vision for the future of NM on a large piece of paper for the purpose of a presentation I was making to our church's elders. It was a critical turning point in the ministry as it turned out. The elders of our church prayed over me and the vision. The picture contained all kinds of bubbles, radiating outside the circle that represented the ministry. They were designated future partners, the tentacles of involvement of others in an emerging work. Each bubble represented the partners God would give us to get this work done. One of the bubbles was called, "suburban church partnerships." Who these partners would be remained undetermined at the time. So when Walt called, I saw the paper with the bubbles on it. Our relationship with Scottsdale Bible Church continued, and as time went on ran into a glitch. Working with us was becoming uncomfortable because we were still the "outreach arm" of the church Open Door Fellowship. This church (and other churches) wanted to partner with a non-profit entity but not another church. Also, SBC wanted to increase its involvement. At this early stage, Darryl Delhousaye (the pastor at the time) imagined every part of his mega church involved with our very tiny non-profit. This signaled the change in status that was to come for NM. Soon we would separately incorporate as a 501c3 in order to accommodate this church's request and many other future requests to partner with us. As elders from both churches began to meet together to draft and codify the partnership and imagine big things for this growing relationship, like a deja vu or the details of a dream remembered, that evening, thirteen years earlier when God said, "this church is going to help you," vividly came back to me.

I'm telling this story twenty-two years after that elder meeting. Our long-time partners and dear friends, Scottsdale Bible Church, just raised $110,000 last week for our capital campaign through a one-time offering; something they do for special causes once a year. It is impossible to describe the myriad of collaborations and support that have taken place year after year over these past three decades from this ONE church. But suffice it to say, all that the Lord whispered to me that night has happened, beyond all

I could have imagined.

This is a unique story of just one important partnership, but NM couldn't do what we do with only one, even very sizable, church. Many partnerships take place that allow us to get done what we do all year long. Partnerships are necessary, in fact, mandatory. Moving forward requires that we work together for the blessing and benefit of our community.

WHO CARES ABOUT OUR COMMUNITY?

The callings and values of Neighborhood Ministries are shared by many others, not in the exact combination, or in the same intensity, and not even from the same source of mission. But scores of people, churches and organizations in Phoenix share a deep conviction and desire to rebuild our troubled communities. Claudia adds, "They believe what we believe – they value the same things we value – they believe in our mission, they believe in our work, they see the need of the community; they know how important our work is." Community building has many success stories. In fact, the more we have engaged in community building the more we look within our own community for the resources needed. John Kretzmann and John McKnight, from their well known *Building Communities from the Inside Out*,[284] reminds us that that is the very place to begin to look for partners.

> Outside help for troubled communities is bleak. Creative community leaders across the country have begun to recognize this hard truth, and have shifted their practices accordingly. They are discovering that wherever there are effective community development efforts, those efforts are based upon an understanding or map, of the community's assets, capacities and abilities. For it is clear that even the poorest neighborhood is a place where individuals and organiza-

tions represent resources upon which to rebuild. The key to neighborhood regeneration, then, is to locate all of the available local assets, to begin connecting them with one another in ways that multiply their power and effectiveness, and to begin harnessing those local institutions that are not yet available for local development purposes.[285]

Isiah reflects on this:

> *I have thought about the question about why Christians don't partner well. There are always people who in churches are called the protectors, they enjoy the little group, there is a fear of bringing others from the outside, a trust factor I guess, plain fear wanting to protect that little environment that God has given them. I see more and more churches who understand how important it is to partner, maybe others don't, but I see the smaller churches who understand that we need to support each other, to expand the body of Christ to include more than us, all working for the same king, I do see that concept changing today, even though it is slow.*

SUBMITTING TO GOD'S META-NARRATIVE

Living out a "for God so loved the world" theological framework, will lead us into the reasons for partnerships and the vision to join God at work, among whomever He has risen to the cause. I am reminded often, that throughout the scriptures God will say that *He, himself,* will do the rescuing, the redeeming, the protecting, the advocating (Ps 12:5.6; Ezek 33:11-16). And that though He desires His own people to join Him, it is He, himself, that is doing what needs to be done. His actions of mercy and justice are the point, He will use whomever is willing, whomever is stepping up to get it done. After all, even the "rocks will cry out," if all were kept silent in worship of our Lord (Luke 19:40). If He can use rocks, he will use all available to His will.

It isn't too far afield to begin the conversation of the "whosoever will" with the object of their concern. We join together to care for humanity in their distressing disguises. Human beings have fundamental human rights, as wholly subscribed to by the peoples of the earth. As Jürgen Moltmann says in *God for a Secular Society*:

> Today the peoples of the earth are entering a shared global history, because they are all mortally endangered, on the one hand by the nuclear threat they pose to one another, and on the other by the ecological crises they share. And the more this global history develops, the more important human rights will become, if we are to build a world-wide human society capable of warding off these perils. Human rights will therefore increasingly become the universally valid framework, capable of winning general acceptance, by which humane policies are judged and legitimated.[286]

It is our human responsibility to care for each other, to eradicate the injustices around us and to collectively do something about our common plight. The fact that our Judeo-Christian heritage requires it of us, makes it that much more determinative. Our reference point for human rights is the theological premise that God assigns to each person, *human dignity*.

> In the prophetic religions, Judaism, Christianity and Islam, the liberty and equality of all human beings is derived from belief in creation – which the American Declaration of Independence also talks about ('endowed by their Creator'). The fact that all human beings are made in the image of God is the foundation of human dignity. Human

beings are intended to live in this relation to God. That gives their existence its inalienable, transcendent depth dimension. In their relationship to the transcendent God, human beings become person whose dignity must not be infringed. The institutions of law, government and economy must respect this personal dignity, which is the endowment of all human beings, if they claim to be 'humane institutions'. They would destroy themselves if they were to treat human begins as objects, things, commodities, or merely as underlings or members of the work force. They would lose their legitimation.[287]

We partner with each other because the cause of humanity warrants it. We work toward the betterment of man-kind (in our local sphere) because the injustices and inequalities of our setting confiscate God-given dignity. There is a resurgence of a term that is helpful here, the idea of the *common good*. Morally bound people ought to care about the common good.

> It is a conviction that the founders of our nation had, and it is one that runs deeply in our Judeo-Christian heritage. It is a vision that rejects personal self-interest as the ultimate end of life and instead invites citizens to understand that their health, personal and moral, is tied to the welfare of all persons within their community, not least of whom are children and those without hope, skills and dignity.[288]

For us, Christians, we can and ought to take it a step further. Partnerships are the vehicle God has designed for His people to accomplish their good works. And that is the meta-narrative: people created for relationship and for community. This is how Marcos describes what partnership looks like to him inside God's meta-narrative:

For me, when I got out of jail, this last time, I didn't expect it, but the friends who ended up being my support team were Ian, Alan, Jeremy, Wayne, and Kit. They saw me, their friend, released from an unjust sentencing and very unhappy. As my friends and mentors, they rallied together to help, even though most of the time didn't know what to do. So they did what came to them, they talked to me, they opened their home to me, Jeremy would take me out and just talk, lending an ear, listening, crying with me, praying with me. This was a very traumatic time in my life, but my team made me feel loved, they gave me someone(s) to lean on, rides to the grocery store, stability when I was having a panic attack, a number of things, so many things. But I have to single out Alan, as far as that goes, who has taught me so much, been such a good friend, taking on this whole project [OpportuniTees] just to help me, and others like me, doing it for no gain, other than to do what the Lord has asked him to do. And then there's Jeremy, mentor, good friend ... I want my son Marcitos to have Jeremy as a mentor. Now my son is developing his own relationships at church, Martha has her own friendships and relationships – Nadine, Pearl, all have their own personal relationships at Neighborhood, we are not only just a church, but our community, our family, we hang out, outside of church, I think you could call this kind of partnership the kind that works.

In the beginning, we see God through a partnership motif. "Let *us* make man in *our* image," God declared (Gen 1:26). And He did. Adam and Eve were created to be the next "us." They were formed to partner and co-steward creation, to work together, empowered by God to fill the earth with life. Their rebellion against their loving heavenly Father began the dominion of separation and estrangement from God and others. But partnership and unity were the original design.

Further, the New Testament teaches the heart of God for all
Christ-followers is for us to dwell in unity despite our differences.
This vision hardly seems possible. Division of every sort is what
we are used to. It is Jesus, Himself, who prays that His body become the "redeemed community working together in unity to be a
tangible demonstration of God's actual power to change hearts. It
is easy to see Jesus' good news message is not just about individual
change, but a total transformation of society and creation."

> *I pray for these followers, but I am also praying for all those
> who will believe in me because of their teaching. Father, I
> pray that they can be one. As you are in me and I am in you,
> I pray that they can also be one in us. Then the world will
> believe that you sent me. I have given these people the glory
> that you gave me so that they can be one, just as you and I
> are one. I will be in them and you will be in me so that they
> will be completely one. Then the world will know that you
> sent me and that you loved them just as much as you loved
> me (Jn 17:20-23).*

The world has probably never seen what this unified body is
capable of. They have many and varied gifts and talents that have
been supernaturally given (1 Cor 12:12-21, 26). They are empowered by the Holy Spirit for love, sacrifice and service. They come
from all walks of life and every culture, and so can assume the
integration into society, simply by who they are and where they
come from. And they have training, specifically designed for
"such a time as this." It behooves us to imagine the capacity of such
a God-ordained army upon the social ills of our communities; for
this imagination opens us up to what partnerships can be and do.
Our world awaits God's love in this incarnation. Panda looks at it
this way:

Our partners help us because they see the mission and vision we have. They want a part of it and we can't do it without their help, it makes things easier to do our mission. Even people with a different faith or even no faith are helping the people in our community, our family; that is helping Phoenix, their helping is not only benefiting us, but it benefits Arizona, even the U.S.

ASSET-BASED COMMUNITY DEVELOPMENT OR CAPACITY-FOCUSED DEVELOPMENT

In too many places, the army of God has been deployed prematurely. These would-be warriors were envisioned onto a place and a people who were unprepared for them. And the message inscribed on their mission was inaccurate: *Go to the needy community. They are without resources and in desperate need of your solutions. There is crime and violence, joblessness and welfare dependency, gangs and homelessness. It is dark and terrible and your "light" is needed.*

Rewind. Picture the same kingdom missioners, but with a different missive: *Partner with the community. It is filled with giftedness and talent. They are not problems to be solved, but partners to be discovered. Investing in them as leaders will bring lasting change. Inside their neighborhoods are all sorts of resources, from schools and hospitals, to parks and businesses. You will find many partners there, people like you, churches and non-profits, all of whom desire what you do and have been faithfully tilling the soil for many years.*

Asset based community development,[289] or Capacity-Focused Development, is an approach that changes the message for service minded partners. This asset approach takes time to craft and as a rule keeps the partners from running head long into a scenario that is bound to do violence to a community. For anxious helpers this waiting to do the "real work" doesn't always translate into producing the map, sadly. But for those that believe that poor communities are filled with beautiful things, the discovery of the assets is well worth it; and in the end partners discover each other and collaborative work that brings success happens.

There is an important byproduct that occurs as a community is mined for its assets. Relationships! Relationships are born first with community members and also with local invested stake-holders, all who care about their community's betterment. This is what makes partnerships sustainable. Trail down a successful partnership that is getting something done and you will find a trusted relationship. Trail down a successful effort that truly brought change, and you will find a solid partnership. Jeremy points out that this is the best way to train young leaders, to use our city as a classroom.

With our summer curriculum for the interns – using our city as classroom – part of this, is honoring our partnerships, honoring the work they have done or are doing; we give them an opportunity to teach and influence these young leaders, and in turn we publically affirm the work they are doing. This approach is contrasted by those in the corporate world, where your competition becomes the enemy – even in churches; we are tempted to behave this way. How do we honor the work they are doing, exposing the work they are doing, all of us working towards the same ends?

WHAT KIND OF PARTNERSHIPS ARE THERE?

1) <u>Church and Community</u>: We continue to practice how to be the church in a community. As discussed before, Neighborhood is fondly called "church" in all its community development expressions by our neighbors. According to Mary Nelson in *Empowerment, A Key Component of Christian Community Development*,[290] the church inside a community has multiple functions that can

and will take place over time: a. Convener – provide a welcoming place and space for people to get together, for resources, around an issue or challenge, fellowship. b. Enabler/Facilitator – work with community leaders and other 'voices' to identify who else should be involved; making connections; thinking through alternative strategies, community meetings. c. Resource provider – provide various resources, money, facilities, holistic ministries, leadership development, employment and human development, connecting to power, business and politics, skills and talents of partners. d. Partner/Advocate – involves community organizing efforts, where community leadership is not overpowered but where honest empowerment is formulated. e. Participant/Recruiter – church becomes a member of community organizations. f. Cheerleader/Encourager – active supporter of what the community is doing, whether the efforts were a result of the church's influence or not.

As a church inside a community, playing these different roles, we have needed to build partnerships for organizational strength, where together with our partners our community's voice can be leveraged and therefore stronger. Ian comments:

> *The reason we got together with our community organizing partners was not to outsource our justice work, but to find allies with whom we could work and with whom we would be stronger. We started Promise Arizona, our current partner and ally in organizing for immigration reform, because of the desire we collectively had to see change happen. This is a key community organizing principle. Together we're stronger, together we have power.*

2) <u>Suburban and Urban</u>: Much has been done and written over the past few decades about the role of suburban churches partnering with urban ministries. Though things are changing

demographically in inner cities (where this model was promoted) as gentrification suburbanizes poverty; there remains a need to describe the partnership of the "haves" with the "have-nots". There is a rule of love that must be honored when wealth and privilege choose a partnership role with a poor community. Mae Elise Cannon, who compiled an amazing resource for justice called Social Justice Handbook, speaks about her experience on staff at mega-church Willow Creek Community Church:

> I learned a lot about partnership in my ministry experience at Willow Creek. It is easy for big churches, or churches with influence, to unwittingly trample on smaller grassroots organizations that are working to bring about effective change from the bottom up. It is rare to see a large church humble itself and give voice to the very people it is trying to help. I don't think most churches are intentionally paternalistic, but this is a trap that churches readily fall into. Paternalism occurs when an organization, group or individuals acts like the parent of another individual or group. The roots of paternalism come from a false theology, often the 'theology of empire'. A theology of empire assumes that people with the most capital, resources and determination will be successful. Empire theology is filled with rulers and despots. Because of their power, affluence and influence, the nations of the Northern Hemisphere often fall into this type of thinking. Theology based on the kingdom of God is opposite of empire theology.[291]

Training volunteers: Much good can happen when suburban partners come humbly to serve a community out of a kingdom of God mindset; much reconciliation, life-long relationships, transformation of character and world-view, exchanging of gifts and hope. But along the way toward that good end, a good deal of training and development are required. We often teach that we wouldn't send a young untrained missionary to a far away country without equipping them with education, language and in some cases years of preparation. And yet, we are willing to deploy a dangerous amount of people, completely uninitiated, with a mindset formed outside of a kingdom paradigm onto another people, unfamiliar to them, and in some cases "labeled" by them. The resources of the suburbs belong to urban partners as a gift exchange from God. How we do this exchange is the challenge, doing it well is the goal. Of our suburban relationships, Susan reflects:

We have a lot of partners. Some of them, like SBC, are a huge help. Rick and Joan Malouf [from SBC] have walked alongside Moms Place from the beginning, who are even now, helping us with very intricate problems regarding the new [Mom's Place] house. He is available right when we need him. I know a lot of folks are like that at SBC. Crisis Pregnancy Center, who because of our partnership gives us for no cost, our curriculum which we use every single week, obviously the benefits to us are great. It is a mutually beneficial relationship, impacting a community they wouldn't have access to. ASU West and Dr. Kelly's class, which provides amazing volunteers, women who come in and understand what we are doing, and this gives them an opportunity to give back, to enter into a relationship they wouldn't have had, we are a good conduit for them to get here. Beautiful mutuality, they give, we receive, we give, they receive.

One more comment on this, there are a lot of partnerships/ relationships where we get to do a lot of receiving, but they never come down here, and need to, because it will change them. These are people who still consider this an unsafe neighborhood. We are regularly challenging them to broaden their horizons. They will benefit by being in this place, will benefit by knowing our families and our kids, and seeing it's not so different. Scratch below and you'll find we are all the same.

3) <u>Church and Para-church</u>: Para-church organizations are Christian faith-based organizations that work outside of and across denominations to engage in social welfare and evangelism, usually independent of church oversight. In Protestant and Catholic theology, para- church organizations are called sodalities,[292] as distinct from modalities, which is the structure and organization of the local or universal church. These range from evangelistic and discipleship ministries (such as InterVarsity Christian Fellowship, Campus Crusade for Christ, Young Life and The Navigators), to political, community organizing and social activist groups, and further welfare and social services, including homeless shelters, child care, and domestic violence, disaster relief programs, and food pantries and clothing closets, and emergency aid centers. It is normal for a group like ours to consider these types of Christian groups natural partners. We share many of the same core convictions and values. Partnerships with para-church entities tend to be strong when: 1) There is a shared core value of partnership. Para-church organizations (as we all) can be myopic, often tethered to the particular vision that gave them life in the beginning, protecting their niche. Often, partnerships outside their chosen arena don't make sense to people who are doing ministry a certain way. 2) The whole realm of competition for people, resources, or visibility doesn't get in the way of a desire to work together. Allowing the partner to take credit for the work done in front of funders or other supporters is a small price to pay for the good work that happened through the partnership. 3) There is a

shared theology and praxis for the work. For a partnership to work the most successfully, partners come together with a crystal clear vision of the "why's" and the "how's". You know you have your perfect partner when you can complete each others sentences. We are always looking for those partners. 4) Relationships are what bond the partnership, tested, loyal, give and take friendships that have stood the test of time. I have often said that a good partnership has a mystical quality, like a marriage. You can't completely define how you got together, but you are glad you did. This reminds Googoos of our radio disc jockey friends, Tim and Willy, who graciously made us recipients of their generosity when they first formed their "fun-dation." At that time they were with KNIX (well known country radio station) and are now with KMLE. She says, "These partners are more like trusted friends, they love the work we are doing for our community, they have love for people that we love; their heart, is to help those who are in need, and so we benefit from that."

4) <u>Public Sector, Government and Education Partners</u>: Jim Touhy, one of the original Directors for the President's Council for Faith-Based and Neighborhood Partnerships under President George W. Bush, was fond of saying that the government needed to partner with faith- grassroots-community-organizations because they can do something the government will never be able to do. "The Government can't love," he would say. As true as that is, and as smart, the reason the government began aggressively partnering with FBO's (faith based organizations) was because they were effective. Amy Sherman, Director of the *Faith in Communities Initiative for Hudson Institute's Welfare Policy Center*, has been at the forefront of this discussion and says it this way:

> Between the programs and resources offered by congregations and religious nonprofits, hundreds of thousands of disadvantaged citizens are being served every year. These

services are being conducted both by large, well-known groups, such as Catholic Charities and the Salvation Army, and by tiny and mid-sized faith-based groups. Any constructive public engagement with the faith sector should be premised on an appreciation of the role FBOs and congregations are already playing as well as clarity about the diversity of groups active on the front lines. There is a small but growing body of empirical research, as to their effectiveness. The anecdotal evidence has been sketched out by a wide number of observers and scholars; there exists a literature review of much of this work.[293]

For those at the ground, this government initiative has changed the tenor of the conversation in ways the President could never have predicted. Most organizations of medium to large have managed at least one public grant since its inception. That element alone brought with it functional accountabilities that many FBO's, ours included, had never had to develop. FBO's capacity was built. The government got what it wanted, to get the job done through grassroots organizations.

The spillover of this good-enough outcome, was the trusted relationships the faith community developed with the public sector. As the White House's OFBCI affirmed and gave credibility to successful organizations, that affirmation opened doors to relationships with other government officials and departments. These relationships have been leveraged for all kinds of good will in matters outside of the original grant arrangement. This good will in turn opened doors to the city, the state, other non-profits, the social service sector agencies, and multiple others.

An example from our story is the growing relationship we have with the Department of Education and ancillary entities that are education focused. We have a true partnership with more than one agency, where there is much give and take. We benefit from funding, training, accountability, best-practice models and resources, and they benefit from an at the ground relationship-laden mission, that does wrap-around about as good as any group they work with. Jeremy emphasizes:

> We partner with large education institutions that have lots of experience, resources and accountabilities, like the Dept. of Ed, First Things First, Murphy, Isaac, and Roosevelt School Districts, and the standardization entity called Quality First. Since Education is something people spend lots of time doing and as Americans we value, there is a shared value for the work it takes to benefit low-income children academically. That's why these groups like to work with us. We bring something they used to do, being embedded in neighborhoods and having relationships in the community; we are smaller and we can engage more outside the box. They appreciate the relationships we have with people, the commitment we have in the community that has to do with education, they see we love our community and we love to see them educated well, which is their value also. We have a posture of learning, desiring to be taught how they've learned to do what they have done, and they are open to us offering the unique perspective we have; and they like our values (#1-9) – actually even this one, though they don't do this value themselves.

Another example is our relationship/partnership with ASU (Arizona State University) which carries a similar value-added arrangement. This partnership began when the university was looking for embedded grassroots organizations that combined long-term relationships with tested models of social service delivery. They had multiple resources to offer, we offered credibility and training. Malissa had a bird's eye view of this partnership for many years:

> *ASU downtown has been such a strategic partner, especially when Debra Friedman was there – allowing us access into the lives of students and faculty, mostly anglos and educated, high income folks who needed to know our kids, and who could in turn help our kids navigate the system. This partnership allowed NM to extend its influence into the ASU world. The mission and values of NM have informed the way students desire to work when they graduate. NM encourages them to build into their personal work ethic an idea of reciprocity, and challenges them to stand alongside and work toward justice. This partnership benefited NM, by providing an easier pathway for our students to transition to ASU. My experience at ASU taught me that the way NM thinks and feels about its work in the community is rare. At ASU we were strategic in exposing key leaders and politicians to this unique method. That allowed NM to make friends with the mayor, Mike Nowakowski, our city council person, and Ed Pastor, our U.S. Congressman. The politicians took advantage of building bridges to new constituents and NM youth began to imagine their future a new way. I am guessing we will have more kids walking into politics.*

5) <u>Businessmen and Donors</u>: We learned early on that once people got involved as volunteers in the mission and built relationships with real people, their money would follow. This philosophy of partnering with donors remains to this day. It is an especially valuable notion today, as younger philanthropists are interested in hands on involvement and want to give more than money. Malissa

says that this reminds her of our partnership with Evergreen Development Corporation:

> *NM doesn't have the money to send all our Dream Act youth to college, we needed partners in the community who value education, hope for the futures of young people, and could come alongside with significant funding to undergird our scholarship program. This was Evergreen Development Corp., who got their young employees involved as mentors to each NM college student; they have been transformed as mentors and have a great meaning for their giving.*

While it makes practical sense, it is also a biblical idea.

And God can give you more blessings than you need. Then you will always have plenty of everything—enough to give to every good work. It is written in the Scriptures: "He gives freely to the poor. The things he does are right and will continue forever." –Psalm 112:9

God is the One who gives seed to the farmer and bread for food. He will give you all the seed you need and make it grow so there will be a great harvest from your goodness. He will make you rich in every way so that you can always give freely. And your giving through us will cause many to give thanks to God. This service you do not only helps the needs of God's people; it also brings many more thanks to God. It is a proof of your faith. Many people will praise God because you obey the Good News of Christ—the gospel you say you believe—and because you freely share with them and with all others. And when they pray, they will wish they could be with you because of the great grace that God has given you. Thanks be to God for his gift that is too wonderful for words. –2 Cor 9:8-15

Jesus' parable of the talents (Mt 25:14-30) describes a man about ready to go on a business trip. He calls his servants and divvies out his possessions. To one he gives five talents, to the next two, and another one. The first two servants invest and use their amount and see it increased. But the one who received just one talent dug a hole and hid what he received. When the master came back to check on his resources, he was pleased with the work the first two had done, by enlarging his investment. "I have set you up for something small, well done faithful servant," he said. "Now I will give you more to take care of." Encountering the one who had a smaller amount, but didn't use it to bless or benefit anyone, his excuse was that his master wasn't to be trusted. The parable ends with the master punishing the faithless and small minded servant. Jesus is telling us about a generous God, who shares his abundance that we might enjoy life abundantly. And yet, all that we have been given is for the abundance of others. When out of fear, insecurity, or distrust, we "bury" our treasure and do not use it for the purposes it was given, we lose everything according to this parable. Partnerships, in order for all involved to be blessed, require a self-giving spirit life. A partnership by its very nature multiplies the original investment (using the image of the parable), but we have to be able to share along the way in order to experience the gain. A great parable for the principles inherent in partnerships.

We have seen this principle active in a new way, lately. Businessmen are enthusiastic about the growing development of social enterprises among non-profits, imagining with us that businesses (if successful) provide a powerful engine for economic and social development for the community, for the non-profit and for all the future employees. When businessmen get involved both as donors and as volunteers in the area they give to in the mission, they are energized by the opportunity to give what they are good at. These gifted doers bring years of honed thinking and skill sets that contribute to our organization's health. Isiah agrees:

> *Well, I can definitely say that if there is another real lesson I have learned here it is in witnessing the blessing of partnerships. I have been able to see tremendous partnerships that work with NM through donors, businesses, contractors, churches, volunteers, I have been amazed with the partnerships that seems like, whatever NM needs God opens the door, people come to us, as partners with resources. It has increased my faith as to what God can do, not only with finances, but with people who want to do and donate, and partner with.*

GRACE RULES – TRUST

A grace rule is the way grace rules. This rule describes a lavish gift from God as experienced in our community. By receiving it, grace rules – leading us further into love and action.

At Neighborhood we have spent many years trying to locate where our different partnerships might fit on a continuum. It helps us make decisions and problem solve. We have identified four kinds or types of partnerships. Some are **utilitarian**, needed for grants or funding requirements. Some are more like a **fan club**, where there is significant appreciation for one another, but there is no commitment which would stand the test of time or change, necessarily. Others are more solid than this; they are **cause-related**. There is a great deal of shared interest and, therefore, more of a long-term need for the partnership; but one or both parties require autonomy and the sacrifice and investment necessary to build a partnership that does life together because of shared values isn't always there. Finally, our goal, is to have **covenant partners**, or soul mates. Though realistically, few partners fit in this category.

There is a mysterious ingredient in a good partnership that I have grappled with for years to try and describe. What is it that allows a partnership to go from a cooperative one that is somewhat self-interested, to one where there is a core self investment? where your gain is mine, and where our work is truly "shared"? These are the covenant partners who by God's grace become people and organizations we do life with. What is this ingredient that takes us down the continuum of partnership relationships? I think it can be identified simply as trust. Somewhere along the way, due to shared life, shared values, shared goals, shared pain, shared hope, something grew. We grew to trust each others hearts and each others motives. Jean Vanier would agree that this gift from God is the secret ingredient: "This is the secret of growth in community. Though it may pass on to us through the hands of others it comes from God. As we gradually discover that God and the others trust us, it becomes a little easier for us to trust ourselves, and in turn to trust others."[294]

How does this kind of trust develop in partnerships? I think it best to receive it as a gift first, from God. Without being too mystical, I think good partnerships are like best-friends. You can't really define exactly why you selected each other, some of the reasons are easy to pin-point. Others, more elusive. Like any relationship they will require some work. It helps when the players are self-aware, thus a little more vulnerable and truthful. Their cards are on the table, so to speak. Their word is their bond. They are in this partnership for the blessing of the community, and as pure as that can be, it pretty well describes what they are about. What helps keep trust unbroken is good communication. Doing the best we, as partners, to not only stay true to the relationship, but discuss frankly the twists and turns along the way or as growth happens how that implicates the partnership in any way.

Though we long for many covenant partners, we love all our partners and desire to continue with them as long as we can. Together we are stronger.

NOTES

284 John P. Kretzmann and John McKnight, *Building Communities from the Inside Out*, (Chicago: ACTA Publications, 1993).

285 Ibid., 6.

286 Jurgen Moltmann, 119.

287 Ibid., 122.

288 Basil Entwistle, *Making Cities Work, How Two People Mobilized a Community to Meet its Needs*, (Pasadena: Hope Publishing Co., 1990), xi.

289 Asset Based Community Development (ABCD's) is a tried and tested model and ought to be a part of the community development organization's toolbox. An excellent resource for the philosophy of Asset Mapping is John P. Kretzmann and John McKnight's, *Building Communities from the Inside Out*, (Chicago: ACTA Publications, 1993).

290 Mary Nelson, *Empowerment, A Key Component of Christian Community Development*, (Chicago: CCDA, 2010), 16-17.

291 Mae Elise Cannon, *Social Justice Handbook*, (Downers Grove: InterVarsity Press, 2009), 98.

293 Dr. Amy L Sherman., "Faith in Communities: A Solid Investment," Hudson Institute's Welfare Policy Center and Director of the Faith in Communities Initiative, 2004.

294 Jean Vanier, *Community and Growth, Revised Edition*, (New York: Paulist Press, 1989), 42.

APPENDIX A
Inside Outs

CHAPTER 2 INSIDE OUT - WELCOME

When God's life inside of us spills out onto others, it is recognizable. Its source is from an upside-down kingdom value system. Choose to cultivate these expressions of God.

The value of Incarnational Love gives us an opportunity to develop a spirit of "welcome." The spirit of welcome can be found throughout the teachings of Jesus. The kingdom of God meets everyone with *God's Welcome*. Jesus told a story (parable) of a wealthy man who was throwing a big dinner party. When it was time for the party to begin he sent his servant out to bring in the invited guests. Most of them had lame excuses. So the man sent his servant back out. Go out to the streets and alleys, down to the river bottom, knock on the homeless shelter, go over the neighborhood and compel them to come! Fill up my house! Say to them, you are welcome, come on in (Lk 14:16-24).

There are other words in the Bible that describe the spiritual formation of welcome that we ought to nurture. *Hospitality*, for example. *Invite*, is another. We like to use the word *Outreach* at Neighborhood, using the image of the shepherd who leaves all ninety-nine and goes after the one lost sheep. Paul implores the Romans to "welcome one another, therefore, just as Christ has welcomed you." (Rom 15:7) "The most basic thought that it seeks to express is important: the will to give ourselves to others and 'welcome' them, to readjust our identities to make space for them, is prior to any judgment about others, except that of identifying them in their humanity."[295]

Alex Canez found a "welcome" at Neighborhood Ministries. He believes it is "because God loves us and we're his children, that's why we feel welcome." He says, "I was welcomed to this place called "home" where I am wanted and loved; it is a place I want to be. This welcome opens into a place of freedom, freedom from evil and wickedness, freedom from fear and worry, from the world, freedom to express ourselves, a place where we don't have to hide our sorrow."

What does it look like to develop a spirit of "welcome"? Here are some disciplines that can be practiced?

> 1) Practice Intruding –
> I have been often accused of intruding. Isiah Oaks re-members his first encounters with me. "The first time she asked us just to come and look. The first mistake is always to come and look. Kit has a way of inviting you in, but never lets you go."
>
> "As his body, the church, through us, members of the body, the living Christ is always intruding, going where he is not necessarily wanted or expected, taking up space where people did not expect God to be. In his earthly ministry, Jesus intruded into the homes of sinners. He showed up at a wedding and caused a scene. He came into places of death, where people hardly knew him, and brought forth unexpected life. Maybe that is one reason people try to keep religion theoretical and spiritual. [But] Christianity is not a "spiritual" religion: it is an incarnational religion. It believes that God has a body that God takes up space, that God will not remain ethereal and vague, distant and detached."[296]

2) Practice seeing Jesus in "his most distressing disguise"— Who better to offer a welcome than to Jesus himself. Unfortunately, this practice gets bogged down with excuses, "not enough time, money or patience." But when you let yourself see Jesus through these disguises, all of a sudden you stop on the way from here to there, cross to the other side of the road, and there you are, face to face with God's opportunity.

3) Practice hospitality –
The Bible in both Testaments teaches us to welcome the stranger and in so doing we practice the biblical form of hospitality. Early on in the scriptures Abraham offers hospitality to three strangers (Gen 18:1-6) only to learn of their holy origins afterwards. The author of Hebrews probably remembered this story and so directs the faithful "to welcome strangers with hospitality, because in doing so, we may be entertaining angels unaware (Heb 13:2). And as has been mentioned previously, Jesus told his disciples that whenever they welcomed and invited in a lowly stranger, they welcomed him (Matt 25:31-46). God does not just suggest we welcome strangers (i.e. immigrants, sojourners, aliens living in the land), he commands it.

4) Practice viewing the Lord's Table as a welcome –
"The reciprocal self-surrender to one another within the Trinity is manifested in Christ's self-surrender in a world which is in contradiction to God; and this self-giving draws all those who believe in him into the eternal life of the divine love." Christians acknowledge this whenever they celebrate and participate in communion remembering that He is "making-space-for-us-and-inviting-us-in."

He invites us in and now it is our turn to be the ones who do the inviting.

CHAPTER 3 INSIDE OUT – THE JESUS PRAYER

When God's life inside of us spills out onto others, it is recognizable. Its source is from an upside-down kingdom value system. Choose to cultivate these expressions of God.

Brenda Salter McNeil in her book *The Heart for Racial Justice* says "it is my firm belief and conviction that reconciliation is ultimately a spiritual process".[297] We need the power and presence of God to break through the generational cycles of racism and injustice. We need a reawakening to the prophetic vision that God desires to bring reconciliation as a defining mark of his people. (Jn 17:21) For this to happen, it will have to begin with a spirit of repentance, renunciation and humility.

Jorge reminds us that "the bottom line is that God did the reconciliation with us when we were sinners." There is no reconciliation possible with other human beings if we are not first reconciled to God. We must begin with a confession of sin, this particular sin, the sin of division, of enmity, of building walls, of hate, of hurt. Ask God for forgiveness and forgive others.

Alex tells this story about DOING the work of reconciliation. About a year and a half ago he was stabbed by a good friend's younger brother. This kid wanted to make a name for himself, and apparently in slicing up Alex, he did. At first, of course, Alex was mad and for a year and a half he always thought about the incident, and on many occasions thought about retaliation. But lots of things have been changing for Alex. He was baptized, he confessed his sin to God and he is walking upright. He attends Bible study and takes care of his family. The other night, during Holy Week, he ran into the guy who stabbed him at Circle K. He saw him at the cash register and stood outside and waited for him to come out. As this kid was leaving the store, he saw Alex outside, waiting. His face turned black. He had no idea what was coming. Alex put out his hand to shake his. What?! He didn't move, didn't say anything, no word. "I forgive you, man", he said. What?! Pause, no words. The kid looked down then muttered, "I'm sorry. I just wanted to make a name for myself." Then Alex said an amazing thing to his stabber. "I forgive you for it because you helped me open my eyes. Things have turned around for me since the stabbing. Thank you, really man, thank you. I am happier now."

Forgiveness, it is the path to reconciliation. First, we must be forgiven by God. Our complicity in all matters of division in our lives is obvious. The blaming and denial must be eliminated. That is only possible through confession and forgiveness. And then we are obligated to forgive others. There isn't another way.

What does it look like to develop a spirit of "reconciliation"? What is a discipline that can be practiced?

Praying the Jesus Prayer

Lord Jesus Christ, Son of God, have mercy on me, a sinner.

The "Jesus Prayer" is an ancient prayer of the church that has stood the test of time. It is "based on Paul's exhortation to pray constantly (1 Thess 5:17) and on the Gospel cries of 'Lord have mercy.' It was shaped by the early Desert Fathers and eventually became a classic form of prayer practiced widely to this day, especially among Eastern Orthodox Christians."[298]   This prayer does two important things.   It leads our thoughts to the life of Jesus Christ, because as the ancients taught, it contains the whole Gospel in brief.   And secondly, it leads us to forgiveness. In humility remembering our helplessness to cure our sin problem, we run to a loving merciful God who has the solution.

We are helpless to cure the divisions in our families, our church, our community, our culture, our world. But God is not helpless. The person who works for reconciliation is the person who has first been forgiven for all acts of division they are responsible for by a merciful God.

Richard Foster in *A Spiritual Formation Workbook*[299] recommends this prayer as a way to practice a "prayer filled life". Following Jesus' example we pray to a tender loving, giving, forgiving Father and receive what we need. He recommends following the tradition of the Eastern Church and repeating this simple prayer over and again each day.

CHAPTER 4 INSIDE OUT - BIBLE STUDY WITH THE LECTIO DIVINA

When God's life inside of us spills out onto others, it is recognizable. Its source is from an upside-down kingdom value system. Choose to cultivate these expressions of God.

There is a spiritual discipline that once cultivated breathes into the wholeness of our lives. For the Scriptures are God breathed and intended to bring us life.

"The Word of Scripture should never stop sounding in your ears and working in you all day long, just like the words of someone you love. And just as you do not analyze the words of someone you love, but accept them as they are said to you, accept the Word of Scripture and ponder it in your heart, as Mary did. That is all ... Do not ask 'How shall I pass this on?" but "What does it say to me?" Then ponder this word long in your heart until is has gone right into you and taken possession of you."[300]

There is a Bible study method that isn't about information gathering or proving a point. It is a chance to engage the Scriptures, not just with our mind, but also our heart, our emotions, our body, our curiosity, our imagination and our will.[301] It's a different kind of engagement, one where our priority is to listen to God relationally. God speaks to us through Scripture and we respond with our heart and soul rather than just our intellect. This approach is called Lectio divina (translated "divine [or sacred] reading"). Lectio divina is a practice of divine reading that dates back to the early mothers and fathers of the Christian faith, rooted in the belief that through the presence of the Holy Spirit, the Scriptures are indeed alive and active as we engage them for spiritual transformation (Heb 4:12).

The Four Movements of the Lectio divina

Prepare: Choose a passage of Scripture no more than six to eight verses in length. Become quiet in God's presence, getting in touch with a desire to hear from God. Read the chosen passage four consecutive times, each time asking a different question that invites us into the dynamic of the move. After each reading, pause for a moment of silence.

First Move: READ. Read the passage once or twice looking for the word or phrase that strikes us, that stands out from the rest, causing a reaction of resonance or acceptance. Remain with the word for a bit.

Second Move: REFLECT. Reflect on the way your life is touched by this word. *What is it in my life that needed to hear this word today?* Staying present with God and not thinking too much about the passage, keep coming back to the word that you have been given.

Third Move: RESPOND. What is your response to God's invitation or challenge? What is your prayer that comes most naturally in response to what you have heard God say? What feelings, big, small or otherwise? What flash of self-knowledge? Conviction of sin? Maybe a great and overwhelming experience of God's love?

Fourth Move: REST. Read the passage one last time and this time rest in God. Receive that you have needed and enjoy God's presence. Resolve to carry this word with you and live it out in the circumstances of today, in the wholeness of today.

CHAPTER 5 INSIDE OUT – COMMUNITY OF THE CROSS

When God's life inside of us spills out onto others, it is recognizable. Its source is from an upside-down kingdom value system. Choose to cultivate these expressions of God.

The beloved community are members of the community of the cross. Meaning that the followers of Jesus are marked by the cross, or at least we should be. Jim Wallace says that "the cross of Christ is both the symbol of our atonement and the pattern for our discipleship."[302]

Jesus tells some stories (parables) in Matthew 18 and 19 about the community of the cross in which disciples embody God's reign and nurture one another. The community of disciples—the church—constituted by God's action, embodies God's purposes. The way of the cross, the way of discipleship, is hard work and is sustainable only through life-giving relationships.

The Spirit of a Child – Matthew 18:2-14
    Who is greatest in the kingdom of heaven? Jesus answered, be like this child (18:2-5). What would a community of cross carrying disciples look like using the image of a child? Relationships of equality come to mind, shared vulnerability and an absence of the world's hierarchical social structure of status, wealth and power. Powerless children are not apt to compete for domination. These relationships will not cause each other to stumble (18:6-9) and are instead devoted to caring for each other (18:10-14). Years later, John wrote to the wider church community, emphasizing that the cross of Jesus expresses sacrificial love (I John 4:17-21). But what does that love look like? "This is how we know what love is: Jesus Christ laid down his life for us. And we ought to lay down our lives for one another (3:16)."

The Spirit of Forgiveness – Matthew 18:15-35
    The basic notion of the term forgiveness involves *release* from situations of indebtedness and enslavement (e.g., the year of Jubilee or release, Leviticus 25). Forgiveness is about releasing the other and the self from revenge, blaming, retaliation, hatred and bitterness. Jesus' teaching requires unlimited forgiveness. The king in the parable does the very opposite. He does not forgive (18:32-34), nor does the forgiven slave (18:28-30). It seems, then, that the parable operates by contrast. The king is not God. The king and his servant exemplify what happens if forgiveness is not the basis for our cross community's relationships. How often do we forgive? We give the same forgiveness we have been given. For such forgiveness, there is no limit (18:21-22).

<u>The Spirit of Release</u> – Matthew 19:23-30

The members of the community of the cross are people who have learned from Jesus about the self-emptying life. The famous text is Philippians 2:5-8, "let the same mind be in you that was in Christ Jesus, who, though he was in the form of God, did not regard equality with God as something to be exploited…." "The self-emptying nature of Jesus on the cross invites us to give up trying to manipulate, coerce, or control God's goodness and to trust that it will be forever available to us in abundance. The self-emptying life allows us to come alongside vulnerable people with our own vulnerability. We cease to be a threat to the powerless because we have given up a need to grasp at power."[303] Jesus tells his disciples that whoever leaves everything for his sake, will receive a hundred fold and eternal life. "But many who are first will be last, and many who are last will be first (19:28-30)."

<u>The Spirit of a Good Shepherd</u> – Matthew 18:10-20

The parable reveals what leadership looks like in the community of the cross. The imagery is one of a shepherd (Psalm 23), a good shepherd. We remember the passage in Ezekiel 34 where God attacks Israel's leaders for failing to represent himself among the people and for damaging them, exploiting them, using them, depriving them of basic resources for their terribly broken lives. By contrast, this parable (18:10-14) presents a shepherd who expresses God's purpose (18:14) of seeking out and caring for the sheep. Such is to be the style of care and vigilance among the community of disciples in protecting one another as God protects them.

The community of the cross is filled with good shepherds who:

> 1. Look upon the harassed crowds as sheep without a shepherd (Mt 9:36) – and step up to provide shepherding

for the distressed and disinherited.

2. Feed the sheep (Jn 21:15-17) – A cross bearing leader hears the words of Jesus to Peter that love for God equates to tending, feeding, nurturing, developing Jesus' lambs.

3. Search for the lost (Matt 18:12-13; Lk 15:4-7) – A leader in this community notices who is missing, recognizes who their flock is and is disturbed when just one is gone. The least, last and lost are the specific targets of God's preferential love, as they are of the community of the cross.

4. Teach the sheep to know the voice of the Good Shepherd (Jn 10:26-29) – The shepherd must first have heard his voice in the silence and in the waiting to be able to usher the next one into that Presence. The community of the cross knows the voice of God and they in turn follow their good shepherd.

5. Protect the sheep from predators (Jn 10:7-18) – Particularly the kind that bring division, disunity and a competitive spirit. The good shepherd protects the sheep from believing the lies that divide the flock.

6. Bind the wounds (Ezek 34:1-16) – As the Good Shepherd does himself, the cross community seeks to rescue, bind, bring healing and restoration to those sheep who have been abandoned, neglected, forgotten and discarded. It is the mark of the community of the cross.

er Teresa of Calcutta. Her lessons for us have also been my lessons
from God. So, I/we learn from M. Teresa about servant leadership.
Who better to learn from, actually? M. Teresa and The Missionaries of Charity have key words (core values) that codified the direction of their servant leadership, and were articulated in what
they called *A Simple Path*.[304] This path is one that she has distilled
from her long experience of working for the love of God with her
fellow human beings. It is composed of six essential steps: silence,
prayer, faith, love, service, and peace. This simple way directs us
on a simple path toward our own servant leadership:

The Simple Path
The fruit of silence is
PRAYER
The fruit of prayer is
FAITH
The fruit of faith is
LOVE
The fruit of love is
SERVICE
The fruit of service is
PEACE

Silence – Silence is the spiritual discipline that allows the servant leader to work from the humble place of dependence. Only God can be and do in and through me. "Be still and know I am God (Ps 46:10)" is a spiritual discipline reference point for Christians throughout the ages, particularly the so-called contemplatives and ascetics. Jesus himself retreated alone for long periods of time with the Father. This discipline has been a hallmark of many Christian leaders. M. Teresa taught that there is no life of prayer without silence,[305] for we cannot find God in noise or agitation.[306] These silences are so practical, not what we traditionally think about the monastic cloistered practice called "silence." The logic for M. Teresa is that these practiced silences give us a new outlook on things, a new way of looking at everything. Jesus is waiting in silence; there he will listen to us. We need silence to touch souls. M. Teresa was famous for saying, "The more we receive in our silent prayer, the more we can give in our active life."[307]

Prayer – Prayer is the spiritual discipline that allows the servant leader its best resource, refuge and place of power, not to mention renewal. For M. Teresa prayer was everything. This giant of a woman considered herself so very fragile, that it was prayer alone that sustained her. She could even find prayer overwhelming. "When the time comes and we cannot pray, it is very simple – let Jesus pray in us to the Father in the silence of our hearts. If we cannot speak, He will speak. If we cannot pray, He will pray. So let us give Him our inability and our nothingness."[308] Her motto was *Love to Pray*. Prayer enlarges the heart until it is capable of containing God's gift of Himself. Ask and seek and your heart will grow big enough to receive Him and keep Him as your own. Another motto: *Pray while you work, Work doesn't stop prayer, Prayer doesn't stop work.*

Faith – The servant leader must learn to trust God. M. Teresa found that the way of faith worked itself out in her life through obedience. Sometimes obedience can exhibit itself as a controlled effort. Yet, she never considered herself in control of this faith that worked itself out in action. She always said, "Faith is a gift of God. Without it there would be no life. And our work, to be fruitful and beautiful, has to be built on faith. Love and faith go together.[309] They complete each other. M. Teresa's theology was married to the passages in the Scriptures where the connection between faith and works (as it pertains to the poor) were articulated. One of the clearest N.T. passages which exposits these is in the book of James chapter two: "…if a man says he has faith, but does not have works? Can faith alone save him? If a brother or a sister is naked and in want of daily food and one of you says to them: go in peace, be warmed and filled, yet you do not give them what is necessary for the body, what does it profit? So faith unless it has works is dead in itself (Jms 2:14-18)." Characteristically M. Teresa taught that even with faith, we do nothing, He does everything. All glory must be returned to him. One of her most quoted statements testifies, "God has not called me to be successful he called me to be faithful."[310]

Love – If M. Teresa is famous for anything it is love. Love for the unlovely and marginalized, the poorest of the poor. What an incredible thing to be famous for, for like the scripture she would often quote from 1 John "you are a liar if you say you love God and you do not love your neighbor (1 Jn 2:9)." What is unique to the understanding of M. Teresa's teaching on love is that our love is defined by how much it is like Christ's love. "I tell my sisters: Let us not love in words but let us love until it hurts. It hurt Jesus to love us: He died for us. And today it is your turn and my turn to love one another as Jesus loved us. Do not be afraid to say yes to

Jesus."[311] She stressed that everyone deserves and needs love. She had an amazing ability to notice the marginalized in the lonely, not just the leper. Suffering people, who had forgotten what human love is, these persons were her specialization. All life is precious, everyone deserves love.

> "You will find Calcutta all over the world if you have eyes to see. The streets of Calcutta lead to every man's door. I know that you may want to make a trip to Calcutta, but it is easy to love people far away. It is not always easy to love those people who live beside us. What about the ones I dislike or look down upon?"[312]

Loving means knowing, touching, continuous care, not giving up. Love has no limit, because God's love is infinite. She often said it's not how much you do, but how much love you put into the doing (into the action). It is the intensity of love we put into our gestures that makes them into something beautiful for God.[313] Do ordinary things with extraordinary love, she taught. We can do no great things – only small things with great love. Works of love are always works of joy. Love is never self-indulgent. But it is always sacrificial.

> "You must give what will cost you something. This, then, is giving not just what you can live without but what you can't live without or don't want to live without, something you really like. Then your gift becomes a sacrifice, which will have value before God. Any sacrifice is useful if it is done out of love."[314]

She had a particular message for the rich, who needed to learn this sacrificial love in their giving to the poor. Don't just be satisfied with giving money; the poor need our hands, our hearts, and our love. We need to touch the poorest of the poor to understand. To know the problem of poverty intellectually is not understanding. It is not by reading, taking a walk in the slums, admiring and regretting that we come to understand it and to discover what it has of bad and good. We have to dive into it, live it, and share it.[315]

Service – Servant leaders serve. Every day, M. Teresa and the Sisters and Brothers of Charity get up very early and begin their common routine of active love. The work is very specific and the target of their active love is the poorest of the poor throughout the world. They act, sacrificially believing that love cannot remain by itself – it has no meaning. Love has to be put into action and that action is service. A mission of love can come only from union with God. Love does not live on words nor can it be explained by words – especially the love which serves God. People who observe others who work among the poor often say, "Doesn't it feel as if your efforts are just a drop in the ocean?" M. Teresa heard this and this was her response.

> "We ourselves feel that what we are doing is just a drop in the ocean. But if that drop was not there, I think the ocean would be less by that missing drop. We don't have to think in numbers. We can only love one person at a time – serve one person at a time."[316]

When asked about the role of government towards the needy and the poor, she would say that governments can't love. Large systemic change was never pressing on M. Teresa. It wasn't in her paradigm. Her view was that each one of us is merely an instrument (a pencil for her) in the hands of God. To be present among the poor, do the work, be available, and be faithful.

Peace – For servant leaders, it is our natural thinking process regarding this way of life, life of service and devotion, to calculate the rewards, rewards like finding purpose and meaning, significance, fulfillment. M. Teresa would say it is enough to find peace:

> "Works of love are always works of peace. Whenever you share love with others, you'll notice the peace that comes to you and to them. When there is peace, there is God – that is how God touches our lives and shows His love for us by pouring peace and joy into our hearts."[317]

Those that know peace can gift it to others. Each suffering person is brought to the Lord, who has the remedy for everything, who can carry the deep woundedness of past hurts. He can bring inner healing, spiritual healing – "the healers and the healed share God's peace."[318] M. Teresa had one message for our world, a message of love and compassion. She embodied a message meant to bring peace to the world through their work:

<u>**ANYWAY**</u>
People are unreasonable, illogical, and self-centered,
LOVE THEM ANYWAY
If you do good, people will accuse you of
Selfish, ulterior motives,
DO GOOD ANYWAY
If you are successful,
You win false friends and true enemies,
SUCCEED ANYWAY
The good you do will be forgotten tomorrow,
DO GOOD ANYWAY
Honesty and frankness make you vulnerable,
BE HONEST AND FRANK ANYWAY

What you spent years building may be
Destroyed overnight,
BUILD ANYWAY
People really need help
But may attack you if you help them,
HELP PEOPLE ANYWAY
Give the world the best you have
And you'll get kicked in the teeth,
GIVE THE WORLD THE BEST YOU'VE GOT ANYWAY[319]

CHAPTER 7 INSIDE OUT - SPIRITUAL WARFARE

When God's life inside of us spills out onto others, it is recognizable. Its source is from an upside-down kingdom value system. Choose to cultivate these expressions of God.

In light of the previous discussion regarding the principalities and powers, we suggest that there is a battle afoot. That "the primary task of the Church with reference to the Powers and Principalities is to unmask their idolatrous pretensions, to identify their dehumanizing values, to strip from them the mantle and credibility and to set free their victims." Well, how does this fight look? How do we, the church, fight against the principalities and powers for justice?

1) Most would agree that the first step toward the engagement with these powers and with injustice is to call out (name them) and move away from apathy. "Words that are opposite of political involvement or social action are: comfort, apathy, default, withdrawal, any type of quietism, (which appearances to the contrary, are forms of political commitment, not options of abstention from politics)"[320]

Jorge describes what moving away from apathy looks like for us:

I think we want to give voice to the ones who don't have means to express their needs. We became the vehicle to give that voice and we are a part of that voice. The role is working among people who are suffering from the oppression, the role our ministry plays is giving voice to the people. Especially, among the whole immigration issue, it is really controversial. Other Christians, have issues with immigration, think we are helping people who broke the law. We are not passive, we are not silent, and we put them in front of the Lord, these big issues. When the body of Christ is silent, they are saying "we are OK, we didn't break the law, we don't want get involved, it is controversial – give to God that which is God, give to Cesar, etc." In other words, the individual approach. "We are about spiritual matters; don't have anything to do with politics."

2) A next step is prayer. Ephesians 6:10-18 rehearses the weapons (armor of God) we have been given to stand against "the schemes of the devil." After recognize the whole outfit of armor has been identified, we are told to pray at all times in the Spirit. We that prayer places us in the inner reaches of the battle. "Be transformed by the renewing of your mind," Romans 12:1-2 says, "live consciously out of tune with the world as it presently is and in tune with the way God intends it to be." Jesus taught his disciples to pray, "Your kingdom come, your will be done, on earth as it is in heaven (Mt 6:10)."

3) Then, become advocates. The scriptures are clear

about our call to stand up for the poor and the oppressed. Paulo Freire understands this part of the fight:

True solidarity with the oppressed means fighting at their side to transform the objective reality which has made them these 'beings for another.' The oppressor is solidary with the oppressed only when he stops regarding the oppressed as an abstract category and sees them as persons who have been unjustly dealt with, deprived of their voice, cheated in the sale of their labor – when he stops making pious, sentimental, and individualistic gestures and risks an act of love.[321]

Advocates are change agents, securing justice through direct engagement, spiritually, socially, legally and politically. "The Bible has spoken to us in the 'wholeness' of our lives, including our political lives. We must attempt to speak about political matters out of minds and hearts disciplined by the word from God. Our political thoughts must be developed to the point where they are fitting ones for people who confess obedience to the will of God."[322]

It is to this point that Jesus refers, though not quite a parable, but certainly a mystery. "Whoever believes in me, as the Scripture has said, out of his heart will flow rivers of living water (John 7:38)." This divine life, filled with the indwelling Holy Spirit, manifests itself in all our ways, walk and words bringing life and healing to many. The advocate, by the very nature of the message, can rely on the hope that out of her will flow rivers of living water. "But as for me, the Lord fills me with his spirit and power, and gives me a sense of justice and the courage to tell the people of Israel what their sins are (Micah 3:8)."

A direct encounter with the principalities and powers, confronted by naming them, prayer and rivers of living water, that's what we need! God is big!

CHAPTER 8 INSIDE OUT – HUMILITY

When God's life inside of us spills out onto others, it is recognizable. Its source is from an upside-down kingdom value system. Choose to cultivate these expressions of God.

Urban ministers seem to have something in common; people accuse us of not being very humble. I don't think it would take many people very long to make a short or long list of the reasons why we get a little bit full of ourselves: really hard work, edgy theology, countercultural lifestyle, you get it. But humility is necessary as part of our Jesus followership, witness and attractiveness. And choosing to become a life-long learner is a great way to develop a God- desired humility. A humble learner is someone who doesn't have it all figured out. Jeremy says it this way:

Learning represents a posture, a learner is someone that is humble, broken, or at least understands the brokenness in them. They are willing to call into question mainstream ideas we take as givens most of the time and that allows us to see how God is working in people and communities long before we got there. And we desire also to be humble enough to learn from our own life, recalling how our history (good and bad decisions) and our cities history (good and bad decisions) influence one another in getting to where we're at.

"Humility signifies, simply, the acceptance of being human; the acceptance of one's human being. It is the embrace of the both-and-ness, both saint and sinner, both beast and angel, that constitutes our being as human. Beginning with the acceptance that being human – being mixed (and therefore sometimes mixed-up) – is good enough, humility involves learning how to live with and take joy in that reality."[323] There are humble people here at Neighborhood.

Marcos is one of them:

> *By giving your life to the Lord, you can walk the straight and narrow, but developing a relationship with Lord does NOT mean all your troubles are going to go away. Because we serve the Lord, it is very comforting to have someone on our side, who is our advocate, who loves us, who wants to be with us, so long as we trust him. As far as putting that into practice, believing what we are saying, I feel that those are the things I am learning.*

And Googoos:

> *Unconditional love is something I receive and something I am learning to give. We don't always do it right, "I'm sorry", is easy to say, but doesn't always cut it. I have to show others that I make mistakes too; it doesn't mean I don't love them, and I don't want better for them. We keep reminding each other, we have lots to learn. Life is an everyday learning process. Unfortunately, it doesn't come with a manual.*

There is a natural connection between learning and humility. Learning puts our focus outside ourselves: on God, on others, on the community and its complex problems, on the goals we desire to see achieved, etc. Madeleine L'Engle, in *A Circle of Quiet*, looks to make this connection:

> When we are self-conscious, we cannot be wholly aware;

we must throw ourselves out first. This throwing ourselves away is the act of creativity. So, when we wholly concentrate, like a child in play, or an artist at work, then we share in the act of creating. We not only escape time, we also escape our self-conscious selves. The Greek has a word for ultimate self-consciousness which I find illuminating: *hubris:* pride: pride in the sense of putting oneself in the center of the universe. The strange and terrible thing is that this kind of total self-consciousness invariably ends in self-annihilation. The great tragedians have always understood this, from Sophocles to Shakespeare. We witness it in history in such people as Tiberius, Eva Peron, Hitler. I was timid about putting forth most of these thoughts, but this kind of timidity is itself a form of pride. The moment that humility becomes self-consciousness, it becomes hubris. One cannot be humble and aware of oneself at the same time. Therefore, the art of creating – painting a picture, singing a song, writing a story – is a humble act? This was a new thought to me. Humility is throwing oneself away in complete concentration on something or someone else.[324]

CHAPTER 9 INSIDE OUT - LAMENT

When God's life inside of us spills out onto others, it is recognizable. Its source is from an upside-down kingdom value system. Choose to cultivate these expressions of God.

Truth-telling, tolerated, celebrated, practiced communally will compel us to learn the spiritual discipline of lament. Lament is the act of taking the time and emotional sweat to recognize the deepest brokenness of our souls, and then mustering the courage to embrace it before God. Lament is an act of love. It recognizes that in order to truly love, one must be truly honest. David the king, and David the psalmist teaches us much about the gut-wrenching, brutal truth-telling that he knew was possible with his God. He knows that if he wants his love affair with God to be true, he must be honest about his anger with God, his accusations of God, his confusion with the perplexing way God sometimes goes silent. Lament is a way of honoring God, of taking Him seriously. It is, as Eugene Peterson says, a way of "making the most of our loss without getting bogged down in it—[it] is a primary way of staying in the story. God is telling the story, remember ... He doesn't look kindly on our editorial deletions."[325]

In our community, we regularly remind each other that our laments are as important to our stories as our hallelujahs. Both have their place, but we are dishonest if we can't find our complaint inside the way in which we tell our story to each other. I was with a friend last night, who spent quite a few years living with us. Her life is very difficult right now. As she told me the truth about all she is enduring, I was able to share in her lament, and in some way shared her burden. Our laments bring us to God, who is ultimately our audience. Walter Brueggemann, in *Prayers for a Privileged People*,[326] offers us this prayer:

ON PONDERING LAMENTS
We celebrate your steadfast love.
We praise you for your mercy.
We count on your faithfulness.
We celebrate and praise and count on.

And then the world does not work right.
We find ourselves unsafe and anxious,

caught up in greed and selfishness,
beset by a culture of violence and threat.

We wonder about the mismatch,
between you and your creation.

Mostly, we trust,
down deep we sometimes do not.
We risk truth-telling
about your absence and silence and withdrawal.

We do such truth-telling, telling it to you,
you ... absent, silent, withdrawn.
You we address, you, our only hope
in this world and in the world to come.

CHAPTER 10 INSIDE OUT - THE HOLY SPIRIT

When God's life inside of us spills out onto others, it is
recognizable. Its source is from an upside-down kingdom value
system. Choose to cultivate these expressions of God.

The wisdom of God, of which the scriptures are filled, of which the Holy Spirit ignites for our remembrance and for our self-giving is for the blessing and benefit of those God has given us to love, which is our community. "A vision of human flourishing – and resources to realize it – is the most important contribution of the Christian faith to the common good."[327]

The resources to realize it ... that is our contribution. Acts 1:8 teaches: "But you will receive power when the Holy Spirit comes upon you. And you will be my witnesses, telling people about me everywhere—in Jerusalem, throughout Judea, in Samaria, and to the ends of the earth." Imagine having the power, and not just any kind of power, to witness verbally and practically, the love, grace and mercy of God. The fruit of the Holy Spirit – love, joy, peace, patience, kindness, goodness, gentleness, faithfulness and self-control – gives credibility that God is at work in us and available for all the resources needed.

How is the power from the Holy Spirit accessed? Better said, what does our relationship with God, the Holy Spirit look like?

- The Holy Spirit makes us heirs of God's power – to love, to serve, to welcome, to forgive.

…true community is a spiritual reality which lies beyond psychology and sociology. Community is a by-product of active love. Community can break our minds and our egos open to the experience of a God who cannot be contained. Community will constantly remind us that our grip on truth is fragile and incomplete, that we need many ears to hear, the fullness of God's word. And the disappointments of community life can be transformed by our discovery that the only dependable power for life lies beyond all human structures and relationships.[328]

- The Holy Spirit hovers and rests in places, on people – and He gives us discernment to see where He is at work.

Our friends from the Street Psalms Community have also taught us to embrace the imagery of God the Holy Spirit "hovering" over chaos,[329] in the same way we see God intimately involved in creation (Gen 1:2). "In the beginning God created the heavens and the earth. Now the earth was formless and empty, darkness was over the surface of the deep, and the Spirit of God was hovering over the waters." Imagine the altered view of our community, when we believe that the Spirit has been way ahead of us. As John Howard Yoder wrote, "God is working in the world, and it is the task of the Church to know how he is working; that is to say, 'Behold, here is Christ. This is where God is at work.'"[330]

- The Holy Spirit is the great minister, helper, teacher, comforter, advocate, intercessor and counselor (Jn 14:16; 7:39; 14:26; 15:26; 16:7).

We hear in Rom 8:26-27, that the Holy Spirit intercedes for us when we don't know how to pray. Could it be that He intercedes when we don't know how to help, and minister, and comfort and advocate? When we feel lost and alone and inept? "We have to realize that this wound [of loneliness] is inherent in the human condition and that what we have to do is walk with it instead of fleeing from it. We cannot accept it until we discover that we are loved by God just as we are, and that the Holy Spirit in a mysterious way is living at the center of the wound."[331]

- The Holy Spirit seals us with a promise – "God put his special mark of ownership on you by giving you the Holy Spirit that he had promised. That Holy Spirit is the guarantee that we will receive what God promised (Eph 1:13-14)."

Jesus told a story (parable) that reveals this Holy Spirit activity both with us, as well as the activity of God in our community. There are two stories, both emphasizing the same truth. Don't despise small beginnings, Zechariah teaches (Zech 4:10). The stories describe a big "bush/tree" that comes from the smallest seed, and a small lump of yeasty dough that bakes a lot of bread. At the time, when I was sealed with the Holy Spirit, my life probably didn't look like it would amount to much, but the seal was a promise given. When we enter into the work of the kingdom of God in our community, it probably doesn't look like it will amount to much, either. But the promise of God, all along, is that the seed and yeast, small as it is, will grow, both in my life, and in our community. Sure, there has been discouragement – but the promise remains.

CHAPTER 11 INSIDE OUT – PETITIONARY PRAYER

When God's life inside of us spills out onto others, it is recognizable. Its source is from an upside-down kingdom value system. Choose to cultivate these expressions of God.

Not too long ago, we were planning a fund-raising event with our partners for one of our programs. These dear friends partner with us despite our faith backgrounds which are very different. Our vision for the year-end goal was more than the previous years and somewhat daunting. This partner looked at me, as we were all squirming under the pressure, and said, "Well, you pray don't you?" Meaning, that's what you bring to the table. They wanted to emphasize that, that this was our contribution, prayer.

Some would argue that prayer, particularly the type that seeks help, resources, provision, answers, rescue, salvation, etc. is the greatest contribution that we can make to our community and our partners. Petitionary prayer is what this is called. And is a very important kind of prayer activity, so much so that prominent theologians have argued for it being the "basis for the other aspects of prayer".[332] For example, "Karl Barth viewed prayer primarily as petition, which he understood as a going toward God, an asking God to give the petitioner what he or she lacks."[333]

For as Stanley Grenz suggests in *Prayer, The Cry for the Kingdom:*[334]

This emphasis on petition indicates that the New Testament writers continued the eschatological orientation of prayer that they saw in Jesus' own outlook. Like the Master, they present prayer as an eschatological activity, the petitioning for the coming of the kingdom into the present. By beseeching God for divine provision in the midst of the brokenness and insufficiency of the present, the Christian community seeks the power of the Spirit for its task of continuing the ministry of the risen Lord, until he returns in glory (see 2 Pet 3:11-12). By petitioning God in the midst of the present experience of persecution and evil that the righteous Judge return in judgment and vindication, the church anticipates the final day of the Lord. In short, the New Testament writers describe the prayer of the community of faith as the cry for the kingdom.

"Petition lies at the heart of prayer, because the kingdom of God must be sought not only by faith and obedience but also by prayer, which includes petition for our human needs ... the language of prayer is ultimately that of crying – a cry that comes after, and goes beyond all talk."[335]

1. Prayer is a request for God to act
2. Prayer is an ongoing conversation with God
3. Pray specifically
4. Pray all the time
5. Pray with persistence
6. Pray alone
7. Pray together
8. Build a life of prayer

This short moment doesn't do the role of petitionary prayer justice, as it relates to partners committed to rebuilding their communities. So we will use this brief discussion to launch a more definitive exercise. Meanwhile, find a good resource to continue building prayer habits that bring this gift to your partnering. Consider Stanley Grenz' book, *Prayer, The Cry for the Kingdom.*

NOTES

295. Miroslav Volf, *Exclusion and Embrace, A Theological Exploration of Identity, Otherness, and Reconciliation*, (Nashville: Abingdon Press, 1996), 29.
296. Quote by Barbara Lundblad, http://jimdoepkenme.wordpress.com/ category/quote/page/8/ (accessed: April 11, 2012).
297. Brenda Salter McNeil, 31.
298. Tilden H. Edwards, *Living Simply Through the Day*, (Paulist Press: 1977).
299. Richard Foster, *A Spiritual Formation Workbook*, (San Francisco: Harper Collins: 1991).
300. Dietrich Bonheoffer, *Life Together*, (New York: Harper Row, 1954).
301. Ruth Haley Barton, *Sacred Rhythms, Arranging Our Lives for Spiritual Transformation,* (Downers Grove: InterVarsity Press, 2006), 50.
302. Jim Wallace, *Agenda for Biblical People*, (New York: Harpercollins, 1976), 68.
303. Kris Rocke, *Geography of Grace*, (Tacoma: Street Psalms Press, 2012), 236.
304. Lucinda Vardey, ed., *Mother Teresa, A Simple Path*, (New York: Ballantine Books, 1995), xxxvii.
305. Dorothy Hunt, ed., *Love: A Fruit Always in Season*, (San Francisco: Ignatius, 1987), 84.
306. Becky Benenate, *In the Heart of the World, Thoughts, Stories, and Prayers, Mother Teresa*, (Novato, California: New World Library, 1997), 19.
307. Ibid.
308. Hunt, 77.
309. Hunt, 19.
310. Ibid.
311. Hunt, 198.
312. Hunt, 159.
313. Becky Benenate and Joseph Durepos, 26.
314. Vardey, 99.
315. Hunt, 224.
316. Hunt, 137.
317. Vardey, 171.
318. Ibid., 172.

319. Vardey, 185 (From a sign on the wall of Shishu Bhavan, the children's home in Calcutta).

320. William Stringfellow, *An Ethic for Christians and Other Aliens in a Strange Land*, (Eugene: Wipf and Stock Pub. 1973), 55.

321. Paulo Freire, 49.

322. Richard J. Mouw, *Politics and the Biblical Drama*, (Grand Rapids: Baker Books. 1976), 12.

323. Ernest Kurtz and Katherine Ketcham, *The Spirituality of Imperfection, Storytelling and the Journey to Wholeness*, (New York: Bantam Books, 1992), 186.

324. Madeleine L'Engle, *A Circle of Quiet*, (Winston: Seabury Press, 1972).

325. Winn Collier, "The Art of Lament," *Relevant Magazine*, http://www.relevantmagazine.com/daily- devotional/26792-the-art-of-lament (accessed April 29, 2012).

326. Walter Brueggemann, *Prayers for a Privileged People*, (Nashville: Abingdon Press, 2008), 139.

327. Miroslav Volf, *A Public Faith, How Followers of Christ Should Serve the Common Good*, (Grand Rapids: Brazos Press, 2011), 63.

328. Parker Palmer, "A Place Called Community," http://www.religion-online.org/showarticle.asp?title=1143 (accessed May 1, 2012).

329. Rocke, Van Dyke, 150.

330. Ibid., 152.

331. Jean Vanier, 288.

332. Stanley J. Grenz, *Prayer, The Cry for the Kingdom*, (Grand Rapids: Eerdmans, 1988), 45.

333. Ibid.

334. Ibid., 25.

335. Ibid., 45.

APPENDIX B
Artist Biographies and
Piece Information

CHAPTER 2 - INCARNATIONAL LOVE PRESENTED BY NATHANIEL GORDNATTAZ

Art Piece: _Front Porch_

Artist Bio

Nate grew up in the neighborhood and became part of NM as a child. He wandered in and out of the programs, sometimes got into trouble, most of the time perked the curiosity of the leaders. He was an enigma. Always up to something Nate has been a delightful surprise, showing great leadership in the summer programs, being a good friend to kids and adults alike, and always being a reminder of all the good in our community. Nate graduated from high school and got one of his first jobs with a Neighborhood partner called Public Allies. Showing an interest in the arts he chose to work with a community group called "Free Arts of Arizona". It was during this time that Nate put together a series of photographs depicting the neighborhood he grew up in, of which this photograph comes. Today, Nate is completing college at ASU and continues in many leadership roles at NM.

CHAPTER 3 - RECONCILIATION PRESENTED BY RALPH MARTINEZ

Art Piece: _Reconcile_

Reconcile reflects artist Ralph Martinez: a little child-like, a prodigal son, telling his story of reconciliation with God. "I have done a lot of rotten stuff, but I am always running back into the arms of God. The message is: 'I'm sorry, I want to start over. I want to push rewind and do it right.' God has accepted me despite all I've done wrong, he accepts the child in me. Whenever I come to church, I always feel like a kid again. Even with all the hurt I've been through."

Artist Bio
Ralph has been a street artist (graffiti) since 1996, of some national renown. He defines his style as "Aggressive Art" describing the role his art plays as social commentary. "Painting some crazy nook in the city, I'm usually painting next to some guy that is living right there, homeless. Jesus was always with the lame, the poor, the broken hearted, and that's where I should be." Ralph wants to use his voice and communicate a message.

CHAPTER 4 – HOLISTIC MINISTRY PRESENTED BY HOPE THRU ART

Art Piece: *Jireh*

Artist Bio
Hope thru Art takes the message of hope and affirmation to the darkest and most dangerous neighborhoods in America. They perform live music and spoken word hip-hop poetry, hand out free books, printed poetry, nature photos, socks, clothing, water bottles and food. They also display art and do street art installations on chain link fences. They believe that creativity is the most commonly spoken language and that it is instrumental as a redemptive platform.

CHAPTER 5 - THE CHURCH PRESENTED BY KYLE MATTHEWS

Art Piece: *Birth Pangs at the Bus Stop*

The point of this painting is to illustrate where the Church is. "In my experience with church, I have learned, that if we are the body of Christ, we must move, learn and grown like a body does. Neighborhood Ministries is a community, in a neighborhood, near the Laundromat and a vacant pay phone. Conversations, enjoyment, and discipleship take place twenty four seven in this neighborhood. We share meals, basketball courts, vehicles, and porches together and with God. The church does not stop when the building is locked up, kids are still outside and mothers sweat 'til the day ends. The relationships built on the property transfer into friendships and into prayers. The painting is a map, a diagram of the intersection of two major streets near the Neighborhood property; 19th Ave and Van Buren. The crosses that elevate from the rooftops of each small structure symbolize the presence of Christ in the homes throughout the neighborhood. The also represent the people alive in the shelter of his wing, hoisting their own cross on their back daily. Pigments of gold reflect the value of the neighborhood itself, the families, and the life that happens here. The green is the growth squeezed slowly from a sponge holding rebirth and renewal in abundance that happens here. The reds and browns reflect the community and the pain that is encountered daily by the beloved people hustling to find hope. The children painted into the satellite are two specific children from this community that at this very moment God sees. When the doors are closed at neighborhood, our Church is not, and our community is but pregnant with miracles."

Artist Bio

Kyle Matthews studied fact and photos as a child by absorbing the

A-Z encyclopedia set he had growing up. He went on to study the tensions in people groups, primarily the between rich and poor, and people of different skin tones. Eyes opened to the neglected and disenfranchised, he moved to Phoenix in 2009 to minister with Neighborhood Ministries. "I believe that God has known the names of every child, mother and father in downtown Phoenix since before the seas were given boundaries. I also believe that our Father has a plan and place for each of them, and therefore I am motivated by the spirit within me to remain with the barrio and to continue to walk."

CHAPTER 6 - LEADERSHIP DEVELOPMENT PRESENTED BY NIKKI VILLEGAS AND XIMENA DANLEY

Art Piece: *No Limits*

Artist Bio
Ximena Danley is a 16-year-old leader at Neighborhood Ministries, which she has attended her whole life.

Nikki Villegas is a case manager with Neighborhood Ministries. She has been on staff since 2004 and also has her hands in Katy's Kids pre-school, mentoring, Kids Life, Hope House and Sunday school.

CHAPTER 7 - JUSTICE PRESENTED BY DERRICK KEMPF

Art Piece: *Overlooking Series*

Artist Bio
Derrick Kempf is a natural-born creator with experience ranging from painting to corporate identity to web design. He enjoys

working with traditional mediums such as acrylics on wood, but spends most of his time creating logos, brand identities, and websites. Drawing cartoons quickly escalated into painting in high school, which then led to art school. He currently works in graphic design at GoDaddy.com. But it is his family and friends who are most valuable to him.

CHAPTER 8 - LEARNING PRESENTED BY ANA MOYA

Art Piece: *Curiosity*

Artist Bio
Ana Moya has been a part of Neighborhood Ministries for many years. She has put her education first her whole life with the goal of becoming a pediatrician. She is currently attending college and is looking forward to medical school.

CHAPTER 9 - RELATIONSHIPS PRESENTED BY STEPHANIE FARWIG

Art Piece: *Joy*
This piece was inspired by a picture of two key participants at Neighborhood Ministries. This drawing is of Irene and Papi, showing the love of a mother for her child—the ultimate relationship.

Artist Bio
Stephanie Farwig has been drawing and painting all of her life. While her professions have been a LPGA tour golfer and a fundraiser for non-profit organizations, her real passion is her artwork. She has the ability to capture people with true feeling or landscapes with absolute clarity. This is what makes her work exceptional.

CHAPTER 10 – COMMUNITY PRESENTED BY CRAIG GOODWORTH

Art Piece: *Liminal Ground*
Liminal Ground is a place-based artwork in a granary/warehouse space in inner city Phoenix. Integrating agricultural and liturgical elements, Craig Goodworth's installation explores the social body. Taking place in the Southwest, where cultures continue to collide and vie for employment opportunities, immigration services, medical care, education and physical spaces to house their indigenous faiths, *Liminal Ground* seeks to engage these tensions.

Artist Bio
Named the Gimilus Chassidim Fellow 2011-2012, Craig Goodworth is an interdisciplinary artist working in a variety of art media including sculpture, prose, found object, and video. Goodworth's art belongs on the Eco tone between desert and city, the spiritual and the material, and the already/not yet.

CHAPTER 11 – PARTNERSHIPS PRESENTED BY MARCO PEREZ

Art Piece: *Working Together*
This piece represents an actual partnership which Neighborhood Ministries has. It speaks to the partnership Marco (the photographer) navigates with Alice Cooper and his foundation, Public Allies and Neighborhood for the benefit of providing high quality dance for the young dancers in our community. This image comes from the Christmas fund-raiser that Alice Cooper and his high powered team produce every year.

Artist Bio
Marco Perez is working with Neighborhood Ministries through a Public Allies partnership, facilitating the dance and arts program.

He enjoys photography, but wants to use it to help others, to tell stories. "I believe there is a lot of purpose and necessity in being good storytellers. So, whenever I do a photo or produce some film, I want to communicate a message for social good. I believe that creativity is an attribute of God that we have been given to share…. When we partake in creativity we are communing with God."

CPSIA information can be obtained
at www.ICGtesting.com
Printed in the USA
JSHW031716260522
26213JS00002B/3

9 780578 287966